Letters to Henry

TOM DENNARD

Cover Photo - Tom, age 3

Cover Design and Photo Restoration by Jonathan Doster

www.jdosterphoto.com

Order this book online at www.createspace.com/3492093

You may contact the author at nldc@bellsouth.net

ISBN: 1453885625
ISBN −13: 9781453885628

This book is dedicated to Irvin Dennard (1936-2009)
I'd give anything if he'd lived long enough to read this book.
He contributed so much to some of the stories, and his spirit was
with me on all the rest.

Me   Irvin

CONTENTS

PREFACE

My daughter, Susan, asked me to write a book for my grandchildren to give them some idea what it was like growing up in Pineview, a small town in southern Georgia. My early years, during the 1940s, were unique times that seem somewhat archaic by today's standards.

After agreeing that I should write the book, it took me a long time to begin. I couldn't decide how the stories should be presented. One day Susan told me she'd found letters her seven year old son, Sutton, had written to his dog in heaven. It occurred to me that this would be the perfect vehicle to write the book. Thanks ever so much, Sutty, for giving me permission to use your idea.

This is not a book about Pineview. It's a book about my growing up in Pineview. Everyone who lived there would have a different story to tell. This is more about experiences that happened to me, rather than a story about the town. Although in reading this, you can't help but get glimpses of what the place was like at that time.

I tried to be truthful to the best of my knowledge and memory. I hope I haven't offended anyone, especially the African Americans, who were such a vital part of my early life. At that time, we referred to them as "nigras," a term my family regarded as being polite. Although today, I'm quite aware it would be considered derogatory. I apologize for that, but I chose to tell these stories as accurately as I could remember them.

In retrospect, the forties in a small, southern town were an ideal time for a young boy to live out his innocence. The entire town was my playground, and the inhabitants acted as my protectors. By having that rare opportunity, I learned to be fiercely independent and discovered the useful tool of how to create things on my own.

Tom Dennard

ACKNOWLEDGEMENTS

There are so many people to thank for giving me information essential to the writing of this book. In addition to Irvin, my cousin, Jamie McLeod Hickman, provided me with invaluable material for many of the stories. My cousin, Angela Evans Burns, was extremely helpful. My classmate, Marvin Talley, reminded me of things that needed to be included in writing this book. My cousin, Jane Lou McLeod Faircloth, was also instrumental in supplying me with helpful information. My sister, Mary Dennard Hungerford, furnished pictures, as well as material and suggestions.

I owe a debt of thanks to my friend, Pete McCommons, Editor of the Flagpole, Athens, Georgia, for reading the book and giving me helpful hints. My friend, Bud Paulding, of Pittsburgh, Pennsylvania, gave me good editorial advice, as did my friend, Mary Lewis of St. Simons Island, Georgia.

I must give special thanks to Stephen and Anne Doster of Nashville, Tennessee, for reading the book and giving me good advice and encouraging words to convince me that the book was worthy of publication.

After creating the cover for my last book, *Born a Ramblin' Man*, Jonathan Doster set out to repeat his delightful and appealing cover for this book.

Thank you ever so much, Jay, for your talent and expertise.

Special thanks to my daughter, Susan Dennard Dunlap, for encouraging me from the beginning to write the book. I am deeply indebted to my grandson, Thomas Sutton Dunlap, for allowing me to use his idea of writing letters to my dog, an ideal vehicle for telling these stories.

And, last, but not least, no book I've ever written could've been completed without the encouragement of my wife, Marie. She has always been my cheerleader, who tries to convince me that I really am a writer, who writes things worthy of publication.

ABOUT THE AUTHOR

Tom Dennard was born in Pineview, Georgia, a small farming community in the heart of Georgia, just like five generations of his ancestors. After attending Davidson College in North Carolina and the University of Georgia Law School, he began a law practice in the coastal town of Brunswick, Georgia. He met Marie Burton of Toccoa, Georgia, at the university. They married upon graduation, and their three children are Susan, Ted, and Jeff, who, together, have produced eleven children. Tom practices law in Brunswick, Georgia, where he specializes in Wills, Trusts, and Estates.

He started the Hostel in the Forest on Highway 82, west of Brunswick. It sits on 133 acres of woodlands, except for the geodesic domes and tree houses, where the guests sleep. Thousands of people go there every year to enjoy the peaceful surroundings. Read about it: *www.foresthostel.com*.

His favorite hobby is mountain hiking, followed by canoeing, working out in the gym, traveling to remote parts of the world, and, of course, writing in his studio at the hostel.

His previously published books are:
Discovering Life's Trails
Buzzards Roost
Born a Ramblin' Man

GLOSSARY OF PEOPLE
IN THE BOOK
(Alphabetized as referred to in the book, usually by first name)

Alice Evans.......Angie's mother. Alice and her husband, Guy, lived directly behind us.

Dr. Augustus Batts........Our family doctor in Hawkinsville

Aunt Alice Thigpen .... My mother's aunt, who lived in Atlanta

Uncle Ambrose Nazareth ....My mother's uncle, who lived on the Hawkinsville-Abbeville highway

Angie....... Angela Evans (now Burns) my cousin, who lived behind us with her parents, Alice and Guy

Annette Conner....... My friend from Finleyson, one grade ahead of me

Audrey Mixon .... The mother of my first-grade girlfriend, Elaine

Bartlett Barker....... A student in school about three years older than I am

Bessie Horne .... A health department nurse and the mother of Jo Horne

Beth Hardy....... My friend from Finleyson, one grade ahead of me

Betty Jean Taylor.......Lived with Sam and Nan Dennard, Nan's niece, two years older than I am

Betty Masters....... My first cousin, about seven years older, daughter of my mother's sister, Nancy from St. Augustine, Florida

Dr. Bill Barton.......Ear, Eye, Nose, & Throat specialist in Macon, Georgia

Bill Masters....... My first cousin, about five years older, son of my mother's sister, Nancy from St. Augustine, Florida

Billy Bloodworth .... Classmate from 1st through 12th grade

Billy Mann.......My first cousin, son of W.D., my mother's brother, five years older than I am

Bob Slade....... About the age of my parents, raised by his Uncle Will and Aunt Carrie Slade

Boots Doster.......Son of Uncle Philetus and Aunt Ida, Papa's sister

Boy....... John Hendley McLeod, Jr., my first cousin, son of Edith and Hendley

Bud Dennard.......Sometimes referred to as Crip. His real name was Hartwell Dennard, my daddy's first cousin, son of my Great Uncle Joe

Charlye....... Referred to as Cudin (Cousin) Char-lye, wife of Rod McLeod, mother of Jane Lou McLeod Faircloth

Christine.......Mr. Clements and Miss Thelma's maid and cook

Clarence Finleyson, Sr........ President of the Bank of Finleyson

(Little) Clarence Finleyson, Jr.......Two years older than I am

Mr. Clements.......Our next door neighbor, father of James and Wilma Nell, owner of Pineviews Drug Store

Dicky Cook....... My friend, who lived with his grand-mother, Mrs. C. K. Cook in Pineview and went to school there. He's six days older than I am

Dinah Hyman.......Lived in Cordele with her mother, Florence, who was Juju's sister, one year older than I am

Miss Dolvin....... Mary K. Dolvin, lived with Nona and owned the Pineview Theater

Dummy.......Angie, Alice and Guy Evans' maid and cook

Duxie....... Edith and Hendley's maid and cook

Edith McLeod....... My daddy's sister

Elaine Mixon....... A classmate from 1st through 12th grade, valedictorian of our class

Elbert Hickman....... from Rochelle, married to my first cousin, Jamie McLeod, daughter of Edith and Hendley

Elinor Smith....... Granddaughter of Mrs. Ware, Pineview's English teacher

Elizabeth Pope....... Lived and went to school in Pineview, six years older than I am, daughter of Mr. Pope, the milkman

Ephraim....... Lived with and cooked for Aunt Ida and Uncle Philet

Ernest Mixon....... Owned a service station in Pineview, father of Elaine

Ethel Finleyson....... Sister of Bernice Finleyson, mar-ried to Leon Finleyson and lived in Finleyson

Evelyn Barfield....... Friend who lived in Finleyson and went to school one class ahead of me

Miss Fanny Clements....... Sister of Mr. Clements, who lived with Miss Thelma and him

Fletcher McLeod.......Juju's husband and Nona's first cousin; Nona's mother was a Wimberley; Fletcher's mother was a Wimberley, and they were sisters

Florence Hyman....... Juju's sister, and mother of Dinah and Mac Hyman, author of *No Time for Sergeants*

Frances Ingram....... From Hawkinsville, married Boy

Mrs. Gammage....... Lived diagonally across from us, mother of Miss Thelma and Lelia

Gayle Talley....... Classmate from 1st grade through 12th grade

Gene Ball....... Student in school about five years older than I am

Goat Lacey....... Delmer Lacey, classmate during grammar school

Grover McLeod....... Hendley and Alice's brother, married to Imogene

Gussie Bragg.......Hendley and Alice's sister, my 4th grade teacher

Guy Evans.......Angie's daddy, Alice's husband, lived behind us

Harry Moore.......Methodist preacher in Pineview, who was blind, son of Bishop Arthur Moore

Hendley McLeod....... Married to Edith, father of Jamie, Sister, and Boy

Henry McLeod....... Son of Charlye and Rod McLeod

Hester……. My caretaker when I was a baby

Herbert Fitzgerald…….From Rochelle, married Wilma Nell Clements

Dr. Hiram Williams…….Ear, Eye, Nose, & Throat specialist in Cordele

Hosey Johnson……. Worked in Papa's cotton gin and Daddy's chauffeur

Aunt Ida……. Papa's sister, married to Philetus Doster

Irvin Dennard, Sr…….. My daddy's first cousin, son of my great Uncle Joe, married to Lillian Lasseter from Rochelle, same age as my daddy

Irvin Dennard, Jr…….. My cousin and best friend growing up, eleven days older than I am

Jack Lawrence……. Lived in the quarters, about the age of Daddy

Jackie Cook…….Sister of Dicky Cook, two years older than I am

Mrs. Alma James…….7th grade teacher, married to Scott James

James Clements…….Son of Mr. Clements and Miss Thelma, lived next door, five years older than I am

Jamie…….My first cousin, daughter of Edith and Hendley McLeod, married Elbert Hickman

Big Jane Lou…….Nickname JuJu, married Fletcher McLeod

Little Jane Lou…….The daughter of Charlye and Rod McLeod, grew up in the home of Fletcher and JuJu, married Bruce Faircloth

Jo Horne…….Classmate, daughter of Allen and Bessie Horne

Joan....... Pronounced Jo Ann, my first cousin, daughter of Ruby and Son Mann, classmate from 1st through 12th grade

Joe L. Dennard.......Papa's first cousin, married to Matibel

Uncle Joe Thigpen.......Married to Mother's Aunt Alice, lived in Atlanta

John Barnes.......Lived in Daddy's camp house as a caretaker when I was little

John Masters.......Married to Mother's sister, Nancy, lived in St. Augustine

John Mitchell.......Married to Mother's Aunt Lena

Josephine Hardy.......First grade teacher, my mother's classmate, lived in Finleyson, mother of Beth Hardy

JuJu.......Jane Lou McLeod married to Fletcher McLeod

Judy Castellow.......Daughter of L.J. (Josh) and Bertha Morgan, Registered Nurse, lived in Decatur, Georgia, married to Frank Castellow

Julius Mashburn.......Lived in Finleyson, father of classmate, Vernon Mashburn, owned the Pineview Theater when I was little

Lelia Gammage.......Sister of Miss Thelma, never married, lived with her mother diagonally across the street

Lillian Dennard.......Wife of Big Irvin, mother of Little Irvin and Lasse

Lizzie Brown.......Wife of Robert Brown who sold barbeque

Loonie Peacock.......Farmer who lived on road to Daddy's farm

Lucille Tippett.......Lived in Finleyson, worked at the bank

Ma Me.......My grandmother and the mother of W.D., Nancy, my mother, and Little Son

Man.......Hosey's son, who married Christine's daughter, Roberta

Mary.......Referred to as Yellow Duxie, washed our clothes and brought them back in a box on top of her head

Mary....... My sister, Mary Mann Dennard, married Ed Hungerford

Mary Dennard.......Daughter of Joe L. and Matibel Dennard, married Ed Lindsey of Atlanta

Mary Mann.......W.D.'s wife and my aunt, lived diagonally across from us

Mary Eliza Ham.......One of my daddy's classmates, who lived next to the Primitive Baptist church on the road to my daddy's farm

Mary John Warren.......Clerked in Nona's store, about five years older than I am, sister of McCall Warren

Martha Syms....... Daughter of Aunt Ida and Uncle Philet, Daddy's first cousin and the same age of him

Marvin Talley.......Classmate from 1st grade through 12th grade

Matibel....... Married to Joe L. Dennard, my sixth grade teacher

Mattie C. Connor.......Lived in Finleyson, sang in the choir, mother of Annette

McCall Warren....... Brother of Mary John, about six years older than I am

Melton Harvey.......Pineview's barber

Midge Doster.......Daughter of Aunt Ida and Uncle Philet

Mildred Malaier.......Sang in choir, my ninth grade English teacher, married to Ronie Malaier, daughter of Dr.Witherington

Miles McKinney.......Pineview's policeman

Mr. Moore.......Reverend Harry Moore, Methodist preacher in Pineview, who was blind, son of Bishop Arthur Moore

Mr. Morgan.......L. J. Morgan (Josh) owned a mercantile store in Pineview, married to Bertha Dennard

Morris Cheek.......Friend of Daddy's who had a small farm between Pineview and Finleyson, member of the Methodist Church

Myrna Broadway.......Classmate from 1st through 12th grade

Nan Dennard.......Married to Sam, mother of Sammy, cook in the school lunchroom

Nancy Masters.......My mother's sister who lived in St. Augustine, Florida

Nona.......Leona Barfield Dennard, my grandmother, Daddy's mother

Nonk Doster.......Norman, son of Aunt Ida and Uncle Philet, my daddy's age

Papa.......Thomas Jefferson Dennard, my grandfather, Daddy's daddy

Pat Palmer.......Classmate in school

Uncle Philet.......Philetus Doster, married to my great aunt, Ida, Papa's sister, lived on a farm on the south side of my daddy's farm

Popcorn.......Jimmy Woods, a classmate

Pope Williams.......Second husband of Wilma Nell Clements, lived in Cordele

Rena.......Nona's sister, married to Syms, lived in Abbeville, had four children: Miriam, William, Martha Lee, and Tom

Robert Brown.......Operated a barbeque café in Pineview

Roberta.......Daughter of Christine, who worked for the Clements

Rod.......Papa's first cousin, married to Charlye, he had five children: Laura, Rose, Square, Jane Lou, and Henry

Rose Marie Bloodworth.......Classmate from 1st through 12th grade

Ruby Mann.......Married to my uncle, Son, had five children and lived with Ma Me

Ruel.......Alice's niece, Angie's first cousin

Sam Dennard.......Daddy's first cousin, son of my great-uncle Joe

Sammy Dennard.......Son of Sam and Nan Dennard

Aunt Sally.......Ma Me's sister, married to Ambrose Nazareth

Sally Williford.......Worked for Mr. Morgan, lived with her sister, Virgie Blue

Sister.......Ann McLeod, daughter of Edith and Hendley, sister of Jamie and Boy

Son....... (Little Son) Joe Walter Mann, son of Ma Me and Granddaddy Mann, brother of Nancy, W. D. and Mama

Syms.......William M. Syms, married to Rena, Nona's
    sister

Miss Thelma.......Postmistress of Pineview, married
    to Mr.Clements, mother of James and Wilma
    Nell,

Thelma Nell.......Thelma Nell Fitzgerald, daughter of
    Wilma Nell Clements and Herbert Fitzgerald

T. O. Conner.......Operated a grocery store in Pine-
    view

Tom Syms.......Daddy's first cousin, son of Syms and
    Rena

Tommy Day Wilcox.......Married to Laura, Rod's
    daughter

Tommy Stalls.......Sharecropper who worked on
    Daddy's farm

Vernon Mashburn.......Classmate from 1st through
    12th grade

Virgie Blue.......Cousin of Papa, whose mother was
    a Blue, lived with her niece, Sally Williford

W. D........Mother's brother

W. F. Stone.......Superintendant of the Pineview
    School

Walt Mann.......My first cousin, son of Ruby and Son
    Mann

Mr. Ware.......Superintendant of the Pineview School
    when Daddy and Mama were in school

Mrs. Ware.......Nora Ware, English teacher at Pine-
    view High School

Wes Conner.......Carpenter who built our house in
    1933, lived across the street from Big Irvin and
    Lillian

Will Slade.......Operated a mercantile store in Pine-
    view, lived next door to Edith and Hendley
William Syms.......Daddy's first cousin, son of Syms
    and Rena
Wilma Nell Clements.......Daughter of Mr. Clements
    and Miss Thelma, sister of James
Mrs. Wilson.......Married to Henry Wilson, Pineview's
    telephone operator
Dr. Witherington.......Pineview's Veterinarian
Yellow Duxie.......Mary, washed our clothes
Zell Mann.......My first cousin, daughter of Ruby and
    Son Mann

PROLOGUE

Marie and I reached a compromise. The best time for me to stay overnight at the Hostel was on Fridays. She knew the Hostel was my favorite place to go. Ever since we opened in 1975, my biggest thrill was to sit around a table, having lively conversations with backpackers from countries around the world. There was no better way for me to learn about new and interesting places to travel.

Saturday mornings meant chore time at the Hostel to do things like raking leaves, cutting dead trees, pruning vegetation, and the like. But my favorite was to wander the trails, bushwhacking gallberry plants and palmettos from the pathway to make them easily accessible for hikers.

One Saturday morning, November 11, 1978, to be exact, found me with heavier things weighing on my mind. I couldn't concentrate on clearing trails for thinking of my daddy. He'd just come home from the Macon Hospital where he'd been confined for over a week. Twenty years of diabetes had played havoc on his body. His doctor had even entertained the possibility of amputating his legs, an option I didn't want to think about.

November 11th was also my parents' wedding anniversary. While it seemed totally unrealistic at the time, I had a nagging urge to make the six-hour roundtrip to Pineview to see him. I called Marie. "What do you think of us riding up to Pineview and taking some flowers to my folks for their anniversary?"

"What are we going to do with the children?" Jeff was ten, Ted was twelve, Susan was fourteen. I knew they didn't want to go. At those ages, they have their own activities planned.

"They'll be O.K.," I said. "We'll just go up for a short visit, take some flowers, maybe some food, and come back later tonight. Can't they go down to Cookie's until we get back?"

Marie, sensing the urgency in my voice, called about a half-hour later and told me she'd made arrangements for the children and would pick me up at the Hostel shortly.

We got to Pineview about three o'clock. Mama met us at the door with a somber expression. "He's not good," she said.

I walked back to the den. He didn't see or hear me. He was absorbed by the Georgia-Florida football game on TV. I hugged him. I could tell he was weak and out of breath.

"I think I'll get in the bed," he said.

That was a not a statement I'd expect to hear from him. He hadn't even asked about Marie. It was no secret in our family. They truly loved each other. They had amazingly similar characteristics, both being classic Libras. He asked me one time in all seriousness, "Does she have any faults at all?"

He stumbled into bed. His breathing was erratic. He seemed to be struggling to inhale.

By that time, Mama was on the phone calling his doctor. Gus Batts had not only been his doctor since before I was born, but also one of his best friends. They bartered their trades. Daddy prepared his income tax returns. He took care of Daddy's healthcare needs.

"They're sending an ambulance," Mama said.

"I'm not going back to that damn hospital," he yelled.

Characteristic of their forty-five years of marriage, she paid no attention to what he said.

Within fifteen minutes, two uniformed medical technicians rang the doorbell. They lifted Daddy off the bed onto a gurney and carried him through the kitchen next to the table where the large bouquet of white daisies we'd brought lay unattended.

I sat beside him in the ambulance holding his hand. His face was chalky-white. The young driver sped away. The last time I saw scenery on that road flying by like that was when I tried to see how fast my daddy's car would go at the age of 16. Occasionally, I looked out the window and caught glimpses of the fields of unpicked cotton. When I was young, no cotton would ever be seen in the fields past September. I tried to comfort my daddy. I could tell he was afraid. I was, too.

Dr. Batts met us at the emergency room of the Hawkinsville Hospital. Mama had driven her car behind the ambulance, and Marie had taken ours. The three of us stood around the table where he lay. His body was painfully writhing as the doctor listened through the stethoscope.

"We need to get him back to Macon as quick as we can. I'll call the doctor up there," he said.

Dr. Batts hopped into the back of the ambulance where I'd been sitting. I rode with Mama in her car, while Marie followed. We quickly lost sight of the ambulance with its screaming siren, traveling at a breakneck rate, and running every red light.

On arrival at the Coliseum Hospital, we hurried through the front door instead of the emergency room. One of my classmate's sisters from Finleyson was working on the reception desk. "You need to go up to the third floor where Dr. Batts will meet you," she said.

When the elevator doors opened on third floor, he was standing in the hallway waiting for us. His sunken face told the outcome without speaking.

"I did everything I could," he said, shaking his head over the loss of his close friend. "We used the defibrillator as many times as we could but never got any response."

"He's dead?" I asked the obvious question.

He directed us into a private room. Mama saw and heard everything, but started talking nonsense like she can do sometimes. "Dr. Batts, do you think we should've taken off his legs? What do you think we could've done? Could we have changed his medicine?"

"Do you realize what he just said?" I stopped her ridiculous line of questioning. "Daddy's dead! Don't you understand, he's dead!" I turned around and rammed my fist into the wall with all the force I could muster. To my knowledge, I'd never done anything like that before in my life. But it just didn't seem possible that my daddy was gone.

Once I calmed down, I searched for a pay phone to call my sister in Houston to tell her the bad news. I couldn't bring myself to say anything more than our daddy was gone.

Even though it was ten o'clock, Marie insisted on making the four-hour drive from Macon back to St. Simons. Being the good mother she has always been, she wanted to make sure the children were O.K. She told me later she cried so much on the drive back, she had to pull off the road several times.

I drove Mama back to Pineview. I guess she was in shock. She never shed a tear. She continued to talk about his health issues over the past month, and what the doctors at the Macon hospital had said about him. She obviously needed to flush out what was on her mind. I let her talk without interruption. Her ramblings seemed more important than anything I had to say.

We'd called some of the family members in Pineview before we left Macon. When we drove into the driveway, a number of friends and family were waiting for us even though it was past midnight: W.D. and Mary, William and Tom Syms, Ruby Mann, and several others.

Daddy had, for years, read the obituaries first thing in the newspaper each morning. He always made the same comment. "If I don't see my name, then I go on about my day." On Monday morning his name appeared. I wondered if he might be reading it over my shoulders and saying something like, "Well, this is it."

At the funeral, the church was overflowing with his friends and our family. His favorite hymns were sung, and he was appropriately buried in the Pine-view Cemetery at the foot of his mother and daddy's grave.

After going back to St. Simons, I called my mother every night to try to get a feel for her reaction. I wondered how she was coping. Was she still in shock? Had it sunk in? I knew she was a tough old bird, but, yet, I still had to reassure myself.

Thanksgiving was only a few days away. Marie and I and the three children arrived in Pineview on Wednesday night, as we'd done for no telling how many years. For Wednesday night's dinner, it never failed that Mama served barbeque and Brunswick stew prepared by Gene Wells.

When she yelled for us to come to the table, we all walked into the dining room to take our usual places. I went to my chair, the place where I'd sat for all 42 years of my life. As I started to sit down, Mama pointed to me, then to Daddy's chair. I looked at her and hesitated. I don't guess I'd ever eaten a meal at this table when Daddy was not there.

I walked around to the head of the table as directed. It somehow didn't seem right for me to take his chair, the only one with arms. Mama looked at me, "Would you ask the blessing?" That was a bit much. It hit me for the first time that I'd inadvertently ascended to the head male member of the family, the patriarch, perhaps. I certainly didn't feel worthy of that distinction. It made me wonder how sons of kings must feel on the demise of their reigning father.

The next morning, in the privacy of the den, while Marie and the children watched the Macy's Parade on TV, Mama and I talked about probating my daddy's will and transferring his assets into her name. Even though I speak about these things almost daily with clients, it seemed unpleasantly awkward to be talking about probating my own father's will.

After being there three days and nights and carefully observing how Mama appeared to be handling things, on Saturday morning she asked me to go with her to his bedroom. "I need you to go through his clothes to see if there's anything you want. I'm going to take what you don't want to Goodwill."

That was one thing I really did not want to do. But then again, I knew it needed to be done for her sake. "I certainly can't wear his shoes," I said. "He wore an 8½, and I wear an 11. And his pants? He wears a thirty-eight. I'm a thirty-two."

"What about his sweaters and jackets?" she tried to encourage me.

"I don't think so, Mama. Why don't I just take a tie?" I thumbed through the rack of what were obviously expensive ties. I found a black one with a sophisticated design that would be nice when I dress-up.

She looked at me with that look I've seen too many times before. As if I were dishonoring his name, she asked, "Is that all you want of your daddy's?" Without a doubt, no one in the world has the power to inflict guilt on me like she could.

"Mama, I really don't want anything else. It just feels awkward. I'm not him. I could never be him. He was who he was. I am who I am."

She'd heard those remarks from me too many times before. After I said it, I wished I hadn't. When I was not at my law office, I wore what my other friends wore: tattered jeans, a T-shirt with the print of some famous rock band, and a pair of worn out sneakers. He, on the contrary, dressed at all times as if he were going to church or to some semi-formal occasion. When he visited us, he was the only person who walked on the beach wearing a coat and tie. In my growing-up years, he always wore a suit, a dress hat, a white shirt, a nice tie, and well-polished shoes.

"All right, if that's the way you feel, I'll just give all of your daddy's things to Goodwill," she said disgustedly. It was her way of punishing me. After a few minutes of silence, she said, "But there's one thing I insist you do while you're here. I want you to go through his chest of drawers." It was completely unnecessary for her to add, "And I think you should do it right now." Every request from her was always urgent.

"OK, Mama, don't worry, I'll go through everything in his drawers in just a second."

She walked out, and I started pulling out drawers. They were crammed to the brim with papers and envelopes and bank statements dating back to kingdom come. He never threw anything away. One manila envelope was marked "Legal Papers." It had a copy of his will and his power of attorney. The rest of that drawer was filled with cancelled checks dated more than five, ten, or fifteen years back. There were numerous current and out of date insurance policies for homeowners, medical, accidental death, cancer, and others.

When I got to the bottom drawer, having filled two cardboard boxes with junk to put in the garbage, I ran across three, large manila envelopes unmarked. I opened the first one and pulled out a stack of letters and cards. There may've been at least a hundred. I poured them onto the floor and started thumbing through them. All of them were from me to him. Postcards, letters from me when I left home for the first time to go to Davidson College, the ones from the University of Georgia, those from the time I was in the army, and all I'd written him since Marie and I married. There were Christmas cards, birthday cards, Fathers' Day cards I'd sent. They were all there. All of them. I got up from the floor, walked in his bathroom, locked the door, sat down on the floor, and cried my heart out. For some unexplained reason, I hadn't shed a tear since he'd died twelve days earlier. But that was the crack in the dam that opened the floodgate.

I stuck my head under the faucet in his bathtub and let cold water run over my hair and face and neck until I couldn't take the cold any longer. Red-eyed, I dried off, unlocked the door and walked out to gather up the letters and cards.

The second envelope was a similar one with all the correspondence from my sister. I put it aside to save for her since she'd planned to come back home for Christmas.

I wondered what the third envelope would contain. I opened it slowly, emptied it on the floor, and began to search the contents. I couldn't believe my eyes. I thought I'd burned them all years ago. But there they were. It looked like all the letters I'd written as a young boy to my dog, Henry, after he'd been run over by a car. When I started writing them, I was convinced Henry was in dog heaven and needed to hear all the news from Pineview. I couldn't believe Daddy had kept them. I crawled up in his bed, fixed the pillows so I could sit up, and began to read.

January 10, 1942

Dear Henry,

I'm sorry you died. I cried when you got run over. You were laying in the road in front of the house when I first saw you. And I miss you so much. I miss hearing you bark at other dogs. And I miss seeing you chase Miss Thelma's cat. Daddy said you smelled bad but you didn't smell bad to me.

I asked Nona if dogs went to heaven. She said of course they go to dog heaven. I ask her if dogs could read in heaven. She said in heaven everything is perfect. She was pretty sure that dogs would be able to read. I asked her if she'd help me write a letter to you. So here it is.

I wanted to let you know I got a new baby sister. Mama and Daddy went down to the Fitzgerald Hospital to pick her up.

A few weeks ago Daddy asked me how would I like to have a new baby in the family. I told him I didn't see as how we really needed one. I got Irvin to play with.

I guess they thought I might want one cause Irvin got a little baby sister last year. But I don't. Irvin's baby sister cries all the time. She throws up on people when they pick her up. She wets her pants and messes up her diapers. Why would anybody want something like that around the house?

Mama and Daddy brought their new baby home yesterday. They said her name is Mary. They put her in a basket looking thing that has a soft pillow inside it. Mama said they put me in it when I was a baby. But I don't remember it.

This baby is pretty ugly. Her face is red looking and she is as baldheaded as my basketball. I can't see a hair on her head. I was worried she might have a crooked nose like that woman who goes to our church. If we had to have a new baby I wish Mama could've at least picked out one that looked better.

Why didn't they get a little boy so I could have another friend to play with besides Irvin? But I guess boys probably cost a lot more than girls and Mama always tries to buy the cheapest thing she can find.

I asked Mama if the baby didn't work out could we send her back and get a new dog instead. She said I'm only 5 ½, and when the baby gets older I'll probably like her a lot better. But I'm not sure I will.

Daddy said we all have to sleep in one bedroom cause it's cold outside and he needs to keep the fireplace burning all night. Sometimes I hear him when he gets up in the middle of the night to throw a few pieces of coal on the fire. It makes a crackling sound like when Mama is cooking popcorn. He said when the weather gets warmer the front room could be all mine if I'd like to sleep up there. I think I do but I'm not sure if I'll get scared trying to sleep up there by myself.

I told Mama I sure hope the baby won't cry too much. She said there is no way it could cry as much as I did. She said she was going to try to nurse the new baby. I'm not sure what that means. She said she didn't nurse me cause she had read a baby book that said that cow's milk was better than nurse milk. She said I screamed all night and all day too. Dr. McAllister from Rochelle had to come see about me a lot of times. He gave Mama a bottle of paregoric to give me so I would sleep all night. Daddy said that every time they would give me a bottle of milk I'd drink it and start screaming. Now that I'm 5 ½ I don't cry when I drink milk but it still makes my stomach hurt and makes me hoarse.

Well, Henry, I hope everything is all right with you up there in heaven and that you're having fun cause things are not really very good down here.

Love,
Tom

April 4, 1942

Dear Henry,

I like to go to Edith's house. Mama lets me go anytime I want to. Edith said she remembers looking out her window and seeing me with a bottle of milk in one hand and a passy in the other coming up the red hill by myself.

I'm 6 years old now and I don't drink milk out of a bottle anymore. And I sure don't take a passy. I quit doing that when I was 5.

At Edith's house I get to play with Jamie and Sister and Boy. Jamie is 20. Sister is 18. Boy is 16. They're a lot bigger than me but I still like to play with them. A lot of times I play chase with Boy. Sometimes we play hide and go seek. I like Boy even if he is 16. His best friend is Henry McLeod. They're the same age and they play together like me and Irvin play together.

Jamie is off at college but she's at home in the summer. Jamie's boyfriend is Elbert Hickman. He's in the war.

When Sister and her friends are at Edith's house they make me put on a dress. Sister turns on the record player. They make me dance with a dress on. I don't like to dress up like a girl. But if I don't Sister will call Dr. Witherington and tell him to come up there and give me a shot. I'll do anything to keep from getting a shot.

Dr. Witherington is a horse doctor. He has an office downtown. Every time I walk by it smells like the bad stink that comes out of our medicine cabinet at home. We don't have a people doctor in Pineview so Dr. Witherington helps out a lot of people when they get sick. He gave me a shot one time. I don't ever want him to give me another one. I think he used a horse needle. It really hurt bad.

I'll write you again sometime real soon.

Love,
Tom

June 4, 1942

Dear Henry,

You remember how me and Irvin sometimes jump on the back of people's cars and they don't even know we're there. I came pretty close to joining you up in heaven the other day.

We jumped on the back bumper of Irvin's mama's car. Some cars we jump on have something to hold on to. But her car didn't. She took off really fast. We wrapped our arms around the back of the car. She was going so fast we started screaming at her to stop. But she had the radio on so she couldn't hear us. We started beating on the back of the car with our hands. She didn't know what the noise was. She thought it was something wrong with the motor. When she stopped we jumped off and ran as fast as we could to Edith's house. We have some really good hiding places inside her barn.

Irvin got a whipping that night when his daddy came home. I wondered why I didn't get one. But I was lucky. Irvin's mama and daddy went out of town. My mama and daddy didn't hear about it until they got back. They jumped on me real good. But I didn't get a whipping.

Mama acted like she was mad about it. "Don't you know you could've been killed?"

I didn't tell her but I thought I was going to get killed, too.

Me and Irvin haven't jumped on anybody's car since. But it's still the fastest way for us to get around town.

Love,
Tom

July 17, 1942

Dear Henry,

Sometimes Mama and Daddy get really mad with me. They tell me not to talk back. How will they know what I think if I don't tell them?

They say I'm a smart aleck. I'm not really a smart aleck but I have to let them know my side of it. If I don't tell them how else will they know?

Daddy says I'd argue with a sign post. But I wouldn't. I wouldn't want to argue with a sign post. Why would I want to do that? But I would argue with Mama and Daddy when they say things that don't seem right to me.

I can tell when they start getting mad. Daddy gets red in the face. Mama swells up. Her hair sticks out on the ends. When I see that I head out the backdoor for Nona's.

Last night Daddy got mad at me about something I said while we were eating supper. He shoved his chair back so hard it almost turned over. I knew he was coming after me. I jumped up and ran out the backdoor as fast as I could to Nona's. He came running right inside her house behind me. But I can outrun him.

He told Nona he had to teach me a lesson.

"Don't you lay a hand on him," she said. I knew I was safe as long as I was with her and Daddy knew it too.

When I was little and couldn't outrun Mama she used to lock me up in the closet when she got mad with me. I'd scream and scream and scream and beat on the door but she wouldn't open it. It was dark in there. You couldn't turn on a light from inside the closet cause the light switch was on the outside. When I got tired of screaming I'd start crying. It was scary in there. After a while Mama would open the door and let me out.

She'd tell me if I didn't want to get locked up in that closet I'd better do what she tells me. She screams at me and tells me I'm going to kill her.

I seem to always get in trouble every time she tells me to do something or not do something. I feel like I ought to have the right to say what I think.

One time when she got really mad with me she dug her fingernails in my arm and made it bleed. I ran across the street to her mama's house where Joan lives.

I showed Joan my arm. She called Ruby and told her mama what had happened.

Ruby asked me if my mama did that to me.

I told her yes.

She said she shouldn't be doing things like that.

I'm not a bad person. I don't drink liquor. I don't smoke. I don't gamble. I've quit cussing now that I'm 6. The preacher said if you don't do those things you'll go to heaven.

So, what do you think, Henry? Am I a bad boy cause I talk back to my daddy and mama? I could always say anything in the whole world to you and you'd never get mad with me.

Well, I guess I better go now. Mama and Daddy think I'm in my room asleep. It's past my bedtime but I needed to tell you what's on my mind.

Love,
Tom

August 9, 1942

Dear Henry

Me and Irvin love to go fishing. Next to going swimming and playing cars that's our favorite thing to do. When school gets out in May we start talking about how we want some fish. Most of the time we go to Cob Creek. It's just a half a mile from town.

We dig earth worms for bait. Daddy showed me how to put a flat stone on the ground in our back yard. He told me to remind Mama to put all her coffee grounds under the stone. That makes a bunch of good earth worms that are fat. It makes the fish want to eat them. We put them in a tin can and stuff an old sock on top so they won't crawl out.

Nona and Papa have a patch of bamboo in their backyard. They make the best fishing poles you can get. When we run out of hooks we have to go down to W.D.'s store to get a nickels worth. We buy a spool of number 8 thread for fishing line. It costs a dime. Then we head out with our bamboo poles over our shoulders walking beside the road toward Cob Creek.

Sometimes we walk in the road and sometimes on the path where the old railroad track used to be. When we get just past the nigra quarters there's a lot of red clay on the side of the road. Sometimes cars slide in the ditch there when its been raining real hard. That clay can get real slippery. When it's like that me and Irvin sqush it up between our toes and roll it into balls to throw at each other. We like getting it between our toes.

Our mamas make us wear shoes to church and Sunday school but that's the only time we put them on in the summer. Mama makes me wash my feet every night before I go to bed. Sometimes it's kinda hard to get all that clay off.

One time when we were walking to Cob Creek Irvin said we ought to hide behind the big clay hill and throw one of those clay balls at the next car that comes by. We had to wait a long time for a car. But finally we saw Miss Colin Slade's long black car headed toward Pineview. She's so short she can hardly see over the steering wheel. Anytime she rides by you can only see the top of her hat through the window. About the time her car went by we splattered the side of it with clay balls.

We then walked on down to Cob Creek and got underneath the bridge and started fishing. We found an old peanut butter jar. We rinsed it out to put the fish in. You hardly ever catch a fish that won't fit in a peanut butter jar.

We'd just about filled up the jar with fish when we looked up and saw T.O. Connor walking down under the bridge.

"What you boys doing?" He acted kinda serious. Usually T.O. is real friendly. He teases us a lot about most everything.

"We just fishing," I said.

"Do your mamas know you're down here?"

"No," I said.

Neither one of us ever told anybody where we were going cause we both just turned 7. We can go anywhere we want to as long as we're home by dark. Our mamas don't care anyway cause they're always playing bridge.

T. O looked at me. "Which one of you threw some clay at Miss Colin's car?"

Me and Irvin both looked at each other. I guess it was the way we looked that made him know we did it.

He tattled on us. When we got home we both got a good spanking from our daddies. After that we never did throw anything at anybody's car ever again.

I knew it was not right to throw that clay ball when we did it. Sometimes me and Irvin get in trouble for doing things we ought not to do. I sure hope it doesn't keep us from getting into heaven.

Love,
Tom

September 12, 1942

Dear Henry,

Mama makes me and my sister drink a cup of coffee for breakfast every morning. I hate it. Mama pours a half a cup of coffee in our cups then fills it up with milk. She puts two spoons of sugar in it.

We always have the same thing for breakfast every day, every day, every day. We can't leave the table until we've eaten all our eggs and toast and grits and drunk all our coffee. The only thing that's different is the meat. Sometimes we have bacon and sometimes sausage and sometimes ham.

When I told some of my friends at school I had to drink coffee every morning they said I was telling a story. But I wasn't. Some of them wanted to know what coffee tasted like. I told them it tastes like medicine.

Mama says we have to drink a glass of milk everyday for dinner and supper. I don't really like milk all that much either. It makes my stomach hurt and makes me hoarse too. Mama says I have to drink it anyway even if it does make my stomach hurt. She says it will make my bones strong and healthy.

I've never seen anybody that likes milk as much as my daddy. He drinks a glass with every meal. He must have the strongest bones of anybody in the world.

The best part of the milk to me is after it has been sitting in the refrigerator long enough for the cream to come to the top. When I get home from school I go to the refrigerator to see if the cream is on the milk. I open the jar and drink it off and lick my tongue around my lips like a cat. When Daddy gets home from work and sees the cream gone he yells and says "Why did you drink all the cream from the top of the milk?" I tell him I just can't help it. It tastes so good.

Sometimes Mama makes apple sauce. I put some in a bowl then take a spoon and scoop the cream off and put it on top of the apple sauce. That's my favorite thing to eat in the whole world.

We've started getting our milk now from Mr. Cheek. He's really nice. He comes in the back door and puts the milk in the refrigerator. He and Mrs. Cheek go to the Methodist Church. That's why Mama likes them so much. Daddy said the reason he's such a hard worker is that he's from north Georgia. They work a whole lot harder than people in south Georgia he said.

We used to get milk from Mr. Pope. I liked him cause he brought the milk on a wagon that has rubber tires on it like a car. He has a board across the front of the wagon that he sits on. He'd stop the mule in front of our house and grab up a quart he'd just milked out of his cows. He brought it up on our front porch and sat it beside the door. Sometimes he'd let me get up on his wagon and ride down the street while he took milk to other houses. I'd sit on the board beside him and wait for him. When

I'd get tired of riding he'd let me get out and walk back home.

Daddy said the milk started tasting bitter cause Mr. Pope's cows got into some bitterweed. Daddy said Mr. Cheek didn't have any bitterweed in his pasture.

I really miss not getting to ride on the back of Mr. Pope's wagon anymore. Every morning when I see him and his mule going by I always wave and yell "Hey Mr. Pope."

My daddy loves buttermilk too. Daddy and Santa Claus are the only two people I know of who like buttermilk. Every Christmas Eve I leave a glass of buttermilk on the mantle where I hang my stocking. The next morning I run in to see what Santa brought and the glass of buttermilk is always empty.

We get buttermilk at our house once or twice a week. Miss Peavy brings it. We call her the buttermilk woman. She parks her car right in front of our house and comes in the front door like a robber. She never knocks or anything. I wish I could lock our front door but it doesn't have a lock on it.

One time I was coming out of the bathroom and didn't have anything on but my underwear. I was walking up the hall to my room and looked up and there she was. The buttermilk woman had opened the front door and had come right in. She scared me so bad. Nobody else was at home but me. She can't hear good and she talks real loud. She always sounds like she's hollering at somebody when she says "Is your mama at home?"

She marches back to the kitchen stomping her feet like she's mad at somebody. She puts the buttermilk in the refrigerator then stomps back out. She always slams the door really hard.

I don't like buttermilk. It's bitter and sour and tastes like yuk. Anyway I wouldn't drink anything the buttermilk woman brought cause she's the weirdest person I know.

Love,
Tom

September 28, 1942

Dear Henry,

Today is Daddy's birthday. He's 38 years old. I'm just 6. Nona wrapped up a handkerchief and put a ribbon on it for me to give him. He said he really liked it. I hope he did.

I used to sing God Bless America to you. And do you remember I had to sing it on the stage at the stadium. I was just 3 years old. I was really scared.

Mama made me do it. I didn't want to. She made me wear my white sailor suit. A lot of school children were there to sing a song or dance or play the piano or the guitar or say a poem or something. I was not even in school. I was the youngest person there.

Mama said it's time for you to go out on the stage. I told her I wasn't going to do it. She said I had to. I knew she meant it. There was no way for me to get out of it.

I walked out on the stage. I could see a lot of people sitting in the chairs and the bleachers. W.D. and Mary were sitting on the front row looking up at me. I could seen Edith and Hendley and Nona behind them. I turned around to walk back to Mama. She pointed her finger at me and had a mean face. I'd seen that face before. I knew I either had to sing that song or get a whipping .

I was shaking. But I sang it all the way through.

     God bless America,
     Land that I love,
     Stand beside her,
     And guide her,
     Through the night with the light from above;
     From the mountains,
     To the prairies,
     To the ocean white with foam,
     God bless America,
     My home sweet home,
     God bless America,
     My home sweet home.

Nona and Edith and Daddy and Mama said I sang really good. But I think they had to say it.

Love,
Tom

October 6, 1942

Dear Henry,

I hope you're enjoying yourself up there in heaven. There's nothing to do in the summer when school's out. I love to go swimming every day. I like to go to the picture show. I work at Nona's store every Saturday afternoon. I go to Sunday School and Church every Sunday. That's about all there is to do in Pineview.

When I woke up this morning I was thinking about nicknames. I don't know a single dog that has a nickname.

Most people call me Little Tom. Papa is the real Tom. Everybody calls Irvin Little Irvin cause his daddy is Big Irvin.

Mama said she didn't like nicknames. She's had one all her life. Her real name is Mary Lou. She said her daddy started calling her Coot when she was a little girl. That's what everybody calls her. Coot. That's been her name all her life. Me and Mary call her Mama. The nigras call her Miss Coot. The only person who calls her by her real name is Mrs. Ware. She calls her Mary Lou.

Mama's older brother is named W.D. His daddy called him Son. Mama's older sister's real name is Ora Edna. Her daddy nicknamed her Nancy. Joe Walter was my Mama's little brother's name.

His daddy called him Little Son. The nigras call him Mister Little Son.

Edith and Hendley's son's real name is Hendley like his daddy. But everybody calls him Boy. The nigras call him Mister Boy.

My daddy's first cousin's nickname is Boots. His last name is Doster. My daddy has another first cousin called Crip. His real name is James Hartwell Dennard. Some people call him Bud.

Henry, I'm glad you don't have a nickname. I like your name just as it is.

Love,
Tom

October 30, 1942

Dear Henry,

How are things in heaven? It's pretty boring down here. I'm sorry you got run over. At least you're up there with Jesus and God.

I want you to know I always wanted to bring you in the house on those cold nights. It really hurt me for you to have to sleep in the garage. You know how Daddy is. He'd never in the whole world let a dog or cat in our house. If I had a house I'd let you stay inside with me as much as you wanted to. You could eat with me. You could even sleep with me.

I had another dog named Pat. She was really nice. But I didn't love her as much as I love you. Pat was white all over. I fed her table scraps just like I did you.

Daddy would get mad at Pat cause she always had puppies. One time Daddy shut her up in the smoke house. I couldn't understand why. He said she had to stay there for a few days before she could come out.

One afternoon while everybody was gone I heard Pat screaming and crying. I ran into the smoke house and there was Goat Lacey's dog. They were hung up. I'd never seen that before. Irvin said that Goat's dog had put his thing in her thing and couldn't get it out. Both of them were hollering like crazy. When Mama came home from playing

bridge she went down town and found Jack Lawrence. He came up to our house and got them
separated. Mama told Daddy about it when he
came home. He was really mad. He stomped out
the back door. He found a lock in the garage. He
nailed it on the smoke house door. He hammered it
so loud and hard I thought he was going to tear the
whole place down. He said it would never happen
again. When I told Goat about what happened
he thought it was funny. He laughed really loud.

A few weeks later Pat had puppies. Daddy said
we had to give them all away. There was a boy
puppy that was really pretty. He was white with
black patches. I begged Daddy to let me keep
him. I told him boy dogs don't have puppies. I
named him Jackie. He was really a good dog. We
used to play together a lot.

One day when I came home from school Mama
said Jackie was chasing a car and got hit. The
wheel didn't run over his whole body. It only got
him on one of his back legs. He was hobbling
around trying to walk. I knew when I saw him what
was going to happen. The same thing that happened to all the rest of my dogs and cats when
they got sick or hurt.

When Daddy got home he put Jackie in the
trunk of the car and drove down to Jack Lawrence's house. Jack shot Jackie the same way he
shot all the rest of my dogs and cats. Daddy always
got Jack to do his dirty work.

Have you seen Jackie up there in heaven? If
you haven't I wish you could meet him. You'd like

him a lot. If you run into him tell him how much I miss him.

A few months later Pat got sick and Daddy had Jack Lawrence shoot her just like all the rest of them. I told Daddy I wish we could take her to a doctor. Daddy said you don't spend money on taking dogs to doctors. The only doctor we have in Pineview is Dr. Witherington. And he's a horse doctor not a dog doctor.

I guess it's a good thing you got run over so you wouldn't have to get shot by Jack Lawrence.

I'll write you later on. Mama is calling me to come to supper.

Love,
Tom

November 11, 1942

Dear Henry,

My baby sister is trying to walk and talk so it looks like to me they've decided to keep her.

Nona is helping me write this just like she did the last letters I wrote you.

Now that I'm 6 I've started to school. I'm in the 1st grade. My teacher is Josephine Hardy. She and Mama were in the same class in school.

I'm learning how to read and write. We read about Dick and Jane and Baby and Spot. Miss Josephine said I could read good. I want to learn to write good so I can write letters to you all by myself.

Today is Daddy and Mama's 9th anniversary. They got married on November 11, 1933. Daddy bought a box of chocolate candy for Mama. She told him he shouldn't have done it. But she sure has been eating a lot of it.

Do you remember my two friends who are not real? One is Dren and the other is Scallop. Dren acts more like me. He's real short. We have a good time playing together. Scallop is bigger than me. He always beats me when we play marbles together.

Daddy took me to see Dr. Batts cause I had a bad cough. He gave Daddy some medicine for me to take. Daddy told him that Mama was worried about me cause I have imaginary playmates.

Dr. Batts told him to tell Mama not to worry. He said I'd grow out of it.

Daddy told him that Mama worries about everything. But he was telling a story cause he worries just as much as she does.

Dr. Batts said he'd heard that children who have imaginary playmates are unusually smart.

Ever since I got back from the doctor I've never talked out loud to Dren and Scallop in front of Mama or Daddy. I guess they think I'm crazy. But I still like to play with them.

Love,
Tom

November 30, 1942

Dear Henry,

Me and Irvin had two fights today. Usually we just have one. He's still bigger than me but most of the time I can beat him. We try to hit each other as hard as we can. Then we grab each other around the waist and see who can throw the other one on the ground.

James and Sammy and Angie were sitting in some chairs on the lawn next to James's house. They saw me and Irvin playing cars in my back yard. James told us to come over there. He said they wanted us to fight so they could watch us. We didn't want to fight cause we weren't mad at each other then. James kept on and we said no. He said he'd give a dime to the winner. We fought pretty hard. We both wanted that dime. I won. Then we went down to Mr. Clement's drugstore. You can buy two strawberry ice cream cones for a dime.

Me and Irvin play cars just about every day. I get the hoe out of the garage and scrape roads in the dirt for our cars to drive on. We make a town by scraping a wide spot. We build our houses out of dirt. We have cars and pickup trucks and a fire engine and a dump truck. We build a house for us then build other people's houses for them. We ride around on the roads with our cars and trucks. We have a fire truck that has to go to people's houses to put their fires out.   We build stores and filling stations too.

Yesterday I hit Irvin in the face and made his nose bleed. He started crying and ran home. His mama called my mama and I got a whipping. She made me go to his house and tell him I'm sorry. He came to the door. I said "Irvin I didn't mean to do it." I started crying then he started crying. We hugged each other and said we'd never fight again. But we did. We fought two times today.

Love,
Tom

December 12, 1942

Dear Henry,

Irvin told me today there's no such thing as Santa Claus. He said that our mamas and daddies are the ones who buy the toys and put them in our stockings and under our Christmas trees. I'm 6½ years old and I've believed all my life that there really was a Santa Claus. Irvin said some of the older boys down town told him. He thinks we ought to play like to our mamas and daddies that we still believe in Santa Claus so we can keep on getting presents.

Me and Irvin were sitting on the front porch talking about it today. Joan came over. You remember she's my first cousin who lives across the street. We told her that there was no such thing as Santa Claus. She got really mad. She said we were wrong cause she knew there was a Santa Claus. She said we were telling stories and we were going to get in some bad trouble. She ran across the street to her house to tell her mama.

In a few minutes, Joan came back. She said her mama told her that we didn't know what we were talking about. She said she hoped Santa heard every word we said. And that we would not get any presents cause we were saying ugly things about him. She said her mama was going to tell our mamas and we'd get a whipping.

I've been worrying about this Henry. Do you think Irvin is right or Joan is right? Could you ask Jesus or somebody up there in heaven? I need to know cause it's only 2 weeks 'til Christmas.

When you ask about Santa Claus see if you can find out about the Tooth Fairy, too.

Love,
Tom

January 9, 1943

Dear Henry,

How are things up there in heaven? They're boring as ever down here.

I'd give anything if I lived in a big town. Nothing happens here. Pineview is so little. We only have 3 long streets and 4 short streets. There's not a paved road in 10 miles from here. Cars make a lot of dust driving down the streets. I don't like it cause Mama makes me sweep the front porch.

I bet every town in the whole world has paved streets and paved sidewalks except Pineview. We just have old dirt paths running beside dirt streets. I wish some day we could have a real paved road going through town with white lines running down the middle of it.

One time when a bridge was out on the Hawkins-ville-Abbeville Highway I saw a Greyhound Bus come right through town. It's the truth. Some peo-ple don't believe it but I saw it with my own eyes. It was a real Greyhound Bus with people sitting in it looking out the window. They were probably thinking who in the world would live in a little town like this.

I lived in Atlanta one time when I was 3. That's when Daddy started to work with the Internal Rev-enue. We didn't live there too long before we moved back to Pineview. All the streets in Atlanta are paved. Every single one of them. And the side-walks too. Atlanta has a zoo with elephants and tigers and bears. I got to ride on the streetcar with Mama when she would go shopping at Davison's and Rich's. Atlanta has a lot of big stores. I wish I could live in a place where there are a lot of things to do.

In Pineview everything is slow. It's the littlest town I know except Finleyson. That's only a mile from Pineview. Old men sit on the benches in front of Sam's store playing checkers with bottle caps. I never saw anyone in Atlanta doing that.

Every Saturday afternoon the nigras come to town riding in wagons pulled by a mule. I never saw anything like that in Atlanta either. Daddy said I may not like living in an old hick town but it's where his family has lived for over a 100 years. It looks like to me if the Dennards have lived here that long they could've built a bigger town than this.

Daddy said Pineview at one time used to be a few miles from where the town is now. It was out on the road toward Bluff Creek. When they put a train track from Hawkinsville to Ocilla the people moved where they could be close to the depot. He said that was about 1900.

All around town is a bunch of cotton fields and peanut fields and corn fields and watermelon patches. Pineview had 2 cotton gins before I was born. Papa owned one of them. He had to close his down when the depression hit. He had a ware-house full of bales of cotton. The price dropped to

5 cents a pound. Daddy said he lost everything he had. Rod McLeod has the only gin now.

Daddy said I should be happy to live around my family. My mama's parents live right across the street from us. My daddy's parents live right behind us. My uncles and aunts live next to them. Mama's daddy died the year I was born. His name was Bill Mann.

Daddy said when he was little Pineview had saloons. That's where men go to drink liquor. He said they all shut down when they had prohibition. He said that means they passed a law that nobody could drink liquor. Daddy said they used to have a lot of fights and bad things going on when they had saloons. I'm glad they don't have them now.

Just about everybody in town goes to church. We have 2 churches. Methodist and Baptist. When somebody in the town doesn't go to church, the people who do go say ugly things about them.

Daddy said I should feel lucky to live in Pineview cause we have a good school. He wants me to get a good education and go to college. Pineview has one of the best schools in the state he said. That's cause Mr. and Mrs. Ware came to town to teach school when my daddy and mama were real little. Daddy said Mr. and Mrs. Ware were the most educated people he ever knew. Daddy took Latin and French in school. They taught him about the Greeks and the Romans. He took calculus and all kinds of really smart things like that. He said everybody in my family went to college. They all may not have finished, but at least they went for a while.

My daddy went to GMC in Milledgeville. It's a military school. Mr. Jenkins from Vienna was the head of the school. Mama went to Wesleyan College in Macon. She studied music. Daddy said people in Pineview feel they're as good as anybody.

But if Pineview is such a good town why do all the other towns have paved roads? Rochelle is 12 miles away. Hawkinsville is 14 miles. Cordele is 23 miles. Abbeville is 18 miles. They all have paved roads. I don't count Finleyson cause it's really not a town. It just has a bank and a grocery store. It's like Pineview. It doesn't have any paved roads either.

Most of the people in Pineview are either Dennards or McLeods. They're all my cousins. Some are 3rd cousins on my daddy's side and 1st cousins on my mama's side.

The nigras live in the quarters. Nona said she didn't ever want to hear me say the word nigger cause that was really an ugly word. I should always call them nigras. That was the nice way to say it she said. Sometimes I hear men downtown calling them niggers. I know better than say that word cause I'll get in trouble.

My mama's last name before she married my daddy was Mann. Some people tease me. They say my daddy married a man.

Henry, I really miss you. I promise you I'm going to write you a letter every chance I get.

Love,
Tom

January 29, 1943

Dear Henry,

Henry, it's that time of year again. Cold enough to kill hogs. Nona said it went below freezing yesterday. Late in the afternoon Daddy wanted me to ride to the farm with him. He didn't tell me what he was planning to do. We drove up to the big house. Several nigra men were sitting on the porch in their overalls. They jumped off the porch when they saw Daddy driving up. One of them said, "We got them hogs in the pen last night, Mr. Ed."

Daddy got out and told me to stay in the car. He walked across the road toward the barn with the nigra men. I could see about ten hogs in the pen oinking really loud. They acted like they were real hungry. A pickup truck was backed up to the hog pen. One of the nigra men had a big sledge hammer in his hand. All of them except Daddy crawled over the fence into the pen with the hogs. The hogs were oinking like crazy. Two of the men grabbed one of the hogs by the back legs and held them up so he couldn't run. The one with the sledge hammer raised it up in the air like he was about to chop some wood. He came down on the hog's head so hard with that sledge hammer the hog fell over dead on the ground. They picked it up and slung it over on the back of the truck.

I got out of the car. It was really cold. The wind was blowing hard. I was walking toward Daddy when he yelled at me to get back in that car right now.

I went back to the car like Daddy said and watched out the back window. The nigra man kept slamming the heads of the hogs with the sledge hammer. The others would throw the dead hog up on the back of the truck. The hogs that hadn't been killed were screaming and yelling and oinking really loud like they were scared to death.

Last night when I went to bed every time I closed my eyes I could see that man hitting those hogs on the head with the sledge hammer. I could hear them oinking and screaming cause they didn't want to die.

When I woke up this morning, I forgot it was Saturday. It's always a good thing when I don't have to go to school. I couldn't find anybody in the house. Then I heard a commotion out back. I looked out the window. Our back yard was full of nigra men and women from the farm. Daddy had driven down there before daylight this morning to pick up the hands in his car. The rest of them sat on the back of the truck with the syrup kettle. When they got to our house they filled up the syrup kettle with water and built a big fire under it. Daddy and Nona were busy setting up tables and getting knives and things. It was so cold. I went back in the house and put on my jacket then went over to the syrup kettle where the fire was blazing to warm my hands.

When the water started boiling, the nigra men began unloading the dead hogs from the back of the truck and tossing them over into the hot water. After scalding the hogs for a while two of the biggest men picked them up out of the water and spread the hogs out on the tables. Nona had an old straight razor that Papa used to use. She started shaving the hair off the hogs.

I asked her where she learned to shave hogs. She said I used to shave your papa all the time.

After Nona got all the hair off the first hog, one of the nigra women started cutting the throat and draining all the blood in a bucket. Nona said in a low voice so no one could hear. Nigras love to eat blood puddin'.

Daddy said they'll eat any part of the hog except the squeal.

I didn't see why the nigras couldn't eat whatever they wanted. They were the ones who did all the work feeding the hogs and killing them and cutting them all up. The only thing Daddy did was buy the feed for them.

They separated the hams and shoulders and sides from the rest of the meat cause that's what has to hang up in our smokehouse. They rubbed it down with salt and wrapped it in strips of cloth. Before Mama cooks supper, she goes out to the smokehouse with a sharp butcher knife and slices off some ham to go in the peas and beans then slices some side meat to go in the turnip greens. Sometimes she fries some slices of the side meat really brown like bacon. Papa calls it streak of lean.

Our smokehouse has pine straw spread out all over the bottom of it. Daddy has to make sure that no rats or roaches or any other things are in there that can eat the meat. After the meat is cured nothing will bother it he said. I guess rats don't like salty meat.

My favorite part of the hog is the tenderloin. Mama cooks it really good with lots of gravy. It's so tender you don't even need a knife to cut it. She makes some rice and puts brown gravy on the rice and it sure is good.

The part of the hog I hate most is the chitlins. They stink so bad. I know you wouldn't eat them either Henry. Nona said they are the hog's intestines. Mama won't cook them and won't let Daddy cook them either cause they smell up the kitchen too bad. He has to go over to Nona's house and get her to cook them. Nona doesn't eat them either but she'd do anything for Daddy cause Mama says he's her baby.

They grind up some of the meat and put hot peppers and sage and salt and black pepper and other stuff to make the sausage. They have to be careful when they take the casings off the intestines cause that's what they use to stuff the sausage in. I love sausage. My daddy hangs the long links about as tall as I am over the smokehouse rafters. Mama goes out in the mornings and cuts off some of the links for breakfast cause Daddy says he has to have meat to eat for all three meals. If he doesn't get sausage for breakfast then Mama has to go to the smokehouse and get some bacon or ham.

The nigras take a big black iron wash pot like Yellow Mary uses to wash our clothes in and builds a big fire underneath it. They chop most of the fat meat off the hogs and cut it up in little pieces. They throw all those little fat pieces of meat into the hot wash pot to make lard. That's what Mama uses to fry all the meat we eat. She makes cakes with lard and biscuits and the crust for pies. I like to eat cracklins that float to the top of the lard when it's boiling hot. They turn really brown. Nona scrapes them out of the pot with a wire basket. Mama and Nona use them to make cracklin bread. That's some good stuff to eat. Daddy likes to pour cane syrup over cracklin bread when he eats it. That's good, too.

Nona likes to eat brains and eggs. She gets part of the brains and gives the rest to the nigras. Sometimes she fixes brains and eggs for me when I spend the night with her. I hate to tell her but it's not all that good. If Daddy wants some brains he has to go over to Nona's house to get her to fix them. Mama won't eat them or fix them.

Daddy likes souse meat too. The nigras take all the rest of the meat inside the hog's head and stuff it together some kind of way. Then they put it in the refrigerator. It looks like it has Jell-O in it. When it gets hard in the refrigerator Daddy slices it and puts it between two pieces of light bread. He dabs some mustard and mayonnaise on it and says it tastes so good. I don't like to eat something that comes out of a hog's head.

It got really cold by the end of the day. Our back yard smelled like dead hogs. Everybody was tired and fussing at each other and had blood all over their clothes and little pieces of meat on their jackets and looked stinking and nasty. I'd had enough of it.

The nigras started gathering up all the blood and some of the chitlins and brains and heart and tail and feet that Daddy gave them. He might've given them some other meat too. They all jumped in the truck and went back to the farm. I helped Nona carry everything she wanted that would fit in her refrigerator. The rest went in our refrigerator.

Daddy said he read in the newspaper that one day there would be freezers where you could freeze vegetables and meat in your own house. That would seem funny cause then you wouldn't need a smoke house.

Mama asked me if I wanted some pork chops for supper. I told her I'd rather have a fried egg sandwich.

Love,
Tom

February 7, 1943

Dear Henry,

Today is Mama's birthday. She's 32. I'm just 6½. Nona wrapped up a handkerchief for me to give her and a birthday card too. I think Mama liked it. Nona said it was a pretty handkerchief. It was good enough to take to church she said. I always try to be nice to Mama on her birthday.

But even on her birthday she always has to ask me if I've been to the bathroom. She said if I missed a day I'd get constipated. And that can cause bad things to happen. Some people have even died Mama said.

Sometimes she acts like she doesn't believe me when I tell her I did go. She will come in and look to make sure I'm not telling a story. If I can't go at all or if it's just a little tiny one she gets the Salapatica out of the medicine cabinet. She puts it in water and stands there until I've drunk it all gone. In about an hour or two I always have to go. That stuff tasted awful. It's so salty. But it's better than her giving me an enema. That's what she usually does when I can't go.

Today she wanted me to take something new called Carter's Little Liver Pills. They're so tiny that even I can swallow them.

When I spend the night with Nona she gives me Exlax. She says it tastes like chocolate. But it really tastes bitter to me. I've had to take so much of it that I don't like Exlax or chocolate either.

A lot of times Mama makes me eat prunes. I like to eat prunes cause then I don't have to worry about going to the bathroom.

Daddy said I should be thankful that all these medicines have been invented. Nona always gave him a dose of Castor Oil when he was little. He said he was glad I never had to take it cause it made him gag.

I don't guess you have to worry about things like that up in heaven do you? I'll be glad when I get there so I won't have to worry about it either.

Love,
Tom

April 16, 1943

Dear Henry,

Mama likes to play the piano. She says she's been playing ever since she was a little girl. When she graduated from high school she went to Wesleyan Conservatory in Macon to take piano lessons. She teaches it to some of the little children in Pineview. She tried her best to teach me. But it always ended up with us getting mad at each other. Daddy said it's because we're too much alike.

Mama got Sammy Dennard to give me piano lessons. I don't mind taking lessons from Sammy. He's a good teacher. But I don't like to practice. When I walk out of his house he says "Practice, practice, practice." But the things he gives me to play will be something by Chopin or Mozart or Beethoven or some guys like that. Daddy said I should be taking boogie-woogie. He's right. I like to play songs like Chop Sticks and Dark Town Strutter's Ball and Alexander's Ragtime Band and things like that.

The worst thing about taking piano lessons from Sammy is that he always likes to have recitals. I hate recitals. I have to memorize a Chopin Etude or Moonlight Sonata or some of those really hard things to play. We always have the recitals at the Baptist Church. All the students have to wait their turn in one of the Sunday school rooms in the back of the church. Irvin and Joan and Betty Jean and Evelyn Barfield and Annette Connor and a bunch of others are all sitting there talking about how nervous they are. I'm usually shaking all over.

When my time comes to play I straighten my tie and button up my coat and walk into the church in front of all those people. The pews are filled with mamas and daddies and grandparents and brothers and sisters. All the students wish they weren't there. I face the audience and say something like "I shall play Etude in E Minor by Frederic Chopin" then I sit down at the piano. I wipe my sweaty hands on my pants leg and start playing. Even though I've played it a hundred times I'm always so nervous. I start playing as fast as I can so I can hurry up and finish.

Mama plays the piano at home a lot. She gave the new piano to my Daddy for his birthday but he can't play a single note. After supper every night Mama has to get my sister to bed cause she's just a baby. While she washes the dishes Daddy goes out to the garage to drink some liquor. Then we all go in the living room for Mama to play the piano. Mama usually wants me to sing something first. She plays some church songs and stuff like that. But I'd rather sing something else. She's been trying to teach me to sing Old Man River cause she really likes that song. I can play it on the piano, but it's a hard song to sing.

After I finish singing then Daddy gets up and stands by the piano. If he's too drunk he just sits in his chair and sings. Mama pulls out the sheet music from the piano bench and plays the songs that he likes. He loves to sing songs like

> I love you truly, truly dear;
> Life with its sorrows, life with its cheer;
> Fades into dreams when I feel you are near;
> For I love you truly, truly dear."

He wants me to clap my hands and tell him how good he sings. If I don't, he gets mad.

He likes to sing "Because God made thee mine I'll cherish thee." He sings that song for every wedding when anybody gets married in Pineview. Sometimes while he's singing I can see tears running down his cheek.

One of his favorite popular songs is,

> I'm going to buy a paper doll that I can call my own,
> A doll that other fellows cannot steal;
> And with the flirty, flirty eyes of those flirty, flirty guys
> Will have to flirt with dollies that are real;
> When I come home at night she will be waiting;
> She'll be the truest doll in all the world;
> I'd rather have a paper doll to call my own,
> Than have a fickle-minded real live girl."

He likes to sing,

> I'll get by as long as I have you;
> Though there be rain and darkness, too;
> I'll not complain;
> I'll see it through."

The sheet music has a picture of Spencer Tracy on it.

Probably his most favorite is,

> Don't throw bouquets at me;
> Don't please my folks too much;
> Don't laugh at my jokes too much;
> People will say we're in love.

The sheet music for that one has Oklahoma written on it. Mama said that's because it's from a Broadway play.

Mama keeps the sheet music to all these songs inside the piano bench ready for him to sing every night. I can play most all those songs by heart, just picking them out, and playing them by ear. I know how to jazz them up when I play them.

Daddy sings them like they're sad songs. It's because he drinks that liquor. Sometimes I get so mad with him for drinking that I don't speak to him. I go in my room and close the door.

Sometimes I cry cause I know he's going to hell. That's what the preacher at church says. "If anybody drinks liquor, they're going straight to hell." I don't know why Daddy can't understand that. I want him to be in heaven with you and me and Nona and Edith and Mama and Mary.

I'll write you again soon.

Love,
Tom

May 17, 1943

Dear Henry,

You remember how Angie sometimes comes out on her back porch and calls me to come over to her house. I really like Angie. She's my friend. Today is her birthday. She's 12. In 13 more days I'll be 7.

When she called me today, I crawled through the hole in my daddy's board fence and went to see her. I like to go in her bedroom. She has pictures of movie stars all over her walls. Her favorite is Van Johnson, but she has pictures of Clark Gable and Cary Grant and Gary Cooper and Humphrey Bogart and Mickey Rooney and Gene Kelly and Cornel Wilde and Montgomery Clift and a whole bunch of others. She has pictures of girl movie stars, too, like Veronica Lake and Betty Grable and Esther Williams and Greer Garson and Barbara Stanwyck and Bette Davis and Vivian Leigh and Irene Dunne and Ginger Rogers and Katharine Hepburn, and some others. I can't even remember all of them. When she joins their fan club, they send her a picture.

Angie sometimes teaches me songs. One of my favorites is:
>Mares eat oats
>And Does eat oats,

And Little Lambs eat ivy
A Kid'll eat ivy, too,
Wouldn't you? Ooh?

Another one she taught me that I like a lot is:
Oh you're ugly,
Man, you're ugly,
You're some ugly child;
The clothes that you wear
Are not in style;
You look like an ape every time you smile;
How I hate you,
You alligator bait you;
Why don't you lay down and die?
You big foot, flat foot, floppy eared too;
How'd they ever get a pair of shoes on you?
Cause you're so ugly,
Man, you're ugly,
You're some ugly child.

Sometimes I try to play songs I like on the piano. Mama says I play by ear cause I never would take the time to learn to read music. I picked out the right hand to Ugly Child and sang it for Mama. She said it was a bad song, and Johnny Mercer never should've written a song like that. But I still like it.

Dummy is the nigra woman who cooks and cleans for Angie's mama while she's out selling insurance. I don't think Dummy likes me. She knows I'm scared of her. She can't talk, and she can't hear. When she tries to talk, she makes sounds like a dog barking. Most of the time Angie can tell what she's trying to say cause Angie says she can read her lips. But I can't.

Dummy always wears a rag tied on her head. Some of her hair hangs down on her forehead. A lot of her teeth are missing. You can see her gums when she's trying to talk to you. She thinks she can talk like everybody else. But nobody except Angie can understand anything she says.

Dummy came to them from Angie's Aunt Ruel. She runs a hotel in Rochelle. She told Angie that one day she went back into the kitchen. Dummy was sitting on a stool peeling potatoes and wearing a prison uniform. Ruel found out she'd been in prison for slitting her husband's throat cause she caught him with another woman.

Ruel knew that Alice needed some help. Alice and Guy are Angie's mama and daddy. Ruel asked Alice if she would like to have Dummy. Nobody knew if she had any family. Some people just saw her walking into Rochelle one afternoon with her prison clothes on. She knocked on the back door of the hotel trying to find something to eat.

Ruel brought her to Pineview. Alice and Guy fixed up a room upstairs in their house for her. Angie said the first night she was there, she pulled all the springs out of the mattress.

Angie got in some big trouble cause she wanted to let her friends hear how Dummy talked. She'd let Dummy talk on the phone to James and Sammy and all her other friends. Nobody could understand a word. She just yapped into the phone like an animal. Mrs. Wilson is the operator. She told Alice that Angie had to stop letting Dummy get on the phone or they were going to have to take the phone away from them.

Angie and Sammy and James like to get me to write plays for them. I like doing that. I always have everybody in the play. When we put it on, Dummy is our audience. She sits on the sofa and laughs and claps her hands. She laughs so hard sometimes we can see tears coming down her face. But she can't hear a thing.

Angie found out that Dummy reads the scripture at her church. Sometimes she holds the Bible upside down. The people in her church like for her to do it cause they think she speaks in tongues.

Angie decided that her and me and Sammy and James ought to go to her church one Sunday morning. I got scared cause a nigra woman started screaming and shaking all over. She got down on the floor and started rolling around. Angie whispered in my ear that if the spirit gets in somebody, it causes a spell that makes them fall out.

When we got back to Angie's house, we went in the living room. We started shaking and screaming and rolling around on the floor like they did. Angie's mama came in and made us stop. She said that was wrong for us to do something like that.

One of Alice's cousin's died and she was sitting at the dining room table crying. Dummy came in and saw her. When you cross your arms and put both hands on your shoulders, that means somebody has died. Alice tried to tell her about it. But Dummy got it in her head that Guy had died. So she started crying, too. Alice couldn't stop her. Dummy went over to Edith's house to tell her. About that time Guy came walking home from his store. He was tired so he laid down on the glider on the front porch. When Dummy came back from Edith's house, she saw Guy laying there sound asleep. Dummy started screaming. She scared Guy so bad, he jumped up. He scared Dummy so bad, she ran off hollering as loud as she could.

Dummy has got a really bad temper. If she gets mad with you, you better watch out. One time James and Sammy and Angie decided they wanted to play a trick on me. They told me to call Dummy a fool. I thought she couldn't hear anything that anybody said, so it wouldn't matter what I called her. But when I looked at her and said, "fool," I could see her eyes getting bigger and her body swelling up. It was like a spell had come over her. She was holding a broom in her hand. She picked it up over her head and came after me trying to hit me. It scared me so bad, I ran out the front door. She chased me down the street. The harder I ran, the harder she ran. She had the broom over her head swatting at me like I was a fly. She didn't catch me though cause I can outrun her. Ever since then, she's always watching me out of the corner of her eye.

Another reason I don't think she likes me is the plum trees on the sidewalk between Angie and Nona's house. There are 3 trees that have the best plums I've ever eaten. There are hundreds of plum trees beside the road when we go to the creek or pappy jack to go swimming. But none of them tastes as sweet as the plums on those trees.

Dummy claims they are hers. She doesn't want anybody else to eat a single one cause she makes jelly out of them. She won't even let Angie have one. When she goes to town to the grocery store or to church, the first thing she does when she gets back is check those plum trees to see if somebody has picked any. She sits in a rocking chair on the side porch of Angie's house holding the broom between her legs. She hides behind the kudzu cause she thinks nobody can see her.

The plums usually get ripe about the time that school is getting out for the summer. At that time of year, she's always sitting on the front porch when the school children walk by. If anybody even looks at one of those plum trees, she starts barking at them like she's going to eat them up. All my friends are as scared of her as they are a mad dog.

Me and Irvin have tried to figure out a way to get some of those plums. Sometimes we slip in Nona's house and scoot down by her bedroom window real low so Dummy can't see us. We keep peeping out the window until she goes back inside the house. When she does, we run out the front door as fast as we can and head for those plum trees. She catches us every time. I guess she sees us from the inside the house. She runs out the door, down the front steps, and starts chasing us down the sidewalk holding that broom over her head. She can run pretty fast, too. But not as fast as me and Irvin.

I guess that's all I wanted to tell you about today, Henry. I'll write more later.

Love,
Tom

June 5, 1943

Dear Henry,

Nancy and John are here to see Ma-Me. Nancy is my mama's older sister. Her real name is Ora Edna, but everybody calls her Nancy. They live in St. Augustine. They have two children named Betty and Bill. Betty is 15. Bill is 13. I'm just 7. They're too old to play with me. Betty doesn't have anybody her age to play with. Bill plays with Billy Mann. He's 12. They play big boy things and don't want me to be around them.

John runs a hardware store in St. Augustine. We like to go to their house to see them. Their backyard is on the river. You can see the town on the other side of the river. When we sit on their back porch at night, we can see the bridge and the lights of the town.

When we were in St. Augustine, they let me walk over the bridge to the picture show. I like going by myself.

Last year, when I was 6, Mama and Daddy put me on the bus at Aunt Sally and Uncle Ambrose's house. I rode all the way to Jacksonville by myself. There were other people on the bus, but I didn't know any of them.

Mama gave the bus driver a good talking to when I got on. She told him he'd better keep a good watch on me. Then she said, "Do you understand me? He needs to sit up here on the front seat beside you. You better not let anybody bother him. And I mean it." I wish she hadn't said all that. I'm 6, and I can take care of myself.

The bus driver said, "Yes, M'am." It's a good thing he didn't say anything else. You don't talk back to Mama when she tells you something.

Every time the bus stopped in a town, I'd get off. One time I bought a bar of candy. The next time I bought potato chips. Later on I bought a Co Cola.

When the bus pulled into Jacksonville, Nancy and John were there waiting for me. They put my suitcase in the car and took me to their house in St. Augustine. I had a good time. I rode back to Pineview with Matibel and Joe L. They'd been to Jacksonville Beach on a vacation.

Last night, Nancy and John ate supper with us. Bill stayed at Billy's house. Betty stayed with Ma-Me. When Mama and Daddy have company, they make me keep my sister on the front porch. They don't want us to come in the house. My sister is only 1 ½. She doesn't know how to talk much. I know what Mama and Daddy really want. They want to get in the kitchen with Nancy and John and drink some liquor. I could hear them talking really loud and laughing a lot. They had all the doors shut.

I was hungry and my sister was too. She started crying. I went to the kitchen and knocked on the door. Mama cracked it open a little bit. I told her we were hungry. I could see glasses with ice in them and a liquor bottle on the table.

We sat down at the dining room table. Mama asked me to say the blessing. I said:

God is great;

God is good;

Let us thank Him for our food;

Amen

Mama and Daddy always try to tell funny stories when people eat with us. I don't like it when they tell about me. Daddy told about the time me and Irvin went to the farm with Papa when we were 3. I've heard him tell that story 100 times before.

Papa always let me sit in his lap and drive his car. He would change the gears and put on the brakes and clutch. He always scraped the gears. Daddy said he couldn't drive real good. Papa chewed tobacco and spit out the window. He let me and Irvin chew tobacco, too. When me and Irvin sat in the back seat, his tobacco spit would blow back all over us. I told Papa to quit spitting that tobacco juice out the damn window. Nancy and John thought that story was funny.

When we got to the farm that day, Papa wanted to walk out in the field where the hands were chopping cotton. Me and Irvin were walking right behind him. All of a sudden I heard Papa yell, "goddammit." There was a snake wrapped around his leg whipping him with its tail. Papa yelled to one of the hands to bring a hoe. A nigra man ran over and pulled the snake off with his hoe. Then he chopped its head off.

The nigra man said, "It's a coach whip Captain."

Papa said, "I know it's a god damn coach whip. The damn son of a bitch was wrapped around my leg."

Papa had on long pants. Me and Irvin had on short pants. We're scared of snakes. I'm glad it didn't get on us.

Papa didn't say a word driving back home. The next thing we knew, Papa swerved the car right over into the ditch. Me and Irvin jumped out the back door. Papa told Daddy I put my hands on my hips and said, "What in the hell have you done now? You've run the god damn car in the ditch." Papa said a bee got into the car and stung him on the leg. That's what made him run in the ditch.

They all laughed. I guess they thought what I said was funny. I didn't think it was funny. The preacher said if you say cuss words you'll go to hell. Now that I'm 7, I don't cuss anymore. But Daddy and Papa still say cuss words all the time.

Every time we have company and eat in the dining room, my sister gets underneath the table and pinches everybody on the foot. When she pinched Nancy and John, they screamed like a rat had bitten them. Mama and Daddy did, too. She doesn't pinch me cause she knows I think it's stupid and dumb. I want to say something at the table about how stupid it is, but Daddy always tells me that children should be seen and not heard.

I'm getting sleepy, Henry. I guess I need to go to bed. Do you sleep a lot up there in heaven?

Love,
Tom

June 30, 1943

Dear Henry,

I don't know why Mama has to play bridge every day. She plays every afternoon. Mondays and Tuesdays and Wednesdays and Thursdays and Fridays. Some people think it's a sin to play cards. Nona said she thought it was.

I've seen Mama and the other women put a dime on the table. I've heard them talk about who wins the money. I haven't asked Nona about it yet, but it sounds like gambling to me. And you'll go straight to hell if you gamble. I know that's true cause the preacher said so.

When I was 3 or 4, Mama took me with her every day where ever they were playing bridge. Sometimes they'd play at Cudin Charlye's house, sometimes at JuJu's house, sometimes at Imogene's house, sometimes at Edith's house, sometimes at Lillian's house, sometimes at Matibel's house, sometimes at Lib's house and sometimes at Mama's house.

I'd play around on the floor under the table where Mama was sitting. Sometimes I'd walk around the table and tell them who had the ace of spades. Mama said I had to quit doing that. She said I could look at the cards, but I couldn't say who had the ace of spades. I thought I was doing them a favor.

Mama dresses up every day to go to the bridge party. She puts on clothes like she's going to church. She likes to wear a dress-up dress, high heel shoes, a hat, and gloves. I don't know why she has to dress up to see the same people every day. I was really glad when Mama said I was big enough to go outside and play on my own. Now I can go anywhere I want to in the whole town.

The only thing I liked about her bridge parties were the refreshments. They had things like cookies and cucumber sandwiches and pimento cheese sandwiches. Mama calls the ones she makes ribbon sandwiches cause she puts pimento cheese on a bunch of pieces of bread and slices it.

They always have coffee to drink or a Co Cola. Coffee smells good in the pot, but it sure doesn't taste good.

One time when I was about 4, I was playing on the floor under the bridge table, and I heard one of the women say something about somebody being pregnant. Mama put her finger up to her mouth and said, "shhh." She pointed to me. All the women acted real embarrassed cause of saying an ugly word in front of me. Mama asked me if I'd heard what had been said. I told her no. But I was telling a story cause I did hear it. I know what it means, too, cause Irvin told me it meant when a woman is going to have a baby. I guess it's a pretty ugly word. But it's probably not as bad as damn and hell and goddam and Papa and Daddy say that all the time.

Another time when I was playing on the floor under the bridge table they started grabbing up the cards and jumping up out of their chairs like the house was on fire. Juju's chair turned over when she was trying to grab up all the dimes. It really scared me.

Somebody was knocking on the door. Mama told me to go and open it. When I did, there was the Methodist Preacher standing there. He wanted to know if my mama was at home. I told him they were playing bridge so he left. Mama said I shouldn't have told him that.

Daddy's always off at work every day while Mama is playing bridge. He doesn't know about them gambling and saying ugly words and telling me to tell the preacher a story. If I tell Daddy about it, Mama is going to give me a spanking. But who should I tell? If Mama keeps on doing those sins, she'll be going to hell like the preacher said.

What should I do, Henry?

Love,
Tom

July 7, 1943

Dear Henry,

How are things in heaven? I sure hope they're better up there than they are down here. It's so boring in Pineview. There's nothing to do in the summertime except go swimming every day down at Pappy Jack or Bluff Creek.

The biggest news is about my watermelon that Mr. Bufford brought me today. He has a farm one mile out of town where the road curves on the way to Daddy's farm. He always plants a big watermelon patch. Ever since I can remember Daddy will stop by to see Mr. Bufford when the watermelons start getting big. He lets me walk out in the field and pick out the one I want to be mine. I always pick the biggest one I can find. Then Mr. Bufford scratches my name on it with a knife.

I always look out in the field every time we ride by to see if I can see my watermelon. When I go to the farm with Daddy or Papa sometimes they will stop and let me walk out in the field to look for it. It's easy to find cause Mr. Bufford has my name on it real big. His watermelons are always dark green so it's easy to find. I get excited when I see T O M painted on the biggest watermelon in the whole patch. He lets me thump it to see if it's ripe. But he can thump it harder than I can.

He lets Irvin pick out one too. But they don't drive by his farm like we do. So I always get there first to get the biggest.

Most all the farmers start picking their watermelons pretty soon after July the 4th. Mr. Bufford always puts mine on the back of his wagon and brings it to our house. When I go out on the porch and see it sitting there it feels like Santa Claus has come.

As soon as Daddy gets home from work he carries my watermelon outside in the back yard to cut it. It's always red as blood when he slices it open. The seeds are real black. Daddy lets me cut the heart out to eat first. I usually run over to Nona and Papa's house to get them to come over to have some. Nona likes watermelon but she likes cantaloupe best.

Mr. Bufford's watermelons are the best tasting ones I've ever eaten.

Henry, I'll write to you later when I have some more news.

Love,
Tom

July 31, 1943

Dear Henry,

You know the bamboo patch next to Nona's house? It's so thick you can hardly get through it. Nona hates it. Papa went fishing down in Darien one time and came back with a bunch of bamboo stalks. He planted them beside their house, so he could always have him a fishing pole. Now it's like a jungle.

Me and Irvin and Dickie Cook built our clubhouse in the back of the patch. We got Nona's ax and chopped down enough bamboo to make a pathway. We wanted it to be as far away as we could get it, so nobody could find it. A clubhouse has to be secret.

We were looking around in the barn and found an American flag and 3 old chairs and a table. Now we have a real clubhouse to hold all our meetings. We had election of officers. I'm the President. Irvin is Vice-President. Dickie is Secretary-Treasurer, but we don't have any money yet.

Joan and Betty Jean and Jackie Cook found out we had a clubhouse. They didn't know where it was. They decided to build them one. They were just trying to copy us. They wouldn't tell us where theirs was. And we wouldn't tell them where ours was.

Yesterday when me and Irvin and Dickie went back to our clubhouse to have our meeting, somebody had broken down our table and chairs. It looked like they chopped them with an ax. The flag was laying down on the ground. We got so mad, we were ready to kill somebody.

I found Nona's ax under her house, and we went searching for the girl's clubhouse. We looked all over the place. Pineview is so little, there's no way to hide anything if somebody wants to find it. We finally found their clubhouse back in the woods between Mrs. Gammage's house and the stadium. The girls had tried to copy us even down to the table and chairs and flag. I started swinging the ax as hard as I could tearing their clubhouse up. When I got tired, Irvin took over. Dickie had his turn. And we leveled it.

We heard the girls coming down the trail toward their clubhouse. When they got there and saw what we'd done, they tried to fight us. Joan jumped on me. She's my first cousin, and she can fight as hard as anybody when she gets mad. Betty Jean is 2 years older than us. She's a lot bigger than Irvin. She started beating on him. Jackie is 2 years older than Dickie. She can beat him up, too. We got a pretty good licking from those girls before we could get out of there.

Joan yelled that they didn't tear up our clubhouse.

I told her that nobody in this whole town would've torn up our clubhouse except them and she knew it.

They were really mad.   We were mad, too. So we ran away.

Henry, could you ask Jesus or somebody up there in heaven if they know who might've torn up our clubhouse?

Love,
Tom

August 23, 1943

Dear Henry,

You'll never guess what happened. I had to be put to sleep and have an operation. I got a butterbean stuck in my throat. I'm not telling anybody about it cause some of the boys have been calling me butterbean. I think it must be impossible to keep a secret in Pineview.

You probably remember how I used to always get food stuck in my throat? It's been going on since I was a baby. Dr. Batts said I have a stricture of my esophagus. He told Daddy I might've gotten hold of some poison like potash or lye or something like that when I was a baby.

When I get choked at Nona's house, Papa always puts a pillow on the floor and gets me to turn somersaults. But it never goes down when I do that.

The butterbean got stuck in my throat last Sunday at dinner. I kept trying and trying and trying to get it down. Mama put a pan in the bed with me Sunday night for me to spit in.

Daddy came in Monday morning and woke me up. He handed me a glass of water to drink. When I took a swallow, the water came right back up. He shook his head. He wanted it to go down as bad as I did.

All day Monday, I had to spit about 300 times. One time when I tried to drink a swallow of water, the butterbean felt like it flipped over. But it just wouldn't go down. When I went to bed Monday night, Daddy said if it hadn't gone down by Tuesday morning, they would have to take me to the doctor. I hate going to the doctor. They always give me a shot or some bad tasting medicine.

Tuesday morning, Daddy came in my room to wake me up to see if it had gone down. I tried to drink some water, but that butterbean wouldn't budge.

Judy Castellow was in Pineview visiting her mama and daddy. She is a nurse in Atlanta. She told Daddy to fix something for me to drink that would make me vomit. Daddy went down to Mr. Clements drug store and got some powdered mustard that you mix with water that's supposed to make you throw up. It wasn't the kind of mustard you put on a hotdog.

Daddy held me while Mama tried to pour that bad tasting stuff down my throat. I gagged and gagged and gagged. But none of it could get past the butterbean.

Edith told Daddy Tuesday afternoon she thought they should take me to a doctor. I cried cause I didn't want to go.

Nona came over and picked up my baby sister. Daddy drove to Cordele for me to see Dr. Hiram Williams. He is an ear, eye, nose, and throat doctor.

We got to his office and had to wait in the waiting room for a long time. Mama had a shoe box for me to spit in every time I had to swallow. When we finally got into his office, Mama told him what had happened. He acted real upset. He said, "You better get that boy to Macon as fast as you can cause he's dehydrated." I didn't know what that meant. Dr. Williams called Dr. Bill Barton in Macon to tell him we were coming.

Daddy drove as fast as he could to the emergency room of the Macon Hospital. Dr. Barton told Mama and Daddy he would have to put a bronchoscope down my throat to get that butterbean out. I didn't know what that meant either. I asked him if it was going to hurt. He said I wouldn't know anything about it until it was over. He wanted to know how old I was. I told him I was 7.

Dr. Barton said, "He's a big boy. He probably doesn't worry about anything."

Daddy said, "Yes, he does. He worries about a lot of things."

A nigra man came in the room wearing a white suit. He picked me up out of the bed and put me on a table and started rolling me down the hall. I was really scared. Mama was on one side holding my hand and Daddy was on the other side holding my other hand.

Dr. Barton came out of the operating room dressed in white clothes. A nurse was with him. He asked Daddy if he liked the looks of his nurse.

Daddy said, "Hell I'm not interested in anything like that right now. I'm just worried about my boy."

The lights were really bright inside the operating room. They strapped me down on the table with some leather straps just like Melton Harvey used to strap me down to give me a haircut. I started struggling to get loose. Before I knew it, they clamped some ether down over my nose. About that time the table I was on started shooting backwards about 100 miles an hour.

The next thing I remember Daddy and Mama were looking down over me. Daddy said the doctor got that damn butterbean out of my throat. He said I could have anything I wanted to eat or drink so long as it was soft. He wanted to know if I wanted some ice cream.

I drank lots of water and ate some ice cream and apple sauce and some oatmeal. It kind of scratched my throat when it went down.

Dr. Barton came in the room and said he had something he wanted to give me. He put the butterbean in my hand.

Daddy said he didn't want to ever see that damn butterbean again.

On the way home, Daddy told Mama, they charged him 75 dollars.

Mama said she'd never heard of anybody charging that much money. She told Daddy that was a whole month of his salary.

I'm sorry Daddy had to pay so much money. I started thinking I could give him $1.50 a week to pay him back. That's how much I make every Saturday working at Nona's store. But it would take a long time.

That's the biggest news I've got to tell you, Henry. I hope everything is good for you up there in heaven.

Love,
Tom

September 30, 1943

Dear Henry,

Every night before Daddy goes to bed he walks out the back door. He stays a little while then comes back in the house. I've looked out the window and seen him peeing. I don't know why he does that. Mama jumps on him and tells him he ought to go to the bathroom. But he won't listen to her.

Last week Daddy got Hosey to come up to the house and build a tall wooden fence. It's about 12 feet high. It goes all the way from the garage to the barn. I asked him why he had the fence built so high. He said he likes his privacy.

He oughta get plenty of privacy with that fence. Nona said it looked like to her he was going to keep an elephant in the backyard.

You'll never believe what he's doing now. He started taking a bath under the hose at night. He tried to get me to go with him. I told him I didn't want to get naked in the backyard even at night. I don't like to take a bath anyway. And if I'm going to take one I sure don't want to use cold water. He keeps a bar of soap on the limb of the china-berry tree. We see him walking out the back door every night holding a towel over his arm. Mama just shakes her head like she doesn't know what to do about it. I told her that all that liquor he drinks has probably driven him out of his mind.

Henry I hope everything is all right with you in heaven. It's pretty crazy down here.

Love,
Tom

November 15, 1943

Dear Henry,

I went with Daddy to the farm today. One of his sharecroppers lives in the biggest house on the farm. His name is Tommy Stalls. I asked Daddy what sharecropper means. He said if they make any money off the crops they get to share the profits with him.

Tommy Stalls has a boy my age named T.J. Sometimes we play together. I like to drink water out of their well cause it tastes really good. Daddy said it tastes sweet. There's a wooden fence around the well so nobody will fall in it. They have a bucket on a rope. They keep the bucket turned upside down on a post. Sometimes Daddy lets me drop the bucket in the well. I can't pull it out when it's full of water. It's too heavy. The water is really cold. On a hot day, Daddy lets me drink all I want then pours the rest over my head.

Daddy gets the hands to plant cane in the spring. He plants two kinds – sugar cane and POJ. The outside of the sugar cane is green and the outside of the POJ is purple. The hands always cut the cane down in November and make syrup. Daddy said he likes the sugar cane syrup better. I asked him what POJ stood far. He said, "Pride of Japan." I thought Japan was an ugly word. We're at war with them. They dropped bombs on Pearl Harbor that killed a lot of our soldiers.

I like it when they grind the cane. The cane juice tastes so good. After the hands cut all the cane, they stack it in a big pile on top of the wagon. They get one of the mules to pull the wagon full of cane behind where Tommy Stalls lives. They hitch up the mule to one end of a really long pole. The cane grinder is in the middle. The mule walks around and around and around in a circle. That's what makes the grinder work. One of the hands puts a stalk of cane in the grinder and the juice comes out the other end in a bucket. I asked Daddy if I could put some cane in the grinder. He said I might get my hand cut off.

They keep a little jar on the ground to taste the juice. It tastes so sweet and good. Daddy always takes a gallon jug home to put in the refrigerator to drink when it gets cold.

I picked up the jar to dip some of the juice from the bucket. Daddy yelled at me. He said don't drink out of that jar. I asked him why not. He said some of the hands might've been drinking out of it. He told T.J. to run up to their house and get a clean jar.

After all the cane is ground the hands build a big fire. They put the heavy syrup kettle on some blocks above the fire. The kettle is really big. I bet 10 people could take a bath in it. They pour the cane juice into the kettle so it will boil and turn into thick syrup.

Daddy lets me taste some of the cane skimmins. He won't let me dip it out though. He tells one of the hands to get me some. He'll take a piece of the peeling from a stalk of cane and skim off some of the white-looking stuff with bubbles in it. It tastes warm and sweet and good. Daddy said the hands like to keep the skimmins. They let it ferment. Then they can get a little drunk on it.

Last weekend we went to Aunt Ida's and Uncle Philet's house. They live on the other side of Daddy's farm. Aunt Ida is Papa's sister. She is kinda fat and laughs all the time. Daddy said nothing makes her happier than for people to come to see her.

Uncle Philet is deaf and wears a hearing aid. Daddy said a lot of times when there are too many people around Uncle Philet will turn off his hearing aid so he can't hear anything. He wears a cowboy hat and cowboy boots. They have chickens and ducks and turkeys and geese and dogs and cats and sometimes pigs that run around in their backyard. At their back door is a big chinaberry tree that me and Irvin climb every time we go there. They have a vegetable garden right next to the house. All their horses live in a barn. They have a smoke house where they store their meat in the winter. They kill a lot of hogs.

The syrup that Daddy makes is for us and Nona and Papa and Edith and Hendley and the hands at the farm. Mama makes pecan pies and syrup pies. We put the syrup on pancakes and waffles and biscuits.

Aunt Ida and Uncle Philet's syrup kettle is bigger than Daddy's. They plant a whole lot more cane than he does. They fill up their syrup kettle several times with cane juice. They have to make a lot of syrup for their family. They have four children plus Big Irvin and all of their grandchildren. They raised Big Irvin from the time he was a little boy after his mama and daddy died. He calls them Mama and Papa but really they're his aunt and uncle. Their real children are name Martha and Midge and Boots and Nonk.

Ephraim is the nigra man who lives with Aunt Ida and Uncle Philet and does all their cooking on a wood stove in the kitchen. He sleeps in a little one-room place they built for him in their backyard. Daddy told me Ephraim's favorite food is cow tail and rice. He also eats a can of sardines every day. Daddy asked him if eating all those sardines didn't leave a bad taste in his mouth. He said anything that good he didn't mind tasting all day.

Ephraim makes biscuits and brings them out there where they are boiling the cane juice into syrup. When they start pouring up the syrup in the bucket, everybody wants to put some of it on Ephraim's hot biscuits. That's the best thing you can eat.

When I get big I want to make syrup and give a gallon to everybody I know.

Love,
Tom

December 18, 1943

Dear Henry,

The gang is what we call our group who goes to the picture show. The Pine Theater has 3 different movies every week. We go on Monday, Wednesday, and Friday night so we can see every one of them.

Mrs. Ware, is the English teacher at the high school. She's really old. Probably about 60. She starts out from her house with a flashlight in her hand and walks down to Angie's house. Angie is 12. She's 5 years older than me. When Angie and Mrs. Ware get to my house, they yell for me. I grab a quarter and run out the front door to meet them.

The next one is James next door to me. He's 12, like Angie. Me and Angie and Mrs. Ware have to yell really loud for him. His mother calls him Jamesey. Sometimes I kid him and yell Jamesey instead of James.

The next one is Sammy. He's 13. He teaches me piano lessons. We have to holler really loud for him too cause he's always late. Then the 5 of us walk down town to the picture show.

Mr. Julius Mashburn prints a calendar of all the coming attractions each month. He hands them out to everybody who goes to the show. I tack the one he gives me on the wall in my bedroom so I'll know what's coming up every week. Mr. Mashburn is the one who owns the picture show. It's next to Mr. Will Slade's store.

On Friday night we always see a western. They have cowboys like Roy Rogers and Gene Autry and Smiley Burnette. I like westerns. But not as much as the serials that they show before. The serials always have something really bad that happens at the end. You don't ever know how they're going to get out of all that trouble. If we didn't go every Friday night, we wouldn't know what's going to happen to the girl hanging on the side of the cliff. She seems to always get off by some miracle. But you never know.

A ticket costs 9 cents for me cause I'm just 7. The rest of the gang has to pay 12 cents. I always get a Co Cola. It costs a nickel. A bag of popcorn costs a nickel, too. It costs me 19 cents every time I go. I always take a quarter then I have 6 cents to put in my piggy bank.

If it's a good picture show with Clark Gable or Betty Grable or somebody like that, the place is full of people. Angie's favorite movie star is Van John-son. That's what she named her cat. I like Betty Grable cause I think she's pretty. James said she has her legs insured for $10,000.

We always sit somewhere in the middle. We don't like to sit up too close or too far back. James said he wishes we could sit in the balcony but that's where the nigras sit.

Sometimes James's daddy goes to the picture show. He always goes by himself and sits in the same seat next to the aisle. He wants to sit in a place where he can get up and get out in a hurry if there's any kissing on the screen.

The saddest movie I ever saw was Lassie Come Home. I cried when Lassie died. The Song of Bernadette with Jennifer Jones was sad, too. But not as sad as Lassie.

I don't like scary movies. If Bela Lugosi is going to be in it then I know it's going to be scary. We saw Frankenstein Meets the Wolfman and The Ghost of Frankenstein. They nearly scared me to death. It's hard for me to go to sleep at night after I've seen a scary show. Sometimes I get out of my bed and slip back to Mama and Daddy's room and go to sleep on the rug next to their bed.

The ones I like best are the comedies. My favorite is Bud Abbott and Lou Costello. Last year I saw Ride em Cowboy and Pardon My Sarong. They were so funny. They're a lot funnier than Laurel and Hardy. I like the Three Stooges, too. My daddy says that Charlie Chaplin was the funniest man who ever lived. But he was in those silent picture shows before I was born.

Angie thought it'd be a good idea for the gang members to have a Christmas party. So, James's mother fixed some punch and refreshments. We had the first party at his house. We played some games like spin the bottle, I spy, and charades.

Sammy's mama is a really good cook cause she cooks in the school lunchroom. When we ate at his house, his mama served some really good cookies and had ice tea to drink.

Dummy cooks for Angie's family. Dummy can't hear or talk. She made a pound cake when we went to Angie's house. Angie made some hot chocolate.

When they came to my house, Mama made tuna fish sandwiches as usual. Every time I have to take sandwiches somewhere, all my friends laugh at me cause Mama always makes tuna fish sandwiches. Last summer when we were unpacking our lunches for the school picnic at Jay Bird Springs, one of the girls in my class said for me to pull out my tuna fish sandwiches. They all started laughing. I was embarrassed. I know Mama must know how to make other kinds cause she fixes pimento cheese sandwiches for her bridge club.

The best party of all was when we went to Mrs. Ware's house. Mr. Ware had a big library with a whole lot of books that make the room smell like leather. She said before he died, he spent most of his time reading in his library. We ate at her dining room table with a white tablecloth and cloth napkins. Mrs. Ware fixed a good chicken dinner with rice and gravy and served us syllabub for dessert. It's kinda like eating foam. Angie told me the next day it had liquor in it. I don't want to drink any liquor cause I want to go to heaven when I die.

Going to the picture show with the gang is one of my favorite things to do. I like our new picture show a whole lot better than the old one. The new one has the sidewalk raised up where you buy your ticket. That makes a good place for us to skate cause you can get up some good speed when you skate down it. I feel like I'm flying by the time I get in front of Mr. Slade's store. He always hollers at us cause he says we make too much noise. Elizabeth Pope told him he ought to put some cotton in his ears.

Our new picture show has soft cushions in the seats. The old one had hard benches. It was where Mr. T.O. Connor used to have his grocery store. Those benches had wooden slats. When you sat on them your butt would slip into the crack. Most of the bigger boys always laid down in the grocery shelves to watch the show. McCall Warren was about 13 or 14. He would lay on the shelf where Mr. Connor used to keep the peas and corn and tomatoes. Boy and Henry would lay on the shelf where they used to keep the sacks of Irish potatoes. I thought when I got to be a big boy, I could lay up there on the shelves, too.

But I never got to lay on the shelves cause Mr. Mashburn built the new picture show. It looks almost as good as the one in Rochelle and Abbeville.

Well, Henry, I guess that's about all the time I've got to write you today. I hope everything is fine with you up there in heaven. When I die I'll be coming to see you.

Love,
Tom

December 25, 1943

Dear Henry,

My daddy loves fireworks more than any child I know. Mama says he's just like a young'un around Christmastime. He sees that I have a good supply of firecrackers, sky rockets, roman candles, cherry bombs and nigga chasers. My stocking is always running over with them. On Christmas morning before the sun ever comes up, he sets off a whole package of firecrackers next to my bedroom window. Then he sets off another package at my sister's window. That's when we get up and run in the living room to see our presents.

I was so happy when I saw what I got for Christmas. I've been wanting an electric football game for a long time but Daddy said he hadn't been able to find one. He said everywhere he went they'd already sold out. When that electric football game was sitting in front of the fireplace I got so excited. This has been the best Christmas ever.

Two bad things happened last night. Irvin came around to my house to shoot some firecrackers that his daddy gave him. Mama and Daddy had gone across the street to drink eggnog with Ruby and Son, W.D. and Mary, and Ma-Me. When we started shooting firecrackers in front of my house, Joan and Zell and Walt came over. My sister came out, too. We were lighting firecrackers as fast as we could and throwing them out in the street. I lit one and before I could throw it, it blew up in my hand. Henry, I believe being shot with a gun wouldn't hurt any worse.

The next bad thing was when Walt set up a sky rocket in the sand. He struck a match and lit it. Before it went off, it tilted over toward Ma-Me's house. The sky rocket flew across the street like a streak of lightning right through the plate glass window. They were all sitting in the living room drinking eggnog. The sky rocket broke through the glass and hit the wall right above W.D.'s head and exploded. They came running out of the living room onto the front porch screaming at us. We told them Walt did it. But they made us quit shooting fireworks, and told us all we all had to go home.

Daddy said, Hell, I thought somebody was shootin' at me. He told me I couldn't shoot any more fireworks until tomorrow. That was O.K. with me. I'd already blasted my hand half off.

Except for those two bad things, it looks like this will really be a good Christmas. Henry, I hope you have a Merry Christmas and a Happy New Year!

Love,
Tom

January 30, 1944

Dear Henry,

Nona said I should always be nice to everybody no matter what color they are. I asked her if she thought nigras would be able to go to heaven. She said anybody can go to heaven if they're baptized and believe in Jesus. I asked her if dogs can go to heaven cause I wanted to make sure you were there. She said dogs go to dog heaven. I hope its not too far away from people heaven. When I get there, I want to see you as much as I can. I wish you could write me a letter and let me know what it's like up there. But I guess I'll just have to wait until I die to find out.

I didn't ask Nona, but I wonder if nigras will have to live in the quarters up in heaven like they do here. Nona taught me to never say nigger cause that's not a nice word to say. You should always say nigra she said when you're talking about colored people. That's the nice way to say it.

Yellow Duxie is a light skin nigra woman. Daddy calls her a high yellow but I don't think that's nice. Yellow Duxie does all the washing and ironing for Mama and Nona. Some people call her Mary. I don't know why she has 2 names.

I like to watch her when she brings the clothes back to our house. She carries them in a pasteboard box on top of her head. She doesn't even hold the box with her hands. I don't know how she does it. If she ever dropped the clothes in the dirt she'd be in big trouble. So far she's never dropped it that I know of.

Sometimes I ride with Mama down to her house in the quarters when Mama takes our dirty clothes to her. She builds a fire under a big black iron pot with some sticks to make the water boil. Mama said she makes lye soap out of hog fat. That's what she puts in the water. She also puts starch in the water to make the clothes stiff. Then she stirs the clothes all around in the pot with a big long pole that's taller than my daddy. After she has stirred the clothes a bunch of times she puts them in another pot that just has water in it. That's where she rinses all the soap out of the clothes. Then she takes the clothes and twists each one in her hands to wring all the water out. She hangs it on her clothes line and clips clothespins over the clothes to keep them from blowing off. She builds a fire in her fireplace inside her house. None of the nigras in the quarters have electricity like white people do. She puts a really heavy iron on the hearth in front of the fire. When it gets really hot she irons all the clothes. She folds the clothes and puts them in a cardboard box and brings them to Mama and Nona. Mama pays her 50 cents and Nona pays her 50 cents.

Hosey is my favorite nigra man cause he's always really nice to me. I don't think I've ever seen him when he was not whistling. He whistles everywhere he goes. He was my daddy's chauffeur. He'd drive Daddy around on his dates with girls before he married my mama. He fixes things for Nona and Papa and Mama and Daddy. He calls Papa "Captain" and calls my daddy "Little Captain." He calls Nona "Miss Leona," and he calls my mama, "Miss Coot." He calls me "little Tom" just like everybody else. Hosey painted the outside of our house one time and painted Nona and Papa's house, too. I like to watch him paint. He whistles really loud when he's painting. Daddy said he preaches at the nigra church down in the quarters on Sunday morning. He has a son that everybody calls Man.

Hosey kills snakes for my daddy and Nona and Papa. He killed a snake in our house. Daddy walked into the living room one day and saw a long black snake lying in the middle of the floor. My daddy is more scared of a snake than a little girl. He ran out the back door and drove down to the quarters to look for Hosey. He found him and brought him back to our house. They had to come in the back door cause Daddy said a long time ago that nigras should never come through our front door. I told Daddy that seemed crazy to me. Every time Mama had the house cleaned by a nigra women she would come in and out of the front door all day long. Daddy called me a smart aleck.

Hosey saw the snake curled up in the corner of the living room. Daddy had gotten his shotgun in case the snake tried to get away. Mama ran to her bedroom and locked the door. I was watching Hosey. He had a hoe. He walked up near the corner of the room where the snake was curled up. It was hissing at him like it wanted to bite him. When

Hosey got close enough, he came down on that snake with the hoe and chopped it in half. Both halves of the snake started wiggling all over the place. Daddy was still pointing his shotgun at the snake. Hosey then hit the snake on the head with the back of the hoe. The top part of the snake stopped wiggling. He got a paper sack out of the kitchen and scooped up both halves of the snake and put it in the sack. Daddy wanted to know what he was going to do with it. He said he was going to bury it in the back yard. Daddy said no hell you're not. He told Hosey to take that damn snake down to the quarters and get rid of it.

The next day Daddy got a ladder and went up on the roof of the house and put a piece of linoleum on top of the chimney. I helped him put bricks on top of the linoleum to hold it down so it wouldn't blow off. He said that no snake would ever come down that chimney again. I ask him if he would take the linoleum off before Christmas so Santa Claus could come down the chimney. He promised me he would.

Daddy wouldn't go up in the living room for days after that. I told him there was no use in him being scared of the snake cause it was dead. He told me to quit being a smart aleck.

Christine works for Miss Thelma and Mr. Clements. She has a daughter named Roberta. Roberta got married to Hosey's son Man at their church in the quarters. James and Sammy and Angie took me with them to the wedding. That's the only time I've ever been to a wedding at a nigra church. I really like the way they sing. They sing really loud. It makes everybody want to dance. I like that kind of music. I've never heard any music at our church that made me want to dance. All the nigras really got dressed up for the wedding. Most of the women wore white dresses and hats. The men wore suits and ties. We were the only white people there. I felt bad cause we just wore our school clothes.

When I was real little Hester was the nigra woman who worked for us. I don't remember too much about her except what mama said cause I must've been about two years old. She said I never wanted to eat my meals in the house. John Barnes who lives at Daddy's camp house built me a little table and two chairs and painted them green. Mama would send Hester out in the back yard with my meals. I always ate on my little table. Mama said I kept wanting to change around where the table was put cause Hester would have to pick up the table and move it to different places all around.

When I work at Nona's store on Saturday afternoons most all the people who come in there to buy stuff are nigras. The women wear a lot of perfume so they smell really sweet. They put Royal Crown hair dressing in their hair. That stuff is really greasy. They can fix their hair all kinds of ways once they put that grease on it.

One Saturday afternoon I went in Sam's store to get a Co Cola. Sam was talking to someone. They were sitting around the wood stove. While I was paying Sam my nickel for the Co-cola a nigra man walked in. Sam's friend got up from the chair where he was sitting and hit the nigra man in the face with his fist as hard as he could. It knocked him down on the floor. I couldn't understand it cause they hadn't said a word to each other. They hadn't argued or anything. I'd never seen that happen before. I ran out the door and told Nona about it. She said the nigra probably owed the man some money.

I told Nona you don't hit somebody just cause they owe you money. That's not right. She agreed with me. I knew Nona would never hit anybody anyway.

I heard some of the older boys in high school laughing and talking about riding down the road on a Sunday afternoon in the summer. They keep slices of watermelon in the floor of the back seat. A lot of nigras are walking on the road coming home from church in their Sunday clothes. The little girls usually have on white dresses and the little boys have on a suit and tie. Those big boys drive by them and throw slices of watermelon at the little children to see if they can hit them. The children scream and run, but when they get hit it really messes up their clothes. Those big boys laugh about it like it's really a fun thing to do. It makes me mad. I don't laugh when they talk about it. I think things like that are wrong.

Irvin told me he heard one time they had a hanging of a nigra man somewhere out in the country. I asked Nona about it and she said she'd never heard of that happening around Pineview.

One Sunday morning at church Irvin told me he heard there had been a big nigra fight downtown the night before. He said there was blood all over the sidewalks. We went down town after church to see if it was true. Sure enough there was a lot of blood on the sidewalks. Billy Mann said it was a big fight. All the nigras were stabbing each other with knives. None of us knew how it got started.

Well Henry that's about all I know about nigras that I can tell you about today. I guess I just wanted to talk with somebody about it. I can always talk with Nona about almost everything but I can talk to you about everything.

Love,
Tom

March 1, 1944

Dear Henry,

I always work at Nona's store every Saturday afternoon. I've been doing that as long as I can remember. I love working with Nona. She teaches me a lot of things I need to know.

Last Saturday Mrs. McDuffie was in the store buying some things. She told Nona, your grandson sure is growing up ain't he?

Nona said he just turned 8 and growing like a weed.

I always thought Mrs. McDuffie was a funny looking woman. Her dress came down to her ankles just above her high top black shoes. She wore black cotton stockings and had her hair tied in a bun like most white women who lived in the country.

It was hot and muggy that day. The weatherman had said it would probably hit 100. After she left, me and Nona sat down. She picked up her Clark Funeral Home fan and began fanning at the gnats that were coming through the back door. Their favorite places to get me are the eyes and ears. When one gets in my eye, Nona gets a Kleenex and picks it out. They're harder to get out when they get in your ears. Nona has to use her hairpin for that.

We knew this would be a busy day 'cause we'd seen a lot of wagons pulling up behind the store.

All the posts for tying mules had been taken. The little nigra children are always dressed up like they're going to church. They were pulling on their mamas dresses trying to get them to hurry up so they could get an ice cream cone or a moon pie and a RC Cola.

The nigra women have to buy groceries cause there are some things they can't raise on the farm. Nona sells them bright colored scarves, underwear, Sweet Peach Snuff, Hoyt's Cologne, and Royal Crown Petroleum Hair Dressing that straightens their hair out.

The nigra women wear dresses that have a lot of colors. The men mostly wear bib overalls and a wide brimmed straw hat. Most of the men chew tobacco and spit on the ground. The women dip snuff and put it underneath their bottom lip. They spit in a tin can. Sometimes I can see a brown streak of snuff juice leaking out of the corner of their mouths.

When the nigras can scrape up enough money, they like to have one of their upper front teeth pulled and put a gold one in its place. That's a really big deal for them. When they first get a gold tooth, they like to smile a lot.

There are benches on both sides of the sidewalk in front of Nona's store. The women like to sit there and talk and laugh a lot. Some of the men go out looking for a bootlegger to buy some liquor. They usually get pretty drunk before the day is over. In the late afternoon when they come in the store, I can smell the liquor on their breath.

Mary John Warren is a high school student. She helps us on Saturday afternoons at the store. I think she's pretty. She has brown hair that comes down to her shoulders. Last Saturday she had on a white blouse and a skirt that Nona thought was too short. It just barely covered her knees. She wears white socks folded down to her ankles and saddle oxfords just like all the rest of the girls in high school.

Nona has had her store since before I was born. Syms furnished her with enough supplies to start her own store in Pineview. She told me she paid him back every penny she owed him. Her store is called The Pineview 5 & 10 Cent Store. That doesn't mean that everything costs a nickel and a dime. There're a lot of things that Nona sells for more than a dollar.

A large white woman came in the store I'd never seen before. She asked me if my grandmother was here. Nona had just walked to the post office.

The lady said she needed a box of Kotex. Nona kept it high up on a shelf I couldn't reach. I didn't know what it was anyway. I asked Nona one time and she told me it was something for women.

I showed the lady where it was. She reached up on the shelf and grabbed a box. When she walked out she said to tell Miss Leona to put it on her bill.

When Nona came back, I told her what had happened. I tried to describe the woman, but Nona didn't know who she was. Nona knew I really felt bad about it. Later on that afternoon she said she remembered who the lady was. But I knew Nona well enough to know she was just trying to make me not feel so bad.

At the end of the day when the sun started going down, the nigra women started loading their children in the wagons and putting all the things they'd bought down beside the children. Then they had to go and look for their husbands. Most of them were probably drunk and would be hard to find. You can't buy any alcohol in Pineview in a store or anywhere else in the whole county. The nearest town that sells liquor and beer is Hawkinsville. But the men get their moonshine from the bootleggers that live around Pineview.

Nona doesn't have a particular time to close the store. We just wait and shut the doors when all the customers have left town. She always pays me my $1.50 salary and tells me to go sit with Papa until she gets home.

Everything is good down here, Henry. I hope it is with you, too.

Love,
Tom

March 30, 1944

Dear Henry,

You'll never believe what happened. The scariest man that me and Irvin know anything about has been seen in Pineview. His name is Leland Harvey. He's the worst criminal in the whole state of Georgia. He has escaped from more prisons than anybody else ever did. My daddy said the prison guards call him Houdini. He said the state quit keeping records of the number of prisons he escaped from. Daddy said one time Leland Harvey was supposed to die in the electric chair. And he escaped by soaping down his body and slipping through the bars.

Daddy said one time Governor Eugene Talmadge made a tour of the state penitentiary. They lined all the prisoners up to meet the governor. He asked everyone of them if he had committed the crime he was in prison for. Every one of them said no. When he got down to Leland Harvey he asked him what he was in jail for. He said armed robbery. The Governor asked him how long was his sentence. He said 150 years. The Governor laughed and said did you do it. He said yeah I did it. The Governor told the guard that he was going to pardon that man cause you shouldn't ever keep an honest man in a prison full of liars. Daddy said the Governor pardoned him. But he was back in jail again before the year was out.

A few days ago he escaped from a prison somewhere around LaGrange. It was written up in the Macon Telegraph that he hopped on the back of a coal truck that had just made a delivery to the prison.

Since he was born and raised in Pineview he came down to Robert Brown's café to eat a barbeque sandwich. Leland Harvey is a cousin of Melton Harvey the barber. I guess he must've come to town to visit with Melton and some of his family. Daddy said he was probably coming around here looking for somebody to loan him some money.

The word went around town like wildfire. It seemed funny to me that nobody called the police to turn him in. I guess they all must be scared of him. All the mothers were getting their children to come in the house. Some people were locking their doors. But we don't have any locks on our doors. Mama said me and my sister had to sit in the house until Leland Harvey left town.

I've never seen a real criminal before. I'd like to see what he looks like since he's so famous. I asked Daddy if Leland Harvey ever killed anybody. He said he didn't know but he'd just about done it all.

I'll be glad when he leaves town. I don't like for people to see my mama walk me to school every day. My friends in school are lucky cause they all get to ride on the school bus. Mama said she wasn't scared of Leland Harvey. I doubt if Mama is scared of anybody. Daddy said she'd fight the devil if he were to walk in our house.

Henry I wanted to tell you about this exciting news. We don't have many things this big to happen in Pineview.

Love,
Tom

April 5, 1944

Dear Henry,

My teacher asked us to write a paper about the person who meant the most to us other than our parents. It was not hard for me to decide. Nona has meant more to me than anyone. I'm going to send you what I wrote.

NONA

I call my daddy's mother Nona. Her real name is Leona. Jamie calls her Kinona. When I was little I couldn't say that so I shortened it to Nona. She told me she didn't like her name cause she thought it was ugly. She was named for her Uncle Leon.

She was born December 2, 1883. Her real name was Leona Barfield. She said her daddy was the constable in Abbeville. In October, 1901 she married Papa. She was 17 and Papa was 22. Papa's real name is Thomas Jefferson Dennard. When they first married they lived on the Pineview-Abbeville road where my daddy's farm is right behind where Boots Doster's house is now.

Papa went to the University of Virginia to learn to be a lawyer. He didn't graduate cause he had to come home. He said he got mixed up with some girl. I'm not sure what kind of mix up he had with her. But it must've been pretty bad to make him have to leave college. He taught school at a little one room schoolhouse near where they lived. When he and Nona got married he ran a saw mill. They had a baby girl named Edith. She was born December 27, 1902. Later on Nona and Papa had my daddy. He was born September 28, 1904. His name is the same as mine except I'm a junior. Everybody calls him Ed, or sometimes Edwin. Everybody calls me Little Tom cause Papa is called Tom.

Papa and Nona moved to Pineview after the town moved from where it used to be. They put the town near the Hawkinsville-Ocilla railroad that had just been built. They had a depot down by the tracks. People started building houses near the depot. Papa and Nona first lived in the house where Irvin and his mama and daddy live now. Then later on they moved in the house behind where we live now.

Daddy and Edith said that Nona is the most independent woman they've ever known. I guess they ought to know since they're her children. I'm not sure what independent means. I think it means she likes to do everything by herself.

She makes her own clothes. She made all her children's clothes. She has made some things for me to wear too. When she walks to her house from her store in the middle of the day to get something to eat, sometimes she'll go back to town in a new dress that she made while she was at home. Mama said Nona could make a dress quicker than anybody she has ever known.

Nona has a little barn behind her house where she keeps her cow. She milks the cow every morn-

ing. She has a big garden and raises all their vegetables. She said she learned how to have a good
garden from her daddy. Mr. Barfield moved from
Abbeville to live with Nona and Papa when he got
old. Daddy said he had the best gardens of anybody in the whole town. I never knew him cause
he died before I was born.

Nona has chickens and ducks and turkeys in her
backyard. I don't like to watch her kill a chicken.
She grabs it by the head and wrings the neck. The
chicken jumps around in the yard until it dies. She
soaks it in boiling hot water and plucks all the feathers off. I don't like to smell the hot chicken feathers,
so I go off and play while she's doing that.

Nona cooks her meals on a wood stove. She
chops all the stove wood. She knows how to swing
an axe just like a man. She has a push lawn mower
she uses to cut the grass in their backyard. She has
a crabapple tree and makes the best jelly of anybody in town. She makes blackberry jelly and may-
haw jelly, too. Mama uses Sure Jell. Nona never
uses that stuff. I like Nona's jelly better cause its
kind of gummy and sticky and tastes so good.

Nona had been the post-mistress in Pineview
until President Harding and the Republicans came
into power in 1920. Daddy said the Republicans
trumped up a lot of false charges against a lot
of the postmasters so they could fire them. They
fired Nona cause they said she had been taking
stamps and using them without paying for them.
She laughed when they told her what the charges
were. She couldn't believe that someone would

tell a story like that just to get her job. She later found out that all the rest of the postmasters in the other towns had been fired for the same reason.

Daddy said that Papa was kinda hot headed. He got really mad about them firing Nona. So he got in his car and drove to Macon to see the head of the post office for the whole state. Papa walked in the man's office and grabbed him by the collar underneath his chin and backed him up against the wall. The man kept saying it wasn't my fault Mr. Dennard. They made me do it. They said I had to get rid of all the Democrats.

Nona's brother in law had a 5 & 10 cents store in Abbeville where he lived. He later put one in Rochelle. When Nona was no longer the postmistress he helped her open a 5 & 10 cent store in Pineview. Nona works in her store every day except Sunday and still does all her chores at home. She teaches the Sunday School class at the Pineview Baptist Church and sings in the choir.

Nona told me that before I was born anytime somebody died in Pineview or even out in the country, Clark Funeral Home in Hawkinsville would come to her house to get her to hold the oil lantern while they embalmed the dead person. She said sometimes they'd come in the middle of the night. I asked her how they embalmed dead people. She said they'd make the family leave the room then they'd put the body on the dining room table or the kitchen table. She'd hold the lantern while the undertaker slit the side of the neck of the dead person. The undertaker would stick a tube in the neck to drain the blood out. She said she'd always take 2 pennies with her to put on the eye lids of the dead person to keep them shut. They drained all the blood out of the body in a large bottle. They'd dig a hole in the backyard to put the blood. They had a hand pump they used to suck all the gas out of the dead person's stomach. Then they'd pump formaldehyde up through the intestines. Nona would be in charge of washing the body and putting on the clothes that the family had laid out if the dead person was a woman.

I asked her how much they paid her to do this. She said they never paid her any money. She just did it cause nobody else would do anything like that but her. She was also one of the women in town they called on for the sitting up. Somebody has to stay with the body night and day after the embalming until it has been buried. The family would sit with the body during the day and she'd sit at night. She said that one time she and Juju were sitting up with Joe L.'s daddy, Mr. J. J. Dennard, right after he died. While they were sitting on the sofa his body was lying on the dining room table beside them. She said all of a sudden his arm jerked and his hand raised up in the air. Juju got scared and went home. Nona didn't leave cause she's not scared of anything.

She always makes a wreath from whatever flowers are growing in her yard and takes them to the funeral of the person who died. She is in the choir that sings at every funeral anywhere close to Pineview.

My mama said Nona was crazy for not charging people for all the things she does. She said she certainly wouldn't do anything like that without charging. I told her that's just the way Nona is. She likes to do things for people.

When girls come from poor families and can't buy clothes, Nona makes dresses for them. Jamie told me that when Annie Belle Pope's daughter Cara Lila was graduating from high school she didn't have a white dress to wear. So Nona made her a long, organdy dress.

I've worked at Nona's store every Saturday afternoon since I was 5. I like to work there. You get to see a lot of people. Mostly nigras. Nona pays me $1.50 each Saturday. Daddy gives me $1.50 allowance every week. Daddy said I should save all my money and buy war bonds. They cost $18.75 and in 10 years they'll be worth $25.00.

I don't spend too much money. I mostly spend it going to the picture show. It costs 9 cents to get in and a nickel for popcorn and a nickel for a Co Cola. I go to the picture show 3 times a week so it costs me 57 cents a week. I buy all my ice cream cones from Mr. Clements for a nickel. Since I've got so much saved up, Papa doesn't have to give me any money to buy my ice creams any more.

Every Saturday night I stay with Nona and Papa. I usually leave the store before Nona closes so I can sit with Papa until she comes home. Me and Papa always snack on sardines and soda crackers until Nona gets there and fixes our supper.

When I was little I'd get two chairs and put them on either side of the living room and play basketball with my rubber ball. Papa would holler real loud every time the ball stayed in the chair. That meant two points for the team. Every time Pineview played New York I'd always try to make sure that Pineview would win.

While I'm playing and Papa is cheering, Nona sits in her chair next to the lamp and reads her Bible and studies her Sunday School lesson. She must be a good teacher. She keeps a shoe box full of letters from soldiers who are fighting in the war telling her how much she taught them in Sunday School. I think that makes her feel real good. She said those soldiers are over there in Europe in a foxhole being shot at by the Germans. She let me read some of the letters. One said, " Dear Miss Leona, I'm over here in the land where Christ was born. I wish to Christ I was in the land where I was born."

After Nona finishes studying her Sunday School lesson, she draws a hot tub of water for me to take a bath. Sometimes it's too hot but she says you need a good hot bath to make you clean. In the wintertime she heats a towel by the fireplace and wraps it around me when I get out of the tub.

Then we listen to the Hit Parade and Judy Cannova and Amos and Andy on the radio. Those are our favorite Saturday night programs. I got a note pad from Nona's store to write down all the songs on the Hit Parade. Sometimes a new song will make it all the way to number one even though it has never been on the Hit Parade before.

I told Nona one time when we were sitting around the fire that if I ever won the 64 Dollar Question on the radio, I'd give all the money to her. She said that was nice of me but she'd rather me give it to somebody who needs it worse.

I love being with Nona and Papa on Saturday nights. We sit by the fire in the rocking chairs. Papa gets up and goes to his room to go to bed. Me and Nona talk a lot. We talk about everything. She tells me stories about when she was a little girl. She said before she married, she lived with her Aunt Belle Reagan in Hawkinsville. They went to the Episcopal Church every Sunday. She said it seemed like church went on for hours and she would get so tired.

When I was little, Nona took me with her one time to Hawkinsville to visit her Aunt Belle. I'd heard Nona talk about her so many times, I felt like I already knew her. When we went into her room she was in the bed. Nona told me she was 100 years old. I've never seen a person who was 100. You'd think she'd be crazy. But she talked to me just like anybody and made good sense.

When me and Nona finish talking, we go to bed. She has two beds in her room. I get the one with the feather mattress. On cold nights she lets me use her slop jar under the bed so I don't have to go to the cold bathroom. She won't let me get in the bed until she holds a blanket up to the fireplace and gets it good and hot. She puts the hot blanket in my bed so I have a warm spot when I sink down into the feather mattress. I always sleep so good at their house. I don't ever get scared.

On Sunday mornings Nona makes me a bowl of oatmeal. While I'm eating it she cooks eggs and toast and cream of wheat and some kind of meat like bacon or sausage or ham. I eat so much it feels like my stomach is going to bust wide open. I usually go home right after breakfast cause she has to get ready to go to Sunday School to teach the people their lessons. Nona goes to the Baptist Church. I go to Sunday School at the Methodist Church with Mama.

I hope I can be like Nona when I grow up. I'm sure I could never be as good as she is. Nona was 60 on her last birthday. I know one thing for sure. She'll definitely go to heaven. I'm going to be the best boy I can possibly be so I can go to heaven and be with Nona when I die.

THE END

Well Henry that was my story. I hope you enjoyed reading what I wrote about Nona. I'll write you more later on.

Love,
Tom

April 12, 1944

Dear Henry,

I spent last night with Nona and Papa. It felt really cool, so Papa built a fire. We sat in front of it like we always do. They have two big rocking chairs covered with cloth that has cotton stuffed inside. They are the softest rocking chairs I've ever sat in.

Papa likes for me to scratch his head. Nona does too. I always go from one chair to the next scratching their heads. Papa gives me a dime if I scratch his head a long time. Then I sit in Papa's lap. I'm 7 but I still like to sit in their laps. I've sat in their laps as long as I remember.

We were rocking and talking. Papa was spitting tobacco juice in the fireplace. Nona was fussing at him. She said quit spitting in the fireplace. I didn't want to hear them fuss so I asked Nona about the picture of her grandmother hanging over the mantle. It's in a wooden frame that has fancy carvings. She's not very pretty. I didn't tell Nona that. Her hair is parted in the middle and slicked down on both side and her ears stick out. She has a big nose and a round face that makes her look like a sad clown.

Nona said her name was Julia Amanda Powell. She lived in Macon and was in the first graduating class of Wesleyan College in the 1840's. She said that Wesleyan was the world's oldest college for women. Nona's grandmother was the first woman to get another degree after she got the first one. Nona said the main thing she could remember about her was that she had knotty feet. Nona said she asked her why her feet were so knotty. She told her that she had to walk all the way to Wesleyan College every day from her home in East Macon. Since she had to walk through the middle of downtown she always wore shoes too little so nobody could see how big her feet were.

I told Nona that was pretty stupid. Why would she do such a crazy thing like that? Nona said it was because she was a real lady.

Nona said her grandmother married Lewis Dawson Wimberly. She made all her family's clothes and was real good at knitting and crocheting. During the War Between the States she taught other women how to sew and knit and crochet. They made sweaters and scarves and gloves and mufflers for the troops.

Nona got up from her rocking chair and went in the closet. She pulled out a cardboard box full of old papers. She brought them back and sat down. She said I'm going to read you some of this letter my granddaddy wrote to my grandmother during the war. I told her I'd really like to hear it all. I like for Nona to tell about things that happened a long time ago.

The letter was written June 21, 1864 from a camp on the Chattahoochee River 8 miles west of Atlanta. I copied it down so I could send it to you.

My dear wife:

I received your letter Tuesday evening last and assure you it was a great pleasure to hear from home, and that you were all doing as well as you are. I'm sorry to hear that little Mattie is not well. Your letters are about the only pleasure I have. No one writes me but you.

We were aroused yesterday morning an hour before day to march to this place which is about 12 miles from our old camp. We marched it in 4 hours. We were sleeping without tents, and it rained all night and is still raining this morning. We are undergoing a great many hardships which are too numerous to mention. But you must not grieve. You must grieve for your bleeding country and think how much better off you are than many a family running from the enemy which comes under my eyes every day.

They are moving us to the enemy lines, but I do not think that any man ought to shrink from duty at the present emergency, for it is my opinion if any man does not shoulder his musket now, he is no friend to his country. So you must not write me despondent letters for I feel confident if I should have to go into a fight, the Lord will protect me from all bullets, and I trust him anyhow. You should do the same, or if it should be my fate to fall in battle, then the Lord will provide for you and my dear little ones.

I am as hardy as I can be, for our meat that we get now is all middling meat and about 4 years old, for it is as rancid as any old meat you ever saw. If you send anything to me by John Humphries, make sure that it be something that he can tote. If it has to be mailed, it will cost as much to get it here as it will be worth. But it's coming from the hands of one that is dearer to me than anyone else makes me appreciate it very highly.

If General Johnston is successful, I will be at home with you soon. If not, there is no telling when we will be turned loose. Hoping to be with you soon, I am as ever, L.D.W. (Lewis Dawson Wimberly)

I asked Nona if her granddaddy got killed in the war.

She said he died a few years after the war from a fever he got in the trenches.

I ask her if he was an old man.

She said he was only 46 when he died. He left his wife with 5 little children to raise – 3 girls and 2 boys. One of the girls was Nona's mama. Her name was Minnie. One of the boys was named Leon, and that's where Nona got the name of Leona.

After her granddaddy died her grandmother became a school teacher. She had to try to make enough money to take care of the children. She moved to Hawkinsville. Nona's mama, Minnie, married Jesse Barfield from Abbeville. That's where Nona was born.

Henry, you probably don't care a thing about all this. But I love to hear stories that Nona and Papa tell me about old times.

Love,
Tom

June 18, 1944

Dear Henry,

How are things in heaven? I bet its really nice up there with all that milk and honey. I'm looking forward to going up there and being with you. But I'm not ready to die yet. I guess you weren't ready to die either. I'm sorry you got run over. I still miss you a lot.

Now that I'm 8 Mama and Daddy let me drive the car to town. If I sit up really straight I can see over the steering wheel. If Mama needs a loaf of bread or something from T.O.'s she sends me to get it. I have to walk. But when Daddy brings the car home he lets me drive the car down town.

I've been driving about a year now. I was 7 when Daddy decided to teach me how to drive. I told him I thought it was about time. He had his own car when he was 12. He didn't know that me and Irvin had already been driving around for a long time. Irvin's daddy has a Ford. He rides the Warner Robins bus to work every day so Irvin's car sits in the garage most all the time. When his mother goes off in the afternoon to play bridge, we back it in and out of the garage. One time Irvin's foot slipped off the clutch and the front of the car hit the back of the garage so hard I thought it was going to knock it down.

My daddy has a 1942 black Buick Special. It's a pretty car. I really wanted Daddy to buy a Super or a Roadmaster instead of a Special but he said those cars cost almost a thousand dollars.

I remember the first time I ever saw Daddy's new car. He was down at Nona's store. He'd stopped there to show it to her. It was so black and shiny. I thought it was the prettiest car I'd ever seen. It was a 2 door car like most everybody else's car in town. I've seen pictures of cars that have 4 doors. Maybe one day Daddy will be able to afford one of them.

Last year Daddy was teaching me how to drive his car. It was hard for me to press the clutch all the way down to the floorboard without sitting on the very front of the seat. When I let the clutch out it jerked and jumped a few times. But I finally got used to what the clutch was supposed to do.

One time I thought I had it in reverse to back out but when I let the clutch out it went forward toward the house into the shrubbery. I had to slam on the brakes to keep from hitting the house. Daddy said goddam. But he says that so many times every day I didn't pay much attention to it.

After I finally got the clutch figured out he had to teach me the hand signals. He said no matter how cold it might be or how hard it's raining you have to roll the window down every time you make a turn to the right or the left. If you're turning left you stick your left arm straight out of the window to let the cars behind you and in front of you know what you're going to do. If you're turning right you stick your left arm out the window and bend your elbow so that your hand is sticking straight up. Then you bend your wrist and point your hand to the right. That way everybody will know you're going to make a right turn. If you're going to stop, you put your arm out the window and point it straight down toward the ground.

Daddy had to teach me how to change a tire cause you're lucky if you go on a trip somewhere and can get all the way back home without having at least one flat tire. There are so many nails in the dirt roads around Pineview. I guess they come from all the horses and mules that pull nigras in wagons.

I learned about changing tires pretty good. You take the jack and the lug wrench and the spare tire out of the trunk of the car. Take the flat end of the lug wrench and stick it in the hub cap to pop it off. The hard part comes when you have to loosen the lugs. Sometimes they're on so tight I have to stand on the wrench to loosen them. Once you get them all loosened, you put the jack underneath the back bumper and start jacking the car up until it starts to lift the flat tire off the ground. That's when you unscrew all the lugs and drop them in the hubcap. Then you got to pull the flat tire off the car and put the spare tire on. Screw the lugs on as tight as you can. Then take the lug wrench and tighten the lugs some more until they are real tight. Put the flat tire in the trunk and take it down to Hardy Gordon's filling station. He'll pull the tube out and patch it. After he patches it he puts the tube back in the tire and then it's as good as new.

Most of the time Daddy lets me drive to the farm. I don't really like going to the farm but I do like to drive. I go with him pretty much every time he goes. Now that he's working for the Internal Revenue he's never at home before I go to bed at night. And he leaves before I get up in the morning. So mostly my driving trips to the farm are only on Sunday afternoons. He usually gets off from work early on Saturdays but that's when I'm working at Nona's store.

Daddy lets me drive to church on Sunday mornings. He said he didn't want me to drive out of town until I'm 9. I'll be glad when I get a little older so I can drive anywhere I want to. I wonder if Daddy will buy me a car when I'm 12 like his Daddy did for him. I guess I'll just have to wait and see.

Henry, I'll write more later.

Love,
Tom

June 23, 1944

Dear Henry,

Mama always makes me get haircuts. I hate getting my hair cut. Yesterday, I promised her I would. A whole lot of men were in the barber shop waiting. Most of them wanted a haircut. Some wanted a shave. Some wanted a haircut and a shave. A few men go to the barber shop to take a shower. I think it costs a dime. I have to pay a dime to get my haircut. When you get to be 12 you have to pay a quarter.

Melton has a long wooden bench where you have to sit to wait for your turn. I got mad yesterday. When it was my turn I stood up. An old man looked at me and said, " I came in before you." But he was telling a big story cause I came in before he did. I thought Melton would say something about it but he didn't.

Mama said when I was little Melton had to tie my arms and legs down in the chair to keep me from jumping up and running out. I remember a little bit about that. He used the leather strap that he sharpens his razor with to tie around my waist. Mama stood beside me threatening me the whole time that Melton was cutting my hair. Finally she told me that I was going to kill her. She said she couldn't stand it anymore.

The next time I got my haircut Cudin Charlye took me. She gets her hair cut there, too. I think she's the only woman I've ever seen who gets her haircut in the men's barber shop. All the men have to watch what they say when she's in there. They usually say things you can't say in front of a woman.

After that Cudin Charlye would come by our house and pick me up every time she got her haircut. She told Mama I acted a whole lot better with her than I did with Mama. That suited Mama just fine.

Mama always gets somebody else to do her dirty work. Every time I get a sore throat she carries me over to Cudin Pauline's house to get my throat mopped out. She pushes me in the door and goes back home. Cudin Pauline takes a piece of cotton, ties it around a stick and then dips it in turpentine. The first time she did it I screamed and she slapped me. So I don't holler anymore. I just suffer through it. She makes me open my mouth and then puts a spoon on my tongue to hold it down. She sticks the cotton soaked in turpentine back in my throat and mops it out real good. It tastes awful and burns too. I'd like to hit her, but I'm scared to after she slapped the tar out of me.

Since I started to school I've been going by myself to get a haircut. Now that I'm 8, I ought not to have to sit on the board that Melton puts over the arm of the chair. Irvin is taller, so he gets to sit on the seat. I asked Melton if I could sit on the seat. He said maybe later.

By the time Melton got to me yesterday there was nobody there except me and him. He likes to talk all the time while he's cutting people's hair. I don't ever say anything.

He told me they're having their summer revival at Friendship Baptist Church at Pleasant View. After not talking for a little while he asked me if I have made myself right with God.

I didn't really know what to say, but I finally said I guess I have. I go to church every Sunday to the Methodist and Baptist churches.

He said going to church is not enough cause many will be called but only a few will be chosen. I thought about that for a minute. I don't know if I'm going to be chosen or not.

When Daddy got home last night, I asked him what Melton meant by that. I'm not sure why I asked him. Daddy probably doesn't even know. I don't think he'll be chosen. He drinks too much liquor and smokes one cigarette after another and cusses all the time.

Daddy said Melton ought to be worried about being chosen.

I asked him why he said that.

He lit a cigarette and blew the smoke in my face. Then he said he'd tell me one of these days.

I told him I needed to know right now, cause there's no telling what might happen to me.

He had a smirk on his face just like he's always telling me to wipe the smirk off my face.

Daddy said when Melton was young he got caught in bed with the policeman's wife. He said when the policeman came home unexpected Melton jumped out the window and ran down the street naked.

Daddy acted like I ought to have laughed. But I couldn't believe what he was saying. That just didn't seem like something Melton would do. I don't really understand stuff like that. I know I would never want to get naked in the bed with a woman. It sounds gross.

Last night before I went to sleep, I laid in the bed thinking about what Daddy said. I bet Melton really is worried about getting chosen. I said my prayers:

> Now I lay me down to sleep;
> I pray the Lord my soul to keep;
> If I should die before I wake;
> I pray the Lord my soul to take.
> And dear God please choose Melton.
> Amen.

I'll write you later.

Love,
Tom

July 8, 1944

Dear Henry,

You'll never guess what happened last Saturday. It was a day I'll remember for the rest of my life. I was working at Nona's store like I always do. Nona told me to go to her house and sit with Papa when the sun started going down.

Papa had already opened a can of sardines. He got out the soda crackers and the Tabasco when he saw me coming in the door. I can eat one every time he hands it to me. I drink a big gulp of water after I eat one. Some people say that Papa drinks liquor. But he never has drunk any in front of me.

Papa asked me if my belly was full. That's what he always says every time he thinks we've had enough. We went out on the back porch to sit in the big rocking chairs they used to rock me in when I was a baby. Papa tells me stories about things he used to do when he was a little boy. I love to hear the stories even though I've heard them a lot of times before.

Papa has been worrying a lot about the war. He doesn't talk much about it. But he sits with his ear right up next to the radio so he can hear all the news about what's going on. The man who gives the news is H.V. Kaltenborn.

Boy is in the war in Germany. Everybody in our family worries about him. Edith and Hendley can hardly talk about it without crying. Every time Papa hears an airplane flying over the house he always walks to the door and looks up in the sky to see if he can see it. I don't really understand why he does that. Sometimes I wonder if he thinks the planes might be carrying Japs or Germans who are going to bomb us.

That night while we sat and rocked and talked, Papa got up from his chair and walked to the back-door. I thought he had heard a plane flying over. Then I heard him falling down those old wooden steps into the backyard. I jumped up and ran to the door. Papa was lying on the ground with his face down in the dirt. The porch was higher than my daddy and he's 6 feet tall. I knew Papa must've hurt himself really bad.

I screamed PAPA as loud as I could. He didn't move. He didn't make a sound. I ran as fast as I could to our house, screaming all the way. Mama was playing the piano and Daddy was singing. Mary is only two years old and was sitting on the floor playing with her dolls.

I screamed out PAPA IS DEAD.

Daddy and Mama jumped up and ran out the backdoor as fast as they could. Mama yelled for me to go get Edith. When I ran out of the backyard there was a big dog standing in the road barking at me. So I ran back as fast as I could to catch up with Daddy. Mama turned around and said she would get Edith.

Daddy ran toward Papa. He was still lying there on the ground just like I left him. I watched Daddy lean over and pick him up. Papa was a big man. He probably weighed over 200 pounds. Daddy scooped Papa up in his arms just like he might be carrying my little sister. He carried him up all ten steps without stumbling. I held the door open for him. Daddy laid Papa on his bed. His eyes were shut and he was not moving at all.

In a few minutes, Mama and Edith and Hendley ran in the front door. Mama said I had to go home to stay with my sister. We'd run out and left her sitting on the floor by herself. I didn't want to leave Papa. Nona and Papa don't have a telephone, so Edith ran back to her house to call an ambulance. It took almost an hour for them to get there from Hawkinsville. They took Papa to the Fitzgerald Hospital. The doctor told Daddy that Papa had had a stroke and it didn't look good. There're only two doctors at the hospital. They're brothers and their names are R.M. Ware and D.B. Ware. Daddy likes R.M. the best cause he is the one who delivered me and my sister.

Papa was never conscious again after he fell. He died Thursday. I was playing cars with Irvin in Nona's backyard when Daddy came to tell me. I cried cause I loved Papa so much. Other than Irvin, he was my best friend. I knew I wouldn't get to drive his car to the farm anymore. I wouldn't get to chew tobacco with him. He wouldn't be telling me any more of his stories about when he was a little boy. I wouldn't get to eat sardines with him on Saturday night. He wouldn't be giving me anymore nickels to buy an ice cream cone. He was gone forever.

The funeral was held this morning in the living room at Nona's house. Nona said it wouldn't be right to have his funeral at a church where he was not a member.

That really scared me. I knew if Papa wasn't a member of a church he wouldn't go to heaven. I wanted him to go to heaven and be with the rest of our family, at least those of us who go to church and don't drink liquor and don't smoke cigarettes or gamble or cuss.

The funeral home put lots of folding chairs in Nona's living room and front bedroom next to the living room. All the chairs were filled with people. A lot of folks stood on the front porch. The nigras were standing out in the front yard. They'd been his good friends just as much as the white people. Some of them had worked with him in his cotton gin. He'd helped a lot of them over the years when he was mayor and on the county commission.

Nona sat in a big chair in the doorway of the bedroom. She had on a black dress and a wide brimmed black hat with a black veil over her face. I sat beside her and cried. But Nona didn't cry. I kept looking but I never saw a single tear come down her cheek. I wondered why she didn't cry. Papa was her husband. She must've loved him. But she didn't cry when he died and I'll never ask her why.

His gravestone says:
THOMAS JEFFERSON DENNARD
BORN FEBRUARY 21, 1879
DIED JULY 6, 1944

I wish I could write on the gravestone that he was the best granddaddy that any little boy could ever have.

I'm sorry to have to write sad things like this to you, Henry. I know you are up there in heaven where everything is good and wonderful. But sometimes sad things happen in Pineview.

Love,
Tom

July 30, 1944

Dear Henry,

One of my favorite things to do is camping out. I like sleeping outside. Me and Irvin sometimes get an old mattress and put it inside the smokehouse to sleep on. We like to eat outside and look up at the stars. We get some of the leftovers out of Mama's refrigerator. But sometimes we like to cook. Daddy has a charcoal stove about the size of a bucket. After you get the charcoal started you can put a frying pan on it or you can put a grill on it if you want to cook some hamburgers or hot dogs. Food just tastes so much better when you cook and eat outside.

Me and Irvin usually slip 2 or 3 of my daddy's cigarettes when he's not looking. We can smoke them while we're sitting around outside. I can't smoke more than one cause it makes my stomach feel sick. Irvin can smoke 2 or 3. I don't like to taste the smoke in my mouth. But it's better than Papa's chewing tobacco.

After we eat, we go inside the smokehouse and get on the mattress and jump up and down. When we get tired we lay down and look up at the hams and shoulders and sausages hanging over our heads. The whole place smells like smoked meat. But we don't care. We like smoked meat. We talk about all kinds of things like our dogs or swimming at Pappy Jack or how we don't get into fights like we used to when we were little. Sometimes we talk about girls but not much.

In the middle of the night it never fails. Irvin gets scared. He says he hears something or sees something or feels something. He always wants to go in the house to spend the rest of the night. I don't think we've ever spent a whole night sleeping outside.

One time he woke me up and said he thought he heard somebody outside walking around. He wanted to know if I could hear it. I told him I didn't hear a thing. We crawled up the side of the wall and looked out through the slats to see if we could see anybody. I couldn't see anything. But Irvin still wanted to go inside the house.

One time we decided to spend the night in the barn instead of the smokehouse. The barn is between our house and Nona and Papa's house. We spent the whole afternoon cleaning up trash and spider webs in one of the corners of the barn to have a place to sleep. We found a set of old bedsprings and got the mattress we always use. We practiced during the afternoon laying on it. It felt pretty good.

Late that afternoon we went down to T O's grocery store and bought a pound of hamburger meat and some buns. The meat cost a quarter and the buns were a dime. We charged it to Mama's account. We went to Sam's filling station to buy some RC Colas. RC's have 12 ounces. I really like the taste of a Co Cola better. But they only have

6 ounces. Mama doesn't have a charge account at Sam's so we both had to pay the nickel out of our allowance money.

We got Daddy's old charcoal grill started late that afternoon when the sun was going down. When Daddy cooks hamburgers he always puts the buns on the grill to get them hot and smoke them a little bit. I got the catsup and mustard and mayonnaise out of Mama's refrigerator. We both ate 2 hamburgers and they were really good, too.

We went inside the barn when it started getting dark and got on the mattress. We talked about a lot of things for a long time. I tried to talk about things that wouldn't make Irvin scared. After we went to sleep Irvin started shaking me. He told me to wake up. He said he'd seen something red going by the barn. I asked him what kind of red thing was he talking about. He said it was like a little red light that was moving right by us. I told him it was probably my Daddy going over to Nona's and Papa's with a cigarette in his mouth. Irvin said it was not my daddy. It was definitely not a person.

All of a sudden Irvin jumped up and ran out of the front of the barn as fast as he could and into the back door of our house. I was running right behind him. After we got in the house I started walking up toward my room so we could get in my bed. Irvin said he didn't think we ought to sleep up there by ourselves. He wanted to sleep on the floor next to Mama and Daddy's bed. We tiptoed into their room and laid down on the rug beside their bed and slept the rest of the night.

Last weekend we decided to do the biggest camp out of our whole lives. We planned to camp out down at Tony Ford about a mile back of Aunt Ida and Uncle Philet's house. We rode the school bus as far as it went then got out and walked about another mile to get to their house.

Ephraim hitched up the mule to the wagon. We put an old mattress in the back of the wagon to sleep on. We got a bunch of food from Aunt Ida's pie safe where Ephraim keeps bread and cake and cookies and stuff. Ephraim picked two ripe tomatoes and pulled up two onions out of the garden. He took some cooked bacon and sausage from the ice box left over from breakfast and put it all in a paper sack. Then we took off in the wagon. Irvin was sitting up on the plank holding the reins.

Irvin wanted to hold the rope to drive the mule cause he said he could do it better than I could. I told him I didn't think the mule really needed much driving cause he'd been down to Tony Ford so many times he knew the way to go without us telling him. When we got there we unhitched the mule from the wagon and tied him to a pine tree with the rope.

Tony Ford is a place where people go to swim. Sometimes they have baptizings down there. It's a creek with cold water and a cleared out spot next to it. We don't go down there very much to go swimming cause we usually go to Pappy Jack or Bluff Creek or the Whirl Hole. They are closer to Pineview than Tony Ford.

Last summer our family had a picnic down at Tony Ford on 5th Sunday when you don't have to go to church. Nona and Juju and Edith and Mama and Daddy and a whole bunch of other people carried some food down there. Before we ate we all jumped in the water except Edith. She didn't want to get wet. That's the only time I've ever seen Nona swimming. She and Juju went in the water with their dresses on cause I don't guess they have a bathing suit. While they were swimming, the bottom of their dresses came up around their shoulders. They looked funny. They swim funny too. When they got out in the water over their heads they paddled their hands up and down really fast like a dog. It made me laugh. We all ate a lot of food and then laid down in the grass. You're not supposed to swim after you eat cause it'll make you have stomach cramps and you might die.

Before me and Irvin go swimming we always throw a bunch of rocks in the water to scare off any moccasins or whatever kinds of snakes that might be in there. I remember one time we went down to Tony Ford to swim. When we drove up we could see a moccasin swimming down the creek right in the center of the stream where we always go swimming. It had its head sticking up really high. Me and Irvin just sort of played around in the edge of the water that day.

After we got the mule tied to the tree, we took off our clothes and jumped in the water. We always go swimming naked unless there are girls around. We swam around until we got too cold and kinda hungry. I started pulling the food out of the wagon. We sat on the ground next to the water and ate until our stomachs couldn't hold anymore.

We jumped up on the back of the wagon when it started getting dark. The mattress was wider than the wagon so it curved up on both sides. Every time we tried to get apart from each other we kept rolling back down the hill. There was just no way not to be jammed up next to each other. A few hours after we finally got to sleep we heard some lightning and thundering. We hadn't even thought about rain. We didn't bring anything with us to keep the rain off. The mule got scared of the lightning and started raring up and down and up and down. The rope broke and the mule took off running as fast as he could back toward the barn. Me and Irvin looked at each other. We didn't have a watch but we figured it must've been about midnight.

Irvin started getting worried. I did too. I told him if it started to rain we could put the mattress under the wagon. The lightning started getting closer. Irvin was scared. I was, too. About that time we saw some headlights coming through the woods. We thought it might be murderers coming to kill us.

When the lights got close enough, we recognized the pickup. It was Boots Doster. He said the thundering and lightning woke him up. He knew he'd better come down and check on us. The rain hadn't started. But we had never been so happy to see anybody in our lives.

He wanted to know if we'd had about enough camping.

We told him we were ready to get back to the house. He wanted to know what happened to the mule. We told him about the mule breaking the rope and running back to the barn.

We jumped in Boot's truck, and he drove us back to Aunt Ida's and Uncle Philet's house.

The old mule was standing by the barn door waiting for somebody to let him back in. He wouldn't even look at me and Irvin. I guess he was embarrassed for being so scared.   Boots opened the gate and let him in, then went in the back door of the house and yelled, "Mama" real loud. Aunt Ida jumped up. Uncle Philet never hears a thing cause he takes his hearing aids out at night. Aunt Ida turned down one of the beds. We jumped in it and pulled the cover up over our heads.

Maybe one of these days me and Irvin will get to spend a whole night outside when we go camping. I'll write you when that happens.

Love,
Tom

August 9, 1944

Dear Henry,

Next to playing basketball my most favorite things to do in the whole world is to put on plays. Do you remember that room in the barn that has a floor in it? Me and Irvin hung up a curtain that goes all the way across the room. We put three boards across some blocks we found under Nona's house to make benches for the audience to sit on. I slipped some of Daddy and Mama's old clothes and hats out of the house for us to wear. Sometimes we get some of Mama's high heel shoes. I always write down what everyone in the play is supposed to say. Joan and Betty Jean play the parts for girls, and me and Irvin play the parts for the boys. We usually practice going over the play several times, then I start going around town to look for some people to watch the play. Usually its only Angie and James and Sammy and Billy that show up.

The last play we put on was called *What Am I Going to Do?* It was about Hitler and his girlfriend. She didn't want to be Hitler's girlfriend. But she didn't know how to get out of it cause she was afraid Hitler would kill her if she left him. Irvin played the part of Hitler. I brushed his hair over his forehead the same way Hitler wore his and made him a mustache out of some of Mama's make up. Betty

Jean played the part of Hitler's girlfriend. Her name in the play was Pootsill Ball. Joan was the maid. Her name was Betty Graybull.

It was supposed to be a comedy. But Sammy stood up and stopped the play right after we got started. He said he didn't like the costume Betty Jean was wearing cause you could see her breast. I came out on the stage and argued with Sammy that you couldn't see her breast cause she didn't have any breast. I told Sammy she's only 10 years old. Sammy got mad and said he was taking Betty Jean home right then. Angie said she didn't like the name of Hitler's girlfriend cause it wasn't nice to say that word.   James and Billy didn't care. They just laughed cause they thought it was funny. Sammy grabbed Betty Jean by the hand and took her home. Angie got up and left so we stopped the play. What else could we do? My play was a failure.

The play we did before that one was really good. Everyone liked it cause Dinah Hyman was in it. She is Juju's niece from Cordele. She and her mother Flossie came over to Pineview to visit Juju cause they're sisters. Me and Dinah decided to put on a play together. Dinah can sing really good and has sung on the stage before. She's 9 years old. I'm only 8.

The play we did was a musical. I think she sang all the songs she knew. I played the part of her boyfriend. I didn't do anything. I just mostly stood up there on the stage and let her sing all the songs to me. Sammy and James and Angie and Billy and

Irvin and Joan and Betty Jean said this was the best play we've ever had.

We've put on about 6 plays so far this summer. Mama hasn't seen any of them. But I heard her bragging to somebody the other day about how good I was at writing plays to be just 8 years old. I'm glad she didn't hear about the reason that Sammy took Betty Jean home cause she'd have given me a good whipping. Even though what Sammy said wasn't true. I also would've gotten a whipping for naming Hitler's wife Pootsill Ball.

That's about all there is to write now. I'll write more later.

Love,
Tom

August 14, 1944

Dear Henry,

You won't believe what a great thing DDT is. It kills everything. And I mean everything. We don't have any roaches or ants or mosquitoes or spiders or any crawly things inside our house anymore. It's the greatest stuff ever invented. I wish we'd been spraying it all over our house forever. Then we wouldn't have to listen to mosquitoes singing in our ears when we're trying to go to sleep.

When you want to get your house sprayed you have to make an appointment with the people who are doing the spraying. They came to our house and told us we had to pull all the furniture away from the walls in every room of the house except the kitchen. There was no way we could pull the stove or the cabinets out cause they are nailed to the wall. We had to cover all the furniture with bed sheets. I helped Mama pull the dressers and chest of drawers and cabinets and everything back from the walls. Then I helped her put the sheets on top of all the furniture.

They told us to get outside the house when they do the spraying. You probably wouldn't want to get the stuff sprayed up your nose. Me and Irvin went in our house about an hour after it was sprayed. It looked like they had sprayed milk all around. There was dried up white looking stuff on the floor next to the walls in every room of our house. It had a funny smell. Even that night after we pulled the sheets off the furniture and pushed it back I could still smell that stuff. I could even smell it when I went to bed. But that's O.K. cause we sure don't have any insects in our house anymore.

Just about every house in the whole town got sprayed. A lot of people in town have been talking about how good it is that they invented DDT.

My little sister is just 2 ½ years old. She started throwing up during the night. I felt kinda nauseated too. Daddy said there could be some kind of virus going around.

Love,
Tom

August 20, 1944

Dear Henry,

I just got back from a trip and want to tell you about it. It all started with a bunch of us sitting around dreaming about how much fun it'd be if we could go to the beach. We were complaining about how the only place we have to cool off in the hot summer is Bluff Creek and the Whirl Hole and Pappy Jack Springs. We wanted to go swimming in the ocean where we could jump waves and all.

There's a girl in my class named Jo Horne. She lives in Finleyson. Her great aunt's name is Nan Bruce. She has a rooming house at Jacksonville Beach. She used to live in Pineview but that was before I was born. Mama and Daddy have taken me and Mary to Nan's place several times to spend a few days for our summer vacation. Her house is not far from the beach.

Angie asked her mama about going but she said we couldn't go unless we had a chaperone. We had no idea who we could get. Angie asked me to see if Nona would go. I didn't want to ask her since Papa just died last month. But she said yes she would go.

Those who wanted to go were Angie and James and Sammy and Billy and Irvin and me and Nona. Sammy is pretty old. He's 14. He still can't drive a car. Nona is really, really old. She's 59 and she can't drive a car either. Plus, she doesn't have a car, even if she could drive. We decided the best thing to do was to take the Greyhound Bus.

Of course there's no bus that comes through Pineview. We just have old dirt roads that no bus could ride on. The nearest place to catch a bus is out on the Abbeville highway where my mama's Aunt Sally lives. Her husband is named Ambrose Nazareth. It's hard for me to say his name. So I've never called him anything to his face. I don't think he has ever called my name either.

The way you have to get the bus to stop is for Aunt Sally to stand out on the edge of the highway and watch for the bus. When she sees it coming she starts waving her white handkerchief up and down so the bus driver will see her. Thank goodness he did. So when it stopped all 7 of us piled into the bus one by one holding our suitcases. All the other people sitting in their seats were looking at us. I bet they were all wondering where we might be going.

The driver said it'd be all right if we waited until we got to Abbeville to buy our tickets. I was so excited I could feel butterflies in my stomach. Angie sat next to Nona 'cause they were the only girls on the trip. Sammy and James sat together. Me and Irvin and Billy sat in the back of the bus where nigras usually sit. But there weren't any on the bus that day.

We bought our tickets in Abbeville to go to Jacksonville. The bus stopped in Fitzgerald, Ocilla, Douglas, Alma, and Waycross. I couldn't believe it but the bus stopped at Stuckey's. That's one of my favorite places in the whole world. Stuckey's sells all kinds of things you can't buy in Pineview like coconut milk and papaya juice and pecan logs. Every time I've stopped there with Mama and Daddy I always get a glass of coconut milk and a pecan log.

Daddy said Stuckey's sits right on the Georgia-Florida line but it doesn't. It's really in Florida and that gets me all excited cause I know that Jacksonville Beach is not far away. I think Mama and Daddy have taken me and Mary to Jacksonville Beach every summer of our lives.

I always remember Daddy talking about taking Mama to Jacksonville Beach for her first time. They got married on November 12, 1933 and went to live with Nona and Papa. Daddy came down with typhoid fever. He was really sick. He was in bed for ten months and almost died. Nona said he sweated so much that almost every time she walked in the room she had to wipe him down with a towel and change the bed sheets. He was unconscious most of the time Nona said.

When he started getting better at the end of the summer he wanted to take Mama to Jacksonville Beach for their honeymoon. He said they stayed in a little one bedroom cabin right next to the ocean. They pushed up all the windows at night to let the ocean air come in to cool them off while they slept. Daddy said that every night they'd have to get up in the middle of the night to take the sheets off the bed and shake them out to get the salt off.

He talked about a fellow who would wake them up every morning yelling fried pies. He would walk up to their window and yell, "fried pies for sale." He said they tried the apple and pineapple and strawberry but the banana pies were his favorite.

After they'd been there a few days, Daddy got blistered really bad from being out on the beach. He hadn't been out of Nona's house for so long he said his skin was as white as cotton. Mama never got blistered. Daddy said its cause she has elephant skin.

Last summer Daddy and Mama took me and Mary to Jacksonville Beach for a week. Edith and Hendley went with their children Jamie and Sister and Boy. I was just 7 and Mary was 2. Boy took me to ride on the roller coaster. Nobody else would ride it except me and him.

One night we took our supper to a picnic ground next to the beach. We ate sandwiches and potato chips and drank ice tea. We were having fun until we heard my sister scream. Daddy ran over and grabbed her up. She had stepped on a piece of glass and cut her foot really bad. Mama went running with Daddy to the car and he was holding Mary in his arms. I stayed with Edith and Hendley while they took her to the hospital to get her foot sewed up.

Well back to our trip. We had to get a beach bus at the bus station in Jacksonville that dropped us off about a half a mile from Nan's Rooming House. It was a long way to have to drag our suitcases. Me and Irvin hardly got inside the house good before we opened up our suitcases and put on our bathing suits. We ran all the way to the beach as fast as we could and didn't stop until we jumped in the water.

There were some funny looking things floating all around in the ocean that looked like pink and blue baby bonnets. I'd never seen anything that looked like that before. The nearest one was about 10 feet away. Any time me and Irvin run after something we always try to see who can beat the other. Irvin is a lot taller and his legs are longer so he got there first and grabbed it up to show it to me. That's when he let out the loudest scream I've ever heard come out of his mouth. You could hear him for miles. He ran out of the water yelling at the top of his voice. I was right behind him. A lifeguard heard him and started running toward him. He tackled Irvin and threw him down on the ground and began rubbing sand all over Irvin's hands and arms.

I wanted to ask the lifeguard what was wrong but Irvin was hollering too loud. Finally the lifeguard said that he'd been stung by a Portuguese Man of War. He wanted to know if I'd been stung too. I told him I hadn't cause if one had stung me I'd be yelling just like Irvin.

I could see red streaks running up Irvin's arms like someone had carved them with a pocket-knife. Other people on the beach began gathering around him. One man said those things have tentacles about 10 feet long.

Sammy and Angie came running toward us. They could tell it was Irvin hollering all the way back down to Nan's Rooming House. The lifeguard took Irvin to the lifeguard station. I ran along behind them. They rubbed Irvin's arms and hands with alcohol and ammonia and some other stuff that I didn't know what it was. I kept thinking that our trip to the beach had been ruined.

Every day after that, me and Irvin went to the Penny Arcade. We played around on the beach making sand castles and stuff like that but we never put a toe in the water for the rest of the trip.

Billy and James have just turned into teen-agers. They're 13 and me and Irvin are just 8. They're always talking to us about things we don't know anything about or care anything about like what boys do to girls and all kinds of crazy stuff like that. They told us they were going down on the board-walk to meet some girls at the Mermaid Lounge that sells cocktails.

Later on me and Irvin were walking on the boardwalk and saw a big sign that said MERMAID LOUNGE - Best Cocktails on the Beach. We decided to go in there and see what it was that Billy and James were talking about. A big man with a mustache was standing behind a bar staring at us. He wanted to know what we wanted.

I told him we wanted one of those cocktails.

He had a funny looking grin on his face. He wanted to know what kind of cocktail we wanted.

Irvin said we just wanted the usual kind. Fruit cocktail.

The man laughed and said something to a woman who was sitting up on a bar stool painting her fingernails. She walked out and after a while came back carrying a paper sack. The man told us to sit down at one of the tables. In a few minutes the woman brought over two bowls and two spoons.

She wanted to know how old we were. We both said 8 at the same time. Irvin asked her how old she was. She said 32. We knew she was pretty old but we didn't realize she was that old.

We ate every bit of the fruit cocktail. Then she brought the bill over to our table. We couldn't believe that he charged us a quarter for just a bowl of fruit cocktail! I told Irvin that was the most expensive fruit cocktail I'd ever eaten. Irvin said they must've added some money on the bill for the music they were playing on the jukebox.

Well, Henry, that's about all I have to tell you about our trip. I'll write more about what's going on in Pineview later.

Love,
Tom

September 15, 1944

Dear Henry,

I just started the 3rd grade. Miss Mary Will Barrentine is my teacher. They say she's a good teacher but she's really hard. I hope she's not going to be too hard. She started off by telling us we had to write a story about somebody. I wrote about Edith. This is what I wrote.

EDITH DENNARD McLEOD
MY 2nd GRADE TEACHER

Last year my 2nd grade teacher was my aunt. She's my daddy's sister. I was glad to have her as my teacher. She's my favorite person except for Nona. A lot of times I would go to Edith's house when I was a little boy and spend the day. It's not very far to get from my house to hers. I just have to walk up the red hill.

Edith was born on December 27, 1902. She is 2 years older than my daddy. She married Hendley McLeod. They have 3 children. Jamie is 22. Ann is the one we call Sister. She is 20. Boy is 18. He has the same name as his daddy but everybody calls him Boy. He is in the Army now fighting overseas in Germany. I'm just 8. All of Edith's children are a whole lot older than me. But I still like to go play with them anyway.

All the students in the class last year called her Miss Edith. That's what I called her too. But really she's just Edith to me. One of the girls in my class asked me why I didn't call her Aunt Edith. I've never called any of my aunts and uncles that way. I've always just called them by their first name.

Edith went off to finishing school to Andrew College in Cuthbert, Georgia when she was 14. The president of the college was her favorite professor. After 2 years he left Andrew to go to Centenary College in Cleveland, Tennessee. Edith and some of the other girls left Andrew and went with him to Centenary.

She spent 2 more years and got a degree in English and dramatics and expression. Nona said she was president of the YWCA. She was president of the student council and she sang in the glee club. Nona and Papa were real proud of what she did in college. After she graduated she married Hendley when she was 18.

My daddy loves his sister. He and Mama go on vacations with Edith and Hendley sometimes. I guess they see each other every day. Daddy said one time he'd do anything in the whole world for her.

He told me when she was little she was scared of the dark. When Nona and Papa would go off somewhere they would get Sam and Bud to stay with Edith and Daddy. Sam and Bud liked to play tricks on them. They liked to see how much they could scare them. Daddy said one of them would go outside the house at night and start scratching on the screen. They got a kick out of making Edith scream.

Edith likes to read books more than anybody I've ever known. Every time I go up to her house she's always reading a book. Her den is full of books from the floor to the ceiling. She's in some kind of book club where she gets a book every month. Sometimes she gives me one of her books to read. They are too hard for me. She gave me a book called The Razor's Edge. I tried to read it. I gave up cause I didn't understand it. She told me she'd like for me to start reading some of Ernest Hemingway's books. He was her favorite author. I told her I thought I might wait until I was a little older. The only books I like to read are adventure books by Zane Grey.

Edith tries to teach me a lot of things when I go to see her. She said I must go to a good college. I have to get the best education I can possibly get if I want to make something out of myself. But I don't know what I want to be when I grow up. Right now that all seems so far away. I can hardly even think about it.

Edith and Sister sometimes play the ouija board. They tell me to wish for something and the ouija board will tell me if it's going to come true. I told them I didn't believe it. They made me ask the board a question. There's a small wooden thing with a point on it. Sister would put her hands on it and I would too. Then the piece of wood starts moving around to different letters on the board to spell out the answer to my question. I told Sister I didn't believe that was true. I thought she was making that piece of wood go to the different letters. She said she didn't have anything to do with where it was moving. Edith acted kind of like she believed it too. I told Nona about it. She said, "Edith makes me tired. Those things are not worth a diddledy squat."

Every day when Hendley comes in from the mail route he always turns on the radio to get some news about the war. Everybody in my family is worried about Boy. We want him to come back home and quit fighting those Germans.

Edith taught me a lot when she was my teacher last year. But she always teaches me anytime I'm around her whether I'm in class or not.

THE END

Well, Henry, I hope you enjoyed what I wrote about Edith. I'll be writing you more later on. I hope you're doing all right in heaven.

Love,
Tom

September 27, 1944

Dear Henry,

I don't know why so many men in Pineview drink liquor. The preacher says you'll go straight to hell if you drink that stuff. Why would anybody want to go to hell?

Some men in Pineview will go off for a few days and no one knows where. When that happens, people always say, "he's probably off on a drunk." Where do men go when they go off on a drunk? Do they find a cave somewhere and sit there with a bottle of liquor and drink 'til they fall over?

I don't think my daddy has ever gone off on a drunk. He just goes out in the garage every night to drink his liquor. Joan's daddy is my Uncle Son. He goes off on drunks every once in a while. They say he goes with a bunch of his friends. My mama always raises some serious cane with him when he gets back. I've heard her yelling at Son that he has a wife and children and needs to be at home taking care of them. I guess she feels like she can say whatever she wants to him cause he's her little brother. But it doesn't do any good. He keeps right on drinking anyway. Mama told me I better not ever drink any liquor. I told her she didn't have to worry about that. I don't like the stuff. Plus I want to go to heaven.

Me and Irvin sometimes go down to Bud's place to get a Snicker. We like his Snickers cause he keeps them in the refrigerator. A lot of times his store is locked up. We try to find out where he is. Somebody usually tells us that he's off on a drunk. We like it when he's there cause a cold Snicker is good in the hot summer time. Some people like Milky Ways better but me and Irvin like Snickers. What we really like is a Mars. But we can't ever get one of them cause they cost a dime.

After we get a Snicker, sometimes we'll slip over next door to Rod's commissary. We crawl up under it so we can hear what they're talking about. If we don't get under the building we just listen in through the back door. Usually, Rod and Fletcher and Mr. Morgan and Grover and John Mitchell and some other men will be in there sitting around drinking liquor. They talk and laugh a lot.

We've heard them tell the story a bunch of times about a stranger who walked into the commissary while they were all in there drinking. They introduced the stranger to my granddaddy. Fletcher said, "This is Thomas Jefferson." Then he introduced Grover. His name is Grover Cleveland. One of them is named Robert E. Lee. Finally the stranger said, "I'm glad to meet y'all. My name is Abraham Lincoln." They laugh really loud when they tell that story.

When Seaborn died, they told Duxie he had cirrhosis of the liver. She told Edith he died of a roasted liver. Seaborn probably drank more liquor than any man in Pineview. I can't ever remember seeing him when he wasn't drunk. I'm sure his liver really was roasted.

Henry, you don't have to worry about me. One reason I'll never drink liquor is cause I want to go up there to be with you so we can play together.

Love,
Tom

October 10, 1944

Dear Henry,

You remember how Daddy was when you lived with us? He never would let you come in the house. He said dogs belong outside. I'm sorry he did that to you, Henry. I would've let you come inside the house anytime you wanted to.

My teacher said everybody in the class had to write some things about our daddies. I'm sending you what I wrote about mine.

MY DADDY

My daddy was born on September 28, 1904. I call his daddy, Papa and his mama Nona. Papa died this year. I loved him a lot.

Daddy has an older sister named Edith. Those are the only two children that Nona and Papa ever had.

Here are some stories about my daddy.

- -

People say my daddy was spoiled rotten. I think they're right. He was 29 before he got married. Everybody in Pineview thought he was going to be an old bachelor.

Mama said when she married him he told her all the things he was not going to eat like turnip greens and sweet potatoes and a lot of other vegetables. Mama said she didn't pay any attention to what he said. She's the type of person who wants to have her way. She said she had him eating turnip greens and sweet potatoes and every other vegetable in just a few months.

He eats some crazy meat that I would never eat. John Barnes lives in Daddy's camp house. He brings Daddy a mess of squirrels. John Barnes knows he has to skin them and clean them cause my mama said she wasn't about to do that. She cooks them with brown gravy. I told Daddy they looked like rats. He told me to shut up.

He likes to eat possums. Mama puts it in the oven with sweet potatoes. Daddy wanted me to taste it. I told him that possums eat dead things plus they look like a cat. He told me to shut up. Anytime somebody gives him a possum he puts it in a little house in our backyard that Wes Connor built for my pet rabbit. When it died, I buried it next to my basketball goal. Daddy said if you feed a possum corn for a week it cleans it out from all that dead stuff it eats, and the corn makes the meat taste sweeter. I told him that was alright but I still didn't want any.

The worse thing he eats is chitlins. They're disgusting. They smell like the worse thing you've ever smelled in your life. It's something you know that if you were to taste it, you'd puke. You remember the time that some chitlins wound up in the table scraps. I put them out in the back yard for you to eat. You sniffed it and walked away.

- -

When Daddy was a little boy he and some other boys were playing across the street from Nona and Papa's house in the neighbor's barn. I don't know how it happened but a horse kicked my daddy in the head. It knocked him unconscious. The boys he was playing with thought he was dead.

Papa sent some of the boys to get the doctors to come quick. Pineview had a bunch of doctors back then. There was Dr. Bruce and Dr. Petway and Dr. Mitchell and Dr. Horne and Dr. Gammage. 2 or 3 came up to Papa's house to look at Daddy. They said his brain was swelling and he needed to have an operation to open up his skull. None of them wanted to do it. They told Papa to call Macon and have the hospital send down a surgeon.

Papa was the mayor of Pineview. That meant he had to keep the town telephone at his house cause nobody else in town had one. It was a big wooden thing that hung on his front porch. If anybody in town got a phone call, Nona had to go to their house and get them to come up to her house. Papa got on that old phone and finally got in touch with the hospital. It's 65 miles to Macon and most of the roads weren't paved back then. The doctor didn't get to Pineview until sometime in the night.

Nona cleared off the dining room table. Papa picked Daddy up and laid him on the table cause he was still unconscious. Nona held the kerosene lantern above his head so the doctor could see what he was doing. I'm not sure what the doctor did but he brought Daddy back to life.

Edith said after that Papa and Nona and everybody else started spoiling him. Nona made sock hats to go over his head to keep dirt out of it. The only thing they had on their minds was that he might die. He didn't. But even today he still has a bad scar on his forehead where that horse kicked him.

- -

Daddy was smart in school. He made an A in all his subjects. Pineview had a really good school. Mr. and Mrs. Ware moved to Pineview when Daddy was a little boy. They had been to college and were really smart. Mr. Ware taught algebra and geometry, and calculus. Mrs. Ware taught Latin and Greek and English and Literature.

Daddy said one time he was in a school spelling bee. After a long time of spelling words he and Mary Eliza Ham were the only ones in the whole school still standing. Mrs. Ware was holding the dictionary calling out the words to spell. Neither one of them had missed a word until Mrs. Ware thumbed through the dictionary to find something hard. She called out the word Xanthine. Daddy was the first one to try. He said he'd never heard of the word. He spelled it Z-A-N-T-H-E-N. Mrs. Ware told him that was wrong. Mary Eliza knew that it started with an X instead of a Z. She spelled it right and won the spelling bee. Daddy said he'd never forget that word for the rest of his life.

He made me look it up in the dictionary. It means a yellowish white purine base found in blood and urine and some plants. I told him I didn't think I'd ever need to know how to spell it since I probably wouldn't ever be using that word again.

- -

Daddy said that winters were a whole lot colder back when he was a little boy than they are now. He said sometimes the sidewalks were frozen over between his house and the school. He had to hold on to a fence to keep from falling down.

Nona bought him a real pretty overcoat out of the Sears Roebuck catalog. He said the first day he wore it some of the boys in his class kidded him about it. He said he took it off and never wore it again.

- -

When Daddy was 12, Papa bought him his own car. It was a convertible. He loved to drive it around and show it off. When he got a little older he started having dates with girls. He had lots of girlfriends in Hawkinsville and Perry and Vienna and Cordele and Rochelle and Abbeville but he never had one in Pineview A lot of women in Pineview said that Daddy was the best looking man they'd ever seen.

Hosey Johnson is a nigra man who is the same age of Daddy. He used to work at Papa's cotton gin in the daytime. At night he was Daddy's chauffeur. He wore a chauffeur's cap and drove daddy on all his dates. I guess it must've really impressed his girlfriends that he had a chauffeur.

Daddy didn't have a special time he had to be home at night like the other boys did. But no matter how late he came in there was always a sandwich and a glass of milk waiting for him by his bed.

He said one time Nona had two of her lady cousins visiting with them. The next morning one of them wanted to know what time he came in last night. He said it made him mad cause he didn't have to tell his mama or anybody else what time he came in.

- -

Daddy likes to kid people and play jokes on them. But Mama says you better not kid him cause he gets mad. He's real bad about kidding fat people. He embarrasses me a lot of times cause he will say something to a fat person in the grocery store like, "If I was as fat as you are, I wouldn't be buying that."

A long time before he married he had a skeleton. It was a real one he got from the Masons. They used it in their initiation. Daddy was a 32nd degree Mason and a Shriner. Papa was too. They went to a lot of secret meetings where nobody knows what they do.

He put a suit on the skeleton with a white shirt and a tie and stuck a cigarette between its teeth. He had it sitting in the backseat of his car. He said he pulled up to a filling station one time to get some gas. A nigra man came out to pump the gas. He asked Daddy if there was anything else he wanted. Daddy said he'd like a Co Cola and told him to ask the man in the back seat what he'd like. When he stuck his head in the window and saw the skeleton he started hollering and ran back inside the station. My daddy thought that was really funny.

- -

When he was a teenager Daddy liked to race his car with his friends. Papa found out about it and told him if he ever did it again, he'd take the car away from him..

One Saturday Nona and Papa went to Macon for the day. There are always a lot of people downtown in Pineview on Saturday afternoons. One of Daddy's friends wanted to race him. So they drove their cars out to Steve Moore's house. The road was about a mile straight all the way to downtown. Some of the people were making bets on who would win.

Miles McKinney was the town policeman. They waited for him to shoot his pistol. When he did, they took off as fast as the car would run. Daddy said he won the race. The people who bet on him were hollering cause they won the money.

Daddy said the first person he saw when he parked his car was Papa. He came walking over to the car where Daddy was sitting. He reached down next to the steering wheel and jerked the keys out. Daddy said neither one of them ever said anything to each other about it. But it was a long time before Papa ever gave him the keys back.

- -

Before my daddy married, one of his favorite places to go was Hot Springs, Arkansas. Sometimes he would take Irvin's daddy with him. One time he took Nonk. I don't know why he liked to go there so much cause Arkansas is a long way from Pineview. I've seen some of his pictures. Daddy always likes to dress up a lot. Most of the time he wears a suit and tie and a top coat and he never goes anywhere without wearing a hat. Some people have said that Daddy was a lady's man. I don't know what that means but I guess it must be a good thing.

- -

Before my daddy got married he used to go to a lot of boxing matches. He still listens to them on the radio. One time he went with my Uncle Syms to Chicago for the world heavy weight boxing fight. He told me that Gene Tunney fought Jack Dempsey. That was in 1927 at Soldier's Field. He said there were over 100,000 people there. He called it the famous long count fight. When a boxer knocks the other one down the referee starts counting to 10. If the one laying down doesn't get up before the referee gets to 10 then the other boxer wins. He said Dempsey knocked Tunney down but the referee didn't start counting cause Dempsey forgot to go back to his corner. By the time Dempsey remembered to go to his corner Tunney got up and beat him.

I asked Daddy what they did up there in Chicago besides going to the fight. He said they went to speakeasies cause this was during prohibition time. You go to a nightclub and knock on the door.

There's a little hole in the door where somebody looks through to see who is knocking. If you look all right they let you in. He said it was against the law to sell liquor so they had to make sure that the police stayed out.

Daddy likes to tell about when he and Syms were driving up to Chicago for the fight. Syms had brought a nigra man from Abbeville who worked for him to be their chauffeur. They called him Jenks. He had on a chauffeur's hat and everything. Daddy and Syms sat in the back seat and smoked cigars, he said. I bet they drank liquor too.

Daddy said while they were riding along they came to a place where men were working on the road. They had to stop. One of the nigra men working close to where they stopped saw the Georgia tag on their car. He yelled out to Jenks. You live down there in Georgia where white people treat you bad.

Jenks said, "Well you see where I is and you see where you is, don't you?"

My daddy liked to tell that story cause he thought it was funny.

- -

When he was young, Daddy worked for Papa at the cotton gin. During cotton season Papa went to the gin every morning at 5 o'clock. He had to get the hands working and tell them what they needed to do. After he got them started he went back home to eat breakfast. Nona would usually cook some ham and eggs and grits and biscuits on her wood stove.

When the depression hit in 1929, Papa had hundreds of bales of cotton stored in his warehouse he had bought and paid for. Cotton was selling for a dollar a pound before the depression and 5 cents a pound after it hit. Papa lost everything he had. Most all the banks closed except the Pineview Bank never did. Daddy said he was proud of Papa for not going into bankruptcy like a lot of men did. After that Nona was the only one bringing in any money. They ate out of Nona's garden, and she milked her cow every day. She started her own 5 and 10 cent store.

Daddy married Mama in 1933 when times were really hard. The first year they lived with Nona and Papa. Daddy had typhoid fever the whole year. After that year, Mr. Clarence Finleyson gave Daddy a job at the bank in Finleyson. He said he learned a lot from Mr. Clarence.

Daddy bought the house where we live in 1934 from Mr. Clements. It cost a thousand dollars. He borrowed the money from Mr. Clarence. Daddy said that was the hardest loan he ever had to pay back cause he didn't make much money. Mama said Daddy would walk the floor at night trying to figure out how he was going to pay their bills. Nona and Papa didn't have any money to give him. Daddy said they lived pretty well before the depression. They had new cars and nice clothes and went on trips. He said one time they went to the world's fair in Chicago. All that came to an end when the depression hit in 1929. Daddy said President Roosevelt had done all he could to help out but it took a long time for things to change.

He said things started getting better for him when he got a job with Internal Revenue Service in 1939. They offered to pay him $75 a month. He'd never made that much money before. They told him he had to move to Atlanta. He said he sure didn't want to do that but there was no way he could turn down that job. I cried cause I didn't want to move from Pineview and Nona and Papa and Edith and Irvin and all my aunts and uncles. Daddy said we wouldn't have to be there too long but he had to go to Atlanta to get trained.

Daddy had a little Ford coupe. We could barely put all our clothes in it. Mama's aunt had a boarding house at 768 Spring Street in Atlanta. I was only 3 years old and I'd never been that far away from Pineview. I'd never seen so many people. They had streetcars that ran on a track down the middle of the street like a train.

One time Mama took me to town to go shopping at Davison's and Rich's. They were the biggest stores I'd ever seen. It was fun to stand up in the seat on the streetcar and pull the cord to let the driver know to stop. Sometimes Mama would forget where to stop, but I never did.

Aunt Alice cooked oatmeal for my breakfast every morning. She and Uncle Joe sat on the porch in rocking chairs and rocked all day long. I played in the front yard, but I didn't have any friends to play with. I could see the Biltmore Hotel from our front porch. That's the biggest hotel I've ever seen.

Aunt Alice had a black cat. I decided one day to put the cat in the refrigerator so it wouldn't run away. Later on Aunt Alice went to the refrigerator to get a drink of ice water and the cat jumped out. It scared her so bad she told me not to ever do that again.

One night Mama and Daddy left me with Aunt Alice and Uncle Joe. They told me they were going to see Gone with the Wind. I asked Uncle Joe if that was some kind of trapeze show where people swing on ropes real high up in the air. He said it was just a picture show.

Every time we went back to Pineview for the weekend, I'd cry when it was time to leave. I wanted to stay with Nona and Papa. I would usually run away and hide so they couldn't find me. They found me one time under James's house. He had invited me to come over for an ant funeral. I asked him if it was a red ant or a black ant. He said it was just a little black ant. We buried the ant and covered it up and put a rock on top of the grave.

It was a happy day when Daddy told me that he was being transferred to the Macon office. That meant we could move back to Pineview. He had to go to and from Macon every day. He could drive it in an hour and a half. It was so good to get back to living in Pineview. I could see Nona and Papa and Edith and Hendley and Ma Me and Jamie and Sister and Boy and Angie and Irvin and Joan and all the other people I loved.

- -

My daddy is a good man most of the time. He's only bad when he drinks liquor and smokes cigarettes and cusses and fusses with my mama. I wish he could make it to heaven to be with the rest of us. But it's not gonna happen unless he changes.

THE END

Henry that was my story about my daddy. I turned it in to my teacher. I made an A, mainly cause mine was the longest one.

Love,
Tom

November 7, 1944

Dear Henry,

You never got to go to my daddy's camp house, did you? I know he wouldn't let a dog ride in his car. I'm sorry about that. You would've loved going there.

Before Daddy got married he built the camp house down at his farm back in the woods next to a spring. He put a barrel over the spring and built a deck to walk out to the barrel. That's where he liked to get his drinking water.

He built a dam so the water would back up and make it deep enough to swim and have a lot of fish. When I go fishing I can catch one every time I drop my hook in the water. Daddy wants me to throw all the fish back. But one time he let me keep some to take to Nona's house for her to fry.

The camp house is made out of logs. It's 2 stories and has 2 bedrooms upstairs and 1 downstairs. It has a big living room downstairs where Daddy has his Victrola record player. You have to wind it up to make it play. He has a lot of records and a box full of needles. You have to put a new needle in every time you play a record. Most of the music is something for old people and not for little boys. One record he likes to play is Caruso. Daddy said he's the best singer in the whole world.

They used to have a lot of square dances at the camp house on Saturday nights. He said there were four men who used to play the square dance music. A lot of people from all around would go there to dance. Daddy said all this was during prohibition when you couldn't buy any liquor. He said he knew a man who lived near Pineview that made it. He'd drive up to their house at night and blow the horn. His wife would stick her head out the back door and say, "Ed you want some stuff?" She'd walk across the highway with a shovel to the field. There was a certain spot where she'd dig and bring up a bottle of moonshine out of the dirt.

We have Thanksgiving dinners and 4th of July parties down at the camp house. All our family likes to go there. Daddy had a putt-putt golf course. He called it carpet golf. There was a shed beside the camp house where he kept the generator so they could have electricity. Daddy had to put gasoline in it and pull a rope to crank it. It made a lot of noise when it was running.

One time Papa let me drive his car with him to the camp house. He liked to go there cause he said it was so quiet and peaceful. When I drove up we went to the front door and Papa couldn't get it open. We walked around to the back of the house. Papa pushed one of the windows up. He picked me up so I could crawl through. He told me to go unlock the front door while he walked around the house to meet me.

I got to the living room and started screaming. There was a big, long, black snake laying on the floor. It scared me so bad. Papa kept ramming the front door with his shoulder until he knocked the door down on the floor. I said, "Papa, I'm sorry you had to knock the front door down, but do you see that snake over there. He got a hoe from the back porch and killed it.

Papa liked to sit on the front porch in the rocking chair and chew tobacco and spit off the porch on the ground. He was tired after knocking that door down. I was sitting on the ground playing and a wasp stung me on the arm so I screamed again. Papa spit out his wad of tobacco and told me to hold it on the place where the wasp stung me. I did, and it finally quit hurting. That was not a very good day.

But there was another day that was worse. Daddy let me drive to the farm. I told him I wanted to go down to the camp house and go swimming. Just before we got there, Daddy yelled for me to stop the car. I hit the brakes with my foot. We both looked at the camp house and couldn't believe our eyes. Somebody had taken an axe and knocked down all the posts on the front porch that made the roof fall in. All the windows had been broken out. The furniture and even the Victrola had been chopped up with an axe. Daddy kept saying "god-dam it" over and over. "What son of a bitch would have done something like this?"

The camp house had been ruined. He told me to come on and let's go. He got under the steering wheel and took off. I knew how much it must've hurt Daddy. It hurt me too. I told him that it would be all right if he wanted to cry. He said he just wanted to find the son of a bitch who did it. He went to the sheriff's office in Abbeville. He talked to Pineview's policeman, Miles McKinney, about it. But no one ever found out who did it or why they did it.

Daddy won't go back to the camp house anymore. He said he couldn't do it cause it broke his heart. Sometimes when I drive him to the farm I walk down to the old broken down camp house while Daddy feeds the cows and hogs. I just have to go look at it. It's all grown up now and the roof has fallen in. It looks real bad. I'm kinda glad that Daddy doesn't have to see it looking like that.

Well, Henry, that's about all I have to tell you about the camp house. I'll be writing you again soon.

Love,
Tom

February 2, 1945

Dear Henry,

I have to go to Sunday school and church every Sunday morning except on 5th Sunday when we don't have church. But we still have Sunday School. At 6 o'clock on Sunday night I have to go to MYF. That's the Methodist Youth Fellowship. I have to go to Sunday night church service at 7:30 after MYF. Then there's Prayer Meeting on Wednesday nights.

On the 1st Sunday of every month we all go to Mt. Pleasant Church. That's the Baptist church of Finleyson. It's in the woods about a mile from town. Daddy calls it Pope's Church. He said that was what he always heard it called. He said he damn sure wasn't going to call it Mt. Pleasant cause there weren't any mountains within 200 miles of Finleyson.

On the 2nd Sunday of every month we all go to the Finleyson Methodist church. It's right there in the town of Finleyson. Finleyson is not real big. It's not as big as Pineview. We have 352 people. That's what the map of Georgia says. Finleyson only has 197. Miss Bernice is in charge of all the music and plays the piano. She's real little and short. I thought she was kin to us but Mama said that her sister was married to Mama's brother W.D. I don't know whether that makes me kin to her or not.

On the 3rd Sunday of every month we all go to the Pineview Baptist Church. It's right across the street from the school house. Sammy plays the piano there and Dr. Chamblee from Ft. Valley is the preacher.

On the 4th Sunday of every month we all go to the Pineview Methodist Church and Mama always plays the piano there.   That church changes preachers about every year or two. So it's hard to keep up with them.

All the same people go to all 4 of the churches and the same choir sings at all of them.

Daddy is a deacon in the Pineview Baptist Church. Mama is in charge of all the music at the Pineview Methodist Church. Daddy is a staunch Baptist and Mama is a staunch Methodist. I go to both churches so I'm not staunch anything.

Nona is a staunch Baptist. Mama's mother I call Ma-Me is a staunch Methodist. Sometimes both of my grandmothers come to our house to eat Sunday dinner after church. We try not to talk about churches and religion and things like that cause Ma-Me and Nona don't always agree on those things.

If a month has a 5th Sunday that's Daddy's favorite Sunday cause we don't have to go to church anywhere. But me and Mama and Mary still have to go to Sunday school even if there's not going to be any church service. Daddy never goes to Sunday school so he doesn't even have to bathe or dress on fifth Sunday. He just stays in his pajamas until we get home.

I'm afraid that Daddy is not going to heaven since he never goes to Sunday School. Worst than that he drinks liquor and smokes cigarettes and cusses. I always pray for him every night when I say my prayers cause I don't want him to go to hell. You and me and Mama and Mary and Nona and Edith and Ma Me will all be up there in heaven. I want him to be there with us.

Nona said Daddy is not respectful when church is going on. When he thinks the sermon is getting too long he starts looking at his watch. He holds his arm up real high so the preacher can see it. I have seen him hold his arm up as high as he can reach and then start shaking his watch. He puts his watch up to his ear to see if it's still ticking. Nona really gets mad with him for doing that.

One time when we were leaving the Pineview Baptist church the preacher was at the front door shaking everybody's hand. Daddy said to him, "Can you come down to my house tonight about 10 o'clock and give that sermon cause I've been having problems going to sleep." That embarrassed me and it made Mama real mad with him for saying that.

One time when the preacher had finished his sermon he called on Daddy to say the benediction. I was sitting right beside him. He got real red in the face. He just said Amen. When we were leaving the church service he told the preacher that he'd better not pull any damn stuff like that again. He said he didn't like to pray in public. Daddy acted like he was real mad so the preacher said he was sorry. I don't know if Daddy stands a chance of ever making it to heaven.

Nona told me that to get to heaven you gotta first get baptized. I don't think she feels like there's any way I could ever get baptized in the right way in the Methodist Church cause all they do is just sprinkle water on top of your head. Nona said to really be baptized your whole body needs to be put down underneath the water. That's what the Baptists do. She called it immersed or immersion or something like that. She said Jesus was immersed by John the Baptist in a big river. When Nona was a little girl she was immersed down at Poor Robin Springs in Abbeville where she lived.

In Pineview all the Baptists get baptized down at Bluff Creek. Nona calls it the Baptizing Hole. She said when Jesus's body was put down under the water he was born again. I didn't really know what she meant by that. She said if I wanted to be born again I'd need to have my whole body put down under the water like Jesus and not just be sprinkled on top of my head like the Methodists do. She said I oughta be about 12 years old before I do that. I'll be 9 this coming May, so I got a long time to wait before I get born again.

When they built the new Baptist Church they put a pool in the front of the church where folks get baptized. That's where James and Sammy were baptized. I guess Irvin will get baptized there when he turns 12. Angie and Billy were just sprinkled down at the Methodist Church. I asked Mama and Daddy about that immersing thing cause I really want Angie and Billy to go to heaven too. Mama said that's the craziest thing she ever heard of.

Of course sprinkling is enough to get you into heaven she said. Daddy didn't have a whole lot to say about it. I guess he didn't know whether to agree with his wife or his mama. He sure ought to know better than disagree with his wife. When she starts raising cane, it's a good idea for everybody to get out of the house. Daddy said you have to watch out for Mama cause sometimes she gets on a high horse and when she gets on that high horse nobody better get in her way.

Papa never did go to any church as far as I know. I asked Nona about why he didn't go to church. She told me he said there were too many hypocrites in the church. I told her that I didn't know what that meant. She said they're people who say one thing and do another. I'm still not sure what that means but I plan to watch out for them the next time I go to church. I asked Nona if Papa ever got baptized and she said that when he was young he went to a tent revival. He told her that was where he got saved. I've been wondering about that since Papa died last year. From what I hear the preachers say you gotta go to church every Sunday if you want to go to heaven.

Every year when I get out of school the last of May, I always have to go to Bible School. One week at Pope's Church in Finleyson and one week at the Finleyson Methodist Church and one week at the Pineview Baptist Church and one week at the Methodist Church in Pineview. We sing the same old songs and do the same old arts and crafts and pray the same old prayers and see the same old people. I get so tired of going to Bible School. It takes up the whole month of June and at the same time we're having revivals at all those churches.

The worst thing happened to me at Bible School at the Finleyson Methodist Church. Miss Bernice is in charge of everything like the singing and playing the piano and all. She asked all of the children to bring a nail to Bible School. That afternoon I looked all over the garage and the barn and inside the house and I couldn't find a nail anywhere. I found one old rusty nail that was bent pretty bad, so I took that.

The next morning she reminded us that nails were what they used to put Jesus on the cross. She asked all the children to stand up and come up to the altar one at a time. She said for each of us to stop by a box and say a prayer for Jesus and put our nail in the box. I walked up to the front of the church when it was my turn. I stopped by the box and said a prayer for Jesus then reached in my pocket to get my nail. But the nail had jammed through the bottom of my pocket and since it was crooked I couldn't get it out. I kept pulling at it and pulling at it and it wouldn't come out. I could hear some of the boys snickering. My face turned red as blood. I kept on pulling at it but I never could get that nail out of my pocket. Everybody started laughing so hard they were about to split their sides. Miss Bernice told everybody to be quiet. She came over and pulled my pocket wrong side out and the nail was still stuck in there. She pulled at it until I thought she was going to pull my pants off. Finally she got it out.

I told Mama that night I was not going back to Bible School anymore. That was it. She said that would be just fine cause if I did, I couldn't go any-where out of the house for 2 weeks. Why is she is so mean?

Surely I'll go to heaven when I die Henry cause there are not many people I know of who go to church as much as I do.

I got to do some homework right now so I'll write more later.

Love,
Tom

March 24, 1945

Dear Henry,

I have to write another paper for my teacher. This time it has to be on our mamas. What can you say about your mama? I've lived with her all of my life. I guess I should know her by now. But it's still hard to write about her.

My Mother

My mother was born on February 7, 1911. Her name when she was born was Mary Lou Mann. I wish she'd had another name. I get tired of people kidding me all the time saying your daddy married a man. They're so stupid. I keep telling them that my mama's name is spelled M-a-n-n. But they just keep saying it. Your daddy married a man.

Mama started spelling her first name Marilu when she went to Wesleyan College in Macon. And that's what she told everybody her name was. But hardly anybody in Pineview knows her first name cause my mama's daddy always called her Coot since the day she was born. She says she hates having a nickname like that. Everybody in the whole town calls her Coot except Mrs. Ware cause she was Mama's high school English teacher. She calls her Mary Lou. Mama said she thought Coot Mann was the stupidest name she'd ever heard of. I guess she was glad to marry my daddy so she could be Coot Dennard instead of Coot Mann.

She went to the music conservatory in Macon and studied piano and organ. When she came back to Pineview she started playing the piano at the Methodist Church. She didn't play the organ cause the church doesn't have one. She's been playing the piano for the church ever since.

My mama and daddy married on November 12, 1933. Edith told me that Daddy had dated girls all over the place. He was 29 and my mother was 23. Edith said she told him that as old as he was it was about time to quit playing around. He needed to settle down and marry a good woman. Daddy told her he didn't know anybody he wanted to marry. Edith told him that he ought to go with Coot Mann cause she was a nice girl. But Daddy thought she was still a little girl cause she had always been a little girl when he was growing up. He was 6 ½ years older than she was. He told Edith that he was scared of her daddy anyway cause her daddy thought he was a playboy. Mama's daddy didn't want his daughter going with anybody like him. But her daddy was a good friend of his daddy so he finally gave in and let his daughter go out with Daddy.

Ruby told me that when I was born Mama never nursed me. She'd read a book that said that mother's milk was not good for babies. So she always gave me a bottle of cow's milk that she heated up in a boiler. Ruby said when I'd drink a bottle of that milk I'd start screaming my head off. She said that every woman in my whole family had always nursed their babies except Mama. They kept telling her that she might shut her baby up if she'd start nursing me. But she never did.

I don't understand my mama and daddy. They fight a lot and yell and scream at each other. One time I saw her hit him over the head with a broom. You'd think they hate each other. But then a lot of times I see them hugging and kissing. That doesn't make any sense to me. But I guess its kinda like me and Irvin. We have a fight just about every day, but we're still best friends.

My daddy says my mama is head strong and hard headed. Plus she has a temper and won't mind. But I think he's just about as bad as she is about those things. He says she is the stingiest woman he has ever known in his life. He said she knows how to squeeze a penny 'til it hollers. I asked him one time why she was like that. He said it was cause she grew up hard. Her mama was like that too. He said, "Her mama can slice a ham the thinnest of any person I ever knew."

Mama makes me go to school every single day no matter how sick I am. There's no excuse for not going to school she says. It's kinda embarrassing cause at the last chapel of the school year I'm the only one who always gets an award for never having missed a day of school. I'd have to be dead to miss school. Knowing Mama, she'd probably make me go to school a few days after I die just to make sure.

The other thing I'm not allowed to miss is church and Sunday School. There's no excuse too good for missing church and Sunday School. She believes that if the church doors are open then I need to be there. The only time I can ever remember missing was when I had the mumps. Even then I got punished and was not allowed to go out of the house for a week except to school. I even had to miss the Pineview-Rochelle basketball game. It's hard for me to forgive her for that.

Her favorite thing to do in the whole world is play bridge. She and some other women play every afternoon Monday through Friday. She likes to dress up and put on pretty clothes and ear bobs and a hat every time she goes to play. One time I asked her why she had to dress up to play bridge. She just sort of looked at me and didn't say anything.

She's always telling me that when I graduate from high school I need to leave Pineview and never move back. That really hurts my feelings when she says that. It seems to me like she doesn't want me around. I don't really understand what she means. I don't want to leave my family and Pineview. It would be scary to live somewhere else by myself.

Sometimes I love my mama and sometimes I don't.

I guess that's about all I can say about her.

THE END

Henry, I hope you're all right up there in heaven and that you have a lot of friends to play with.

Love,
Tom

April 26, 1945

Dear Henry,

I'm glad today is Memorial Day. School lets out at 11 o'clock to go clean up the cemetery. All the students walk from the school house. But it's not very far. Some of the parents are there to show us what to do. We have to hoe the weeds away from the graves and clean up any trash and pull up weeds that are hard to hoe and whatever else needs to be done to get the cemetery looking good.

April 26th is Confederate Memorial Day. The state banks and state workers all get a holiday. But the federal banks and federal workers all have to work. My daddy works for the federal government so he has to work today. He gets off on May 30th. That's yankee memorial day. It's also my birthday. I used to get kidded about that. They called me a yankee. That really made me mad. That's about the worst thing you can call somebody if you live in Georgia. They kid me about living in town too. Everybody else in my class except Irvin and Joan lives in the country. I'll be 9 next month so I'm getting big enough not to pay any attention to all that kidding.

All the rest of the mothers get to the cemetery around 12 o'clock. They bring sandwiches and drinks. That's the best part. By the time you've been working in the hot sun for an hour you're starved. They have iced tea and pimento cheese sandwiches and banana sandwiches and peanut butter and jelly sandwiches and pineapple sandwiches and of course Mama always brings tuna fish sandwiches. That's another thing that makes my friends laugh at me.

We got the cemetery all cleaned up, Henry. We ate a good lunch and had to go back to school at 1 o'clock.

Love,
Tom

June 18, 1945

Dear Henry,

Friday night was the last night of the revival at our church. Daddy said he sure was glad cause he had a belly full of being revived. The first week of June we went to the revival at the Pineview Baptist Church. That's Nona's and Daddy's church. We have to go to the morning service and the night service every day for a week. Then the second week of June the Finleyson Methodist Church had its revival. The third week was Pope's Church. That's the Baptist church in Finleyson. And then the fourth week was the Pineview Methodist Church where Mama has to play the piano. Revivals take up the whole month of June every year. Plus Mama makes me go to Bible School for a week in the mornings at each one of the four churches. So I'm getting kinda like Daddy. I've had a belly full of going to church too. I wanna start going swimming every day and playing outside. I've had to miss going to the picture show at night and all kinds of things I like doing.

I asked Nona why we have so many revivals. She said it's kinda like taking a tonic. In the springtime we all have to take a dose of Castor Oil and Black Strap Molasses. I can tell you that's some horrible tasting stuff. She said a tonic rejuvenates the body after a long cold winter. And that's what a revival does to your spirit. Your spirit needs reviving and good singing and good preaching will do it every time, she said.

Every church always has a preacher from somewhere outside of Pineview and Finleyson like Americus or Cordele or Fitzgerald or Dublin or somewhere like that to come preach the revivals. A lot of times they bring in someone from another town to lead the singing too. And when the revival is at the Methodist and Baptist Church in Pineview we have to have the preacher and the singer eat dinner with us before the service starts. Mama said it's not whether you want to do it but it's because you have to do it.

The singer at the Methodist Church last week was from Cochran. He was an older man. About 30 I'd say. He could really sing loud too. By the time we had sat down good, he would yell out for everybody to stand up. Stand up for Jesus, he said. Then he started singing without Mama playing the piano. Everybody joined in without even opening up the hymn book:

> Stand up, stand up for Jesus,
> Ye soldiers of the cross;
> Lift high His royal banner,
> It must not suffer loss;
> From vict'ry unto vict'ry,
> His army shall He lead,
> Till ev'ry foe is vanquished,
> And Christ is Lord indeed.
> Stand up, stand up, for Jesus,
> Ye soldiers of the cross;

> Lift high His royal banner,
> It must not suffer loss.

About half way through the hymn Mama finally found page 224 and started playing as hard as she could to try to keep up with him. Then when the last word was sung of that hymn, he'd start right into singing another one. Poor mama had no idea which page to turn to. This time he was singing so loud, you could've heard him all the way to Finleyson.

> What a wonderful change in my life has been wrought,
> Since Jesus came into my heart!
> I have light in my soul for which long I had sought,
> Since Jesus came into my heart!
> Since Jesus came into my heart,
> Since Jesus came into my heart,
> Floods of joy o'er my soul like the sea billows roll,
> Since Jesus came into my heart.

Mama finally found page 84 where that hymn is. She found it just before we sang the last line. I knew what page it was on cause that's one of my favorite hymns. I found it before Mama did. I started to run up there and tell her where it was but I didn't. It just wasn't fair to Mama that he didn't tell anybody what page the hymns were on. He'd just started singing another one right after he finished the one we had been singing:

> Onward, Christian soldiers,
> Marching as to war,

With the cross of Jesus,
Going on before!
Christ, the royal Master,
Leads against the foe;
Forward into battle,
See His banner go!
Onward, Christian soldiers,
Marching as to war,
With the cross of Jesus,
Going on before!

I kept trying to motion to Mama that Onward Christian Soldiers was on page 85 right next to Since Jesus Came Into My Heart.

He then started singing again:
I was sinking deep in sin,
Far from the peaceful shore,
Very deeply stained within,
Sinking to rise no more;
But the Master of the sea
Heard my despairing cry,
From the waters lifted me,
Now safe am I.
Love lifted me

Every time the congregation would sing the words, "Love lifted me," W.D. would say, "even me."

Love lifted me - Even me.
When nothing else could help,
Love lifted me. Even me.

Mama said W.D. couldn't carry a tune in a bucket if he had to. And she ought to know cause he's her brother.

The singing went on for about 30 minutes and poor Mama was so flustered she didn't know what to do. About that time the preacher walked up into the pulpit. His stomach was kinda round and poked out over his belt. He had on a coat and a red bow tie. The front part of his head was bald but he had hair in the back of his head. His shirt was wet from sweating so hard. But it wasn't near as wet as the song leader's shirt. His clothes looked like he'd just jumped in Pappy Jack Springs. It was definitely hot that night. W.D. and Morris Cheek had pushed the windows up as high as they would go. Everybody in the church was fanning as hard as they could with their Clark Funeral Home fans.

The preacher looked over at Mama and told her that we will now have a special to be sung by the choir.

Nona and Edith and Matibel and Lillian sing soprano. Miss Bernice and Miss Ethel sing tenor. Mattie C and Cuddin Charlye and Mildred Malaier sing alto. They sing at every church service in Pineview and Finleyson and at every funeral anywhere around.

Mama started playing and they started singing:
All hail the pow'r of Jesus' name!
Let angels prostrate fall,
Bring forth the royal diadem,
And crown Him Lord of all,
Bring forth the royal diadem,
And crown Him Lord of all.

Daddy said that there is no Methodist preacher alive who would forget to pass around the collection plate at least once if not twice. While W.D. and Morris Cheek passed around the collection plate the choir sang really soft:

Into my heart,
Into my heart,
Come into my heart, Lord Jesus;
Come in today,
Come in to stay,
Come into my heart, Lord Jesus.

The preacher started preaching about how you got to love Jesus if you want to go to heaven. Holland Wilson was sitting on the back seat and came out with a loud, "Amen brother."

Then the preacher said, "You gotta follow the Ten Commandments if you want to go to heaven. That's right. You can't go outside this church and start taking the Lord's name in vain. If you do you're doomed."

I knew then that Daddy was doomed cause he can't even say a sentence without a damn or a hell or a goddam.

"You can't commit adultery," the preacher said in a louder voice looking all around in the congregation like he might be trying to spot somebody who was guilty. I don't even know what adultery means but whatever it is I certainly don't want to do it.

"Thou shalt not covet thy neighbor's house he said even louder. Thy neighbor's wife and thy neighbor's manservant and maid servant nor his ox nor his ass nor anything that is thy neighbors." Irvin was sitting next to me and he started giggling when the preacher said ass. That made me start giggling too. We were giggling so hard the pew started shaking. Then I looked up in the choir and saw Edith and Nona staring at me. That's when I shut up in a big hurry.

"Which had you rather do?" The preacher hollered. "Had you rather burn in hell for eternity or had you rather live in a mansion in a land flowing with milk and honey?" I wasn't sure about living where milk and honey are flowing all over the place but I know one thing for sure and that is I don't want to burn in hell.

The next day I asked Nona how long was eternity. She said it's forever and ever and ever. How could there not be an end? Doesn't everything have to end sometime? She said there's no end to eternity. No end at all. It just goes on forever. That really started worrying me a lot.

That night I couldn't go to sleep worrying about eternity lasting forever. I just couldn't understand how that could be. I got real scared thinking about it like I do when I see a Frankenstein movie. I got so scared I started sweating even though I had all the windows up and Daddy had the fan on. I slipped back to Mama and Daddy's room. He was snoring real loud and sounded like a hog. My sister was asleep in her bed. She's only 3 years old so there's nothing she could do. I shook Daddy. He started grunting and snorting. He finally looked around at me and said "What's wrong with you."

I told him I was scared.

What're you scared of?

Eternity.

What the hell are you talking about boy?

Eternity is what I'm scared of. Nona said there's no end to eternity. It just goes on forever and ever and ever.

What kind of damn nonsense is she putting in your head?

How is it possible that time can just go on forever and ever without ending? There has to be an end sometime. Doesn't it?

Just get the hell over here in the bed with me and go to sleep. We'll talk about eternity tomorrow.

But we didn't talk about tomorrow nor the next day nor the day after that nor any other day. And I still haven't been able to figure out eternity.

The preacher kept on talking that night about everything you could do that would land you in hell but I didn't hear another word he said after I started thinking about eternity. I just couldn't get my mind off of it. Then I heard the preacher say to the singer. "Brother J.T. you got a hymn for us to close our service with tonight?" Then he looked over at Mama and said in a really sweet sounding voice. "Miss Coot, Brother J.T. has had you all flusterated all week hasn't he?"

Mama laughed acting like she wasn't but I knew she was.

"Brother J.T., now you give Miss Coot the page number of the hymn we gonna sing and I bet I know what it's gonna be too."

The singer started thumbing through the pages and then said, "Let's take our Cokesbury Worship Hymnal and turn to Page number 151 – Just As I Am."

The preacher said, "That's the one I hoped you'd pick, Brother J.T." The preacher wiped his forehead with his handkerchief to get all the sweat off that was dripping in his eyes and started saying in a low voice. "If there's any one of you here this evening who has been sinning and wants to change your life. If there's anybody here tonight who needs to find out more about Jesus. If there's anybody here who does not want to suffer hellfire and damnation but wants to live in heaven with Jesus in a land flowing with milk and honey. If you have a tug in your heart and want to get to know God better. If you want to be saved then you need to walk down that aisle during the singing of this hymn and grab my hand and say Preacher I want to know Jesus. I want to be saved. So while Miss Coot is playing the piano and Brother J.T. is leading the congregation in this wonderful old hymn want you come. I beg you to come." Then he turned and looked at Mama. She started playing and everybody started singing:

> Just as I am, without one plea,
> But that Thy blood was shed for me,
> And that Thou bidd'st me come to Thee,
> O Lamb of God, I come! I come!

Most of the time nobody ever goes down the aisle except Effie Fountain. She always goes down the aisle at every church service to be saved no matter whether it's a revival or not. Irvin says she's crazy as hell. I don't know if she's crazy or not but she's definitely not quite right. I bet she has gone down the aisle a hundred times to shake the preacher's hand when he gives the call. Nobody in the church ever pays any attention to her.

I'm so glad it's now July and all the bible schools and revivals are over so things can sort of get back to normal. Henry, if you run across anybody up there in heaven who can give you some information about eternity, I sure do wish you'd let me know. It's been bothering me and keeping me awake at night ever since the revivals ended.

Love,
Tom

July 10, 1945

Dear Henry,

I've just had the worst time I've ever had in my whole life. I told Mama I did NOT want to go to Dooly Campground. But no. She made me do it. She kept saying you're 9 years old and you've never ever been to camp. But I don't want to go to camp I kept telling her. She said that Billy and Angie and Little Clarence Finleyson were all going and that I would meet a lot of young people from Methodist Churches from all around. I told her I didn't want to meet people from Methodist Churches. I didn't care where they were from. Why do I have to do this I kept arguing with her. Irvin's mother was not making him go to camp.

She wouldn't have it any other way but her way. I had to go. I told her I was not packing my suitcase. So she packed it for me. Angie's mama picked up me and Billy. Angie sat in the front seat with her mama. Me and Billy sat in the back. Miss Bernice was going to take Little Clarence.

Alice drove us to Vienna and then on the other side of town was Dooly Campground. It was a miserable looking place. There were ugly bunk rooms for boys and bunk rooms for girls and a cafeteria. A place they called the tabernacle was a building where they held the church services and vespers and all that. It had a roof but no sides and a dirt floor and a whole bunch of benches.

We had to get up really early and go to sunrise services at the tabernacle every morning and go to vespers every night. A lot of singing and praying and preaching went on. I'd just spent the whole month of June going to revivals at all 4 churches in Pineview and Finleyson. It looks like to me that should've been enough church to take care of me through the summer.

Every day we had to do arts and crafts and make stupid little bracelets and cut out animals from construction paper and dumb things like that. We strung them together with a long cord like it was going to be some kind of Christmas tree decorations and hung them around the room. But it wasn't Christmas. It was July.

We had to go out on hiking trails all around the property and the lake where there were mosquitoes and red bugs and ticks. I don't like hiking. That's not something I want to do.

One of the boys in my bunkroom got a red bug on his thing. They called his mama and daddy to come get him. That started me to thinking that might be a good way to get home. But then I changed my mind.

Our group leader came into the bunk room every night before lights out to hold good night prayers. I prayed the hardest I've ever prayed in my whole life that the week would hurry up and get over with.

Little Clarence is 11 and Billy is 14. They don't want me hanging around with them cause I'm only 9. Angie is 14. She wouldn't mind me being around her. The only thing is that she is a girl and they had girl things to do all day long. I only got to see her in the cafeteria at mealtime and at sunrise service and vespers.

The food was OK I guess. My favorite thing to eat in the world is fried chicken and they never had it the whole time I was there.

One night just before lights out some of the older boys in the bunk room decided they were going to take me on a snipe hunt. I didn't know what a snipe hunt was so I told them I didn't want to go. They decided they were going to take me anyway. They were dragging me out the door but I was saved. Mr. Masters saw us. He's the head man at the camp. He yelled out, "You boys better get back in that bunk house right now and go to bed." I laughed to myself cause I was saved from the snipe hunt at least for that night.

The camp lasted a whole week from Saturday to the next Saturday. But by the time Wednesday came around I didn't think I would make it to Saturday. I wrote a postcard to Daddy to come get me. I knew Mama wouldn't do it.

On Thursday night after supper a wonderful thing happened. I walked out of the cafeteria and that's when I saw the best sight I'd ever seen. Mama and Daddy and my little sister were standing there by Daddy's black Buick. I ran to them and hugged them as hard as I could.

An older woman who was one of the heads of the camp came out to speak to Mama and Daddy. I think she and Daddy must've known each other cause they were talking real friendly like. I heard her say to Daddy, "I'm afraid Tom has been a little homesick these past few days." She didn't know the half of it. "He wanted to call y'all," she said, "but we have a rule against calling home during camp."

We got in the car and started home. Mama didn't say a word. She acted all disgusted like and mad that they had to come pick me up before camp was over. After a while Daddy said, "It's OK, son. They made me go to camp when I was a boy and I came home early too." I could see Mama rolling her eyes around like she wanted to say that she didn't want me to be like my daddy. She has told me a bunch of times that she wants me to be stronger than he is.

I thought a lot about those things while we were driving back home that night. This might've been the worst time in my life, but maybe when I get older, I might want to do some stuff like they were doing in camp. Someday I may like to do some arts and crafts and maybe I might want to go hiking sometime. But for now I'm satisfied just to stay at home and do what I like to do like playing basketball and going swimming and going to the picture show and playing cars with Irvin.

Love,
Tom

July 29, 1945

Dear Henry,

The most fun thing to do in the summer in Pineview is to go swimming. It's either Bluff Creek or Pappy Jack or the Whirl Hole. If any girls want to go that means we have to go to either Bluff Creek or the Whirl Hole cause boys don't wear bathing suits at Pappy Jack. If Angie or Joan or Betty Jean are with us, they always want to go to Bluff Creek. They say there're too many snakes at the Whirl Hole.

The Whirl Hole has a rope swing and a platform that you can crawl up on to swing out over the water. That's really fun. Sometimes when I'm holding on to the pipe swinging out over the water I think about what James told me. He said that a boy swung out over the water one time and dropped into a bed of moccasins. He was screaming as he went down. They pulled his dead body out and it had over 100 moccasin bites. I always think about that when I'm swinging out over the water.

One time Walt Mann was in the Whirl Hole trying to swim. He was just a little boy. He grabbed me around the neck 'cause he thought he was going to drown. When he grabbed me around the neck with a death grip we both went down. He was choking me so bad I thought we were both going to drown. James saw us and pulled us out.

If it's just me and Irvin we usually ride with Bud to Pappy Jack. Some people call him Crip. He keeps a bar of soap on the limb of a tree. He can reach it but me and Irvin can't. He doesn't like anybody messing with his soap. He starts cussin' if his soap is not exactly where he left it the last time he was there.

Bud is pretty old. I don't know how old but he's got to be at least 40. He hasn't ever been married. Nona said he has never been right ever since a rattlesnake bit him picking plums when he was a little boy. He got so crazy they had to send him off to Milledgeville.

One Saturday afternoon I was working at Nona's store and we didn't have any customers. I told Nona I'd be back in a minute. I went down to Bud's store to get me a cold Snicker. Mr. Clements keeps his candy out on the counter. I like to eat one when it's really cold in the hot summertime.

When I told Nona where I'd been she jumped on me for going down there to Bud's place. I didn't know why she was so upset about it. She finally told me that Bud had a woman he was keeping upstairs in his bedroom over the store. I told Nona that I didn't see a woman while I was down there. I wasn't sure why Bud would want to have a woman upstairs in his place unless she was his wife. From the way Nona scolded me, I knew that having a strange woman upstairs must be a really bad thing.

A lot of times me and Irvin go down to Bud's store in the late afternoon when it's real hot. He always goes down to Pappy Jack to take a bath. If we go too early he tells us to come back later. He says when he takes a bath at Pappy Jack, he wants to stay cool for the rest of the night.

Bud makes me and Irvin sit in the back seat. He sits up front by himself. He never talks to us. Sometimes Irvin will ask him a question cause he's Irvin's uncle. But half the time he won't even answer it. The only time he ever says anything is when we do something he doesn't like. Then he'll yell at us to quit doing whatever it is we're doing. One time I was twisting the knob on the window. He pulled the car over to the side of the road and said a bunch of ugly cuss words to me.

Sometimes John Mitchell goes with us to take a bath. He's married to my mama's Aunt Lena. One day we were all standing in the shallow part of Pappy Jack soaping up our bodies when a water moccasin came up out of the boil and swam right through John Mitchell's legs. He hollowed like he'd been bit, but he wasn't. Me and Irvin and John all jumped out of the water as fast as we could. We had soap in our hair and all over our bodies but none of us wanted to go back in the water to wash it off. Bud didn't care. He rinsed the soap off before he got out. I guess he figured being bit by a moccasin couldn't be any worse than being bit by a rattlesnake. Me and Irvin and John Mitchell put on our clothes and rode home with soap in our hair and soap caked all over our bodies.

Pappy Jack is where me and Irvin learned to swim when we were 5 years old. Boy and Henry sometimes took us down there to play around in the shallow part while they went swimming. That was before they had to go off to the war. They're 10 years older so they were 15. They liked to play a game with us. One of them would stand up on the bank and throw us in the middle of the spring. The other one would be down in the water to grab us when we came up. It was kinda like a ballgame except me and Irvin were the ball.

One time Boy threw both of us in at the same time. When we came up, Henry was standing over in the shallow part. We were both screaming, "We can't swim, we can't swim." They were laughing and saying, "Either swim or drown." I was gagging from swallowing water. Irvin was too. We both paddled as hard as we could and finally made it to where we could stand up. From then on, we've been swimming ever since.

We were really mad at Boy and Henry for doing that to us cause we knew we could've drowned like Little George Hill did when he dived off the highest bank in Pappy Jack. His head hit a sandbar and broke his neck. That happened before me and Irvin were born but we've been hearing that story ever since we can remember.

Sometimes I like to go to Bluff Creek to swim 'cause there's a log across the creek that you can swim to. It's fun to sit on the log or stand up on it and dive off. Since I learned how to swim I can swim to the log and sit on it with the big boys like James and Sammy and Billy.

All the Baptist churches around Pineview use Bluff Creek to baptize people when they join the church.

When we go to Bluff Creek to swim on Sundays, a lot of times we have to wait for the preacher to finish baptizing people. He stands in the water with his clothes on about waist deep. He holds the person's nose and says some words and leans them backwards down into the water. When he brings them up out of the water everybody starts clapping and saying Amen and Hallelujah.

One time when we were down there watching people get baptized, the preacher dipped a boy down in the water and he didn't come back up. He swam off and went to the log. None of the people knew what to say. They didn't clap or say Amen or Hallelujah or anything.

Nona wants me to be baptized in the water so I will go to heaven for sure. My mama and her mama feel that sprinkling water on your head is all you need.

Henry, if you ever run into Jesus or God, I wish you'd ask them about that.

Love,
Tom

August 15, 1945

Dear Henry,

Did you get the news the war is over? When Angie told me about it we got in her mama's Lincoln Zephyr and picked up James and Sammy. We rode all over town blowing the horn. Everybody is excited that the soldiers will be coming home. Boy has been in the Army in Germany. He already got home last week cause the war in Europe has been over for 2 or 3 months. Henry McLeod got home from the Navy. He gave me his sailor's cap. I've been wearing it every day.

I'm just 9. Boy and Henry are 19. I still like them even though they did throw me and Irvin in the middle of Pappy Jack when we were 5 and told us to swim or drown. I don't know how long they've been fighting in the war. It must've been 2 or 3 years. I asked Boy what it was like to fight in a war. He told me he didn't want to talk about it. He said he would teach me some German he learned over there. He made me repeat it over and over until I memorized it. Alles kaput in Deutschland! Das ist gut! Das ist gut!

I taught Irvin how to say it. He laughed cause he thought I said "ka-poot." I told him it was kaput not poot. It was sorta halfway between poot and put. Boy said it meant all is over in Germany. That is good. That is good.

Daddy told me that the war got over cause we dropped atom bombs on Japan. I saw it last week on the newsreel at the picture show. It looked pretty awful. Those bombs killed a lot of people. Daddy said it was their fault cause the Japs are the ones who started the war when they bombed Pearl Harbor.

I wish Papa was still alive. He would be so happy to know that the war is over. He spent a lot of time listening to the news on the radio every night. He had a big radio that sat on four legs like a cabinet. It's taller than I am. Every night after supper he always pulled his chair up to the radio and put his head down next to it so he could hear every word that H.V. Kaltenborn said. Papa said he gave the best news of anybody. Papa needed to know what was going on in the war since his grandson was fighting over there in Europe. Papa said if we didn't win this war we'd all be in big trouble. He said if we lose the war, Hitler would come over to America and take over our country.

I've got something to tell you that I never did tell Papa or Nona or anybody else in the whole world. You're the first one to hear this. You have to promise you won't tell anybody in heaven cause it's a big secret. I've known for a long time that Mama and Daddy are German spies. I was searching around in their closet one day looking for something. I found a book that had Germany written on it. They never knew that I found that book. I'm sure they were trying to hide it. I noticed that every night after supper they always wanted me and Mary to go up in the living room while they sit at the kitchen table. They shut all the doors so we can't hear them talking. I know they must've been talking about Hitler and the war and stuff. I wanted to tell somebody about it but I wasn't sure who to tell. Now that the war is over, it's probably too late to turn them in.

I guess we won't be having any more blackouts. I'm glad about that. Since Mr. Clements is the mayor, he always had to go out in the middle of the street at night and shoot his pistol 3 times. That meant that everybody in town had to turn all the lights off. Daddy would light a candle. We'd sit around the radio and listen to our favorite programs. Daddy said it's a good thing that all the towns turn out their lights. If German planes fly over they won't know there's a town there to bomb. Sometimes I wonder if Daddy or Mama might try to turn on some lights to send a signal to those planes. I don't know why the Germans would want to bomb Pineview. Especially since they probably know that they've got spies living down here.

Maybe now me and Irvin can get some good balls to play with and some good cars too. During the war all the balls were made out of synthetic rubber. Those things are so hard if you got hit with one, it'd kill you. We've been having to play baseball and softball with them cause all the rubber had to be used in the war. Our cars have been made out of wood instead of metal since the war got started. It sure will be good to get some new balls and new cars.

Gasoline has been rationed too.   Sugar is rationed and a lot of other things. You have to have a book of coupons to buy gas and sugar. Every time Daddy goes down to Sam's store to buy some gas, Sam comes out to our car. Daddy always tells him he wants 10 gallons. Sam takes the handle next to the gas tank and starts pushing it back and forth to pump gas up into the glass thing. There's a bunch of numbers on it that shows how many gallons you've pumped into it. When the gas reaches the mark that has 10 written on it, he stops pumping. Daddy always gets out and looks to make sure that Sam pumped the gas up to the right mark. Then Sam puts the hose into the gas tank on the car and drains all the gas out of the glass thing into the car tank. Daddy has to tear our 10 gallons worth of stamps out of the ration book to give him. Gas usually costs about 18 cents a gallon. So Daddy pays him $1.80.

Nona sent me to T.O.'s store to buy her a 5 pound bag of sugar the other day. She gave me a dollar and her ration book. T. O. handed me the sugar and tore out the coupons. When he gave me the change for the dollar, I ran out the door holding the sugar. I was running along the sidewalk back to Nona's store and stumbled. I fell down and the bag of sugar broke open and spilled on the sidewalk. I felt so bad. Nona was going to use the sugar to make some crabapple jelly. When I told her what had happened, she walked with me down to where the sugar was spilled on the sidewalk. We tried to pick up as much as we could. You can't afford to waste things like sugar. There are a lot of crabapples on the tree behind Nona's house. And she makes the best crabapple jelly of anybody in the world. It's real sticky like glue. But when you get some out of the jar and put in on your toast in the morning, it's the best thing I know of.

A few years ago, me and Irvin were downtown and saw a man in front of W.D.'s store up in Bob Slade's face cussing him and calling him a slacker. The mean old man started hitting him. Bob was pushing him back. The man kept yelling slacker and hitting him. Bob kept trying to push him away. But they fought all the way across the street to Mr. Will Rhode's filling station before somebody separated them. Irvin said it was because Bob Slade didn't go to fight in the war. I asked Irvin why he didn't go. He didn't know. We figured it had to be a good reason cause Bob's a good man.

I told Daddy about it, and he said that somebody had tried to say that to him too. Daddy didn't go to the war either. Daddy said only the boys who were between 18 and 35 were drafted in the service. He was 37 when the war broke out and had 2 children. So he got a deferment. Other people don't like it when men don't go to fight in the war. I'm glad Daddy didn't have to go cause he might've been killed. I don't want people to think he was a slacker. Irvin's daddy didn't go to war either so it's not like everybody went. It was only men who were younger than Daddy and Big Irvin that had to go to war.

Wilma Nell's husband got killed in the war. His name was Herbert Fitzgerald. They had a little baby girl named Thelma Nell. She's about the same age as my sister. Before Herbert went to the war, he rode a motor cycle and wore a leather jacket. I thought he looked pretty cool. Wilma Nell got the telegram that he'd been killed. She was living with Miss Thelma and Mr. Clements cause they're her mama and daddy. James is her brother.

Wilma Nell got something in the mail that had black ribbons hanging on it to put in their front window. Every day I walk by their house on the way to Mr. Clements drugstore to get an ice cream, and I always look at those black ribbons hanging in the window. Miss Fanny is Mr. Clements sister. She lives with them and has a wooden leg. She rocks on the front porch every day singing church songs like *Amazing Grace* and *Just as I am* and *What a Friend We Have in Jesus* and songs like that. It seems kinda scary when I see her rocking in the chair with her wooden leg and hear her singing those hymns. She sounds like she's singing through her nose. I've started walking to town up on the street where Edith lives where it's not so spooky.

My cousin William Syms was in the war too. He lives in Abbeville with his mama and daddy. His mama's name is Rena. She is Nona's sister. He had to come home from the war before it was over cause Daddy said he got shell shocked. I don't know what that means. But he stays in his room all the time and won't come out. We go to see them sometimes on Sunday afternoons. But we never see

William cause he's locked up in his room. Daddy said he was on Normandy Beach where there was a lot of killing. The last time we went to see them, Rena showed us William's Purple Heart. You get a Purple Heart if you've been wounded in the war. Daddy said that William had shrapnel in his head. That's the reason he got the Purple Heart and sits in his room.

One of the best things about the war being over is that Elbert will be coming home. Jamie will be so glad about that. I'll never forget when Jamie told Edith that Elbert was coming home on a furlough, and they were going to get married. I was at Nona's house when we heard about it. We both started crying. Jamie was Nona's first grandchild. Edith always said that Nona loved Jamie more than anybody else until I came along. Nona said she's just a little girl. She's only 21. I told Nona that she was just 17 when she got married. She said she should've known better.

The wedding was going to be in Edith's living room. Daddy and Papa were crying too. They loved Jamie better than anybody. She spent a lot of time with Nona and Papa when she was little. Edith had Sister and Boy to take care of. So Jamie would stop off from school. She'd play at Nona's house and sometimes spend the night with them. Daddy was living there before he married. So he and Jamie were really close too. He called her Jim.

Jamie asked Daddy to sing at her wedding cause he sang at everybody else's wedding. He told her he felt like he'd be singing at a funeral.

Edith said Daddy couldn't do it cause he'd break down and start crying right in the middle of it.

Dr. Chamblee was the preacher at the wedding. They wouldn't let me go in the living room cause I was just 6. I had to stay in the kitchen with Duxie. Jamie's wedding was March 16, 1943. When Elbert came down from Portsmouth Virginia where he was stationed Daddy and Papa were sitting in the living room. They didn't speak to him when he came in. Edith said they were sulking. I don't know what that means but it must mean something like they didn't want Jamie to get married to Elbert.

Me and Duxie were peeping through the doors to try to see what was happening in the living room during the wedding. Elbert had on his Navy uniform and looked really nice. Jamie had on a pretty white dress. When me and Duxie were peeping in there Dr. Chamblee was preaching some things to Jamie and Elbert and getting them married.

After the wedding Edith had some wedding cake and punch and sandwiches to eat. I could hardly eat anything cause I was so sad. We waved goodbye as they drove off in Elbert's car heading to Virginia. Everybody in the whole family was crying.

I'm sorry this was such a long letter Henry but there's a lot to tell about the war and how glad we are that it's over.

Love,
Tom

Sept 30, 1945

Dear Henry,

Miss Gussie Bragg is my teacher this year in the 4th grade. I think she's kin to me somehow. But I don't know exactly how. We got 27 pupils in our class. She makes us sit in alphabetical order according to our last name. That makes me have to sit in the last desk in the back of the room. It's O.K. with me though. I don't want the teacher to always know what I'm doing.

She makes us answer the roll call with a bible verse. All us boys like to say the shortest one we know. "Jesus wept" is the shortest verse in the Bible. But Irvin always gets that one cause I comes ahead of T.

Miss Gussie says we ought to say a different one each day. But most of us boys don't know all that many. She forgets anyway. The smart girls in the class say those long ones like – "For God so loved the world that He gave His only begotten Son that whosoever believeth in Him shall not perish but shall have everlasting life." All us boys just kinda look at each other and roll our eyes when the girls say those long ones like that. They're always trying to brown nose the teacher.

I was writing you this letter to tell you I got a whipping yesterday. At recess some of us boys were playing underneath the school building. There's a bunch of old boards stored under there. Some of them have tar on them. While we were playing I got some of that old black tar on my pants. One of the girls told on me. So Miss Gussie gave me a whipping with a paddle. I tried my best not to cry. I might have. But only just a little bit. I couldn't understand why I ought to get a whipping for something like that. They were my pants that I got the tar on. It didn't hurt anybody else.

After Papa died, Nona divided her house up into 3 parts. Nona lives on one side. Miss Gussie lives on the other side. Miss Dolvin lives in the middle. Miss Dolvin came to Pineview from Talbotton, Georgia. She's the one who bought the Pine Theater. I like her a lot. I get to see her at the picture show every time I go on Monday and Wednesday and Friday night. Sometimes when I go over to Nona's house, Miss Dolvin gives me the schedule of picture shows for the whole month. I'm the first one to get it besides her. I always run it over to show Angie and James and Sammy. They're really glad when I show it to them so they can see what's going to be on.

Miss Gussie is divorced. She's the only person I've ever known who has gotten a divorce. She got it when she was living in Hawkinsville. Nobody in Pineview has ever gotten a divorce even though they might've wanted one. Nona said Miss Gussie was married to Lowell Bragg. He's the horse doctor in Hawkinsville. Nona said she got the divorce cause of his drinking.

Her name before she married was Miss Gussie McLeod. She is Angie's mama's sister. And Hendley's sister, too. She plays the piano in chapel every day at school. She has a piano at Nona's house that used to be an old player piano. But that part doesn't work anymore. Sometimes when I go over to Nona's house, Miss Gussie teaches me some things on the piano. She taught me how to play Glow Worm. But I can't play it as good as she does. She knows how to make her right hand ripple the notes. That's hard for me to do. In the summertime she eats a lot of watermelon. I guess that must be her favorite food.

Nona told me not to worry about the whipping. She said Miss Gussie has been kinda nervous ever since she got her divorce. She said I ought to just overlook it. I've thought about it a whole lot. I guess I can overlook it since she's nervous and all that. But that's the first whipping I've ever gotten from a teacher so far.

Love,
Tom

October 5, 1945

Dear Henry,

Elaine Mixon was my girlfriend in the first grade. She was the best reader in the whole class. I liked the way she read when she'd say, "Look Jane. See Spot run. Funny, funny Spot." She could read that as good as any grown person.

Miss Josephine Hardy was our first grade teacher. She was really strict. If you misbehaved you had to go stand in the cloak room. You had to stay there until she told you to come out. One day I was talking in class. She made me go stand in the cloak room all by myself. I told Mama about it cause she said Miss Josephine was in her class in school. I thought she might go talk to her and raise some cane about putting me in the cloakroom. Mama said if I misbehaved she should've given me a whipping.

When I was in the first grade I missed not seeing Elaine during Christmas holidays. So I told Daddy I wanted to go see her. He laughed and said, "Hell's bells son you're only 6. Don't you think you're a little too young to be calling on a girl?"

I told him I didn't see anything wrong with it. But I didn't know where to go cause I didn't know where she lived. Daddy said he knew Audrey and Shorty Mixon. They live out in the country near Pleasant View. Daddy couldn't take me cause he was working every day. He told Edith to let me spend the night with them. Then I could go out on the mail route with Hendley the next morning to see her.

Edith woke me up early before the sun came up and fixed me and Hendley some eggs and grits and bacon and toast. Edith didn't make me drink a cup of coffee like Mama does. She let me drink some orange juice. I sure do like that better than coffee.

I told Hendley I was real proud to have an uncle like him who was a rural mail carrier. He laughed. We got in his new white Pontiac and went to the post office. Miss Thelma Clements was already there when we walked in. She's the postmistress. She said to Hendley, "I see you've hired some help with all this Christmas mail." He laughed and told her that he was taking me to see my girlfriend.

I waited while Hendley sorted out the mail. I was nervous cause I'd never had a real girlfriend before. I put on my best school clothes, and Nona picked out a Christmas present and wrapped it up for me to give to Elaine.

I was real excited when me and Hendley left the post office and went out on the mail route. It was still dark cause the sun hadn't even come up. We had to stop at every mail box for him to put the mail in. There was a whole lot of mail cause of Christmas cards and packages. I helped him as much as I could. He would tell me the name of the people who lived in the next house. I would get their mail out of the front seat and hand it to him. He'd pull the car up to each box and shove their mail in. Then he'd drive on to the next one. Three or four times people had put Christmas presents in the mail box for Hendley. They were wrapped up in nice Christmas paper. He opened each one. The present I liked best was the paper plate with different kinds of cookies. Hendley said it'd be OK if I slipped one out through the wrapping paper and ate it. I did eat it, and I told him it sure was good. He said he didn't want one.

I got really nervous when Hendley told me the next house was Elaine's. It was not a pretty house. It was kinda small. Hendley told me we'd get out and go inside. I could feel my stomach tingling a little bit when I got out of the car. He knocked on the door. In a little while a big woman wearing a bathrobe opened the door.

Hendley said, "Good morning Audrey."

"How're you Mr. Hendley?"

"Here's your mail."

"Who've you got there with you?"

"I brought Tom. He was hoping he might get to see Elaine."

"Y'all come on in," she said. "Don't pay any attention to the house. It's a mess. I think Elaine is still in the bed, but it's time for her to get up."

Her mama was kinda big. Elaine is little and skinny. I've seen her daddy before cause he drives a school bus. His name is Ernest. But everybody calls him Shorty except Fletcher and he calls him the Little Toy Man.

Me and Hendley backed up to the fire and stood there trying to warm up cause it was cold outside. In a few minutes Elaine came walking in the room. She still had on her pajamas and her hair was all messed up. When I looked at her, I knew that I still wanted her to be my girlfriend even if she just had on her pajamas. I didn't say anything. I just handed her the present. Her mama said, "Can't you say thank you?" So she said, "Thank you," and started ripping the paper off the box like she was in a hurry to see what it was. She looked at the little box of chocolate covered cherries that Nona had picked out. I could tell she liked them by the look in her eyes. But she didn't say anything. I was really hoping she would like them cause that candy cost me half of my allowance.

Hendley said, "We better get going. We need to get on with the route."

After we left I was staring out the window a lot and not helping Hendley like I should. He had to remind me more than once the name of the people in the next house. He said, "You don't seem to be paying attention like you were before you saw Elaine."

I told him I was sorry cause I had my mind on something else.

One time later on, we were playing games at recess where everyone had to get in a circle and hold hands. I jumped as quick as I could to stand next to Elaine. I got to hold her hand for the first time and the only time. It never happened again.

In the second grade I changed girlfriends. I didn't like Elaine anymore cause I liked Gayle Talley better. She was the prettiest girl in the class. Edith was my teacher. She asked me who my girlfriend was. I told her it was Gayle.

When I was in the third grade Miss Mary Will Barrington was my teacher. I decided it was time to change girlfriends again. When Miss Barrington asked me who my girlfriend was I told her it was Joan. She said, "You can't have her as a girlfriend cause she's your cousin."

Just cause her daddy is my mama's brother, I don't see what that's got to do with her not being my girlfriend? I decided I'd keep her as my girlfriend anyway and just not tell anybody.

Now that I'm in the fourth grade, I figured it was time to have a new girlfriend. The one I really like the most is Jo Horne. But Irvin already got her to be his girlfriend. I was thinking about Myrna Broadway or maybe Rose Marie Bloodworth. Right now I'm not sure. I like having a girlfriend. But I've never held a girl's hand. I don't have the nerve to do anything like that. I saw McCall Warren kiss Betty Horne in the mouth on the hayride last Christmas. They were 13. I don't think I'd ever want to kiss a girl on the mouth. What do you think about that, Henry?

Love,
Tom

November 14, 1945

Dear Henry,

Do you remember the Balls that live behind Mrs. Gammage and Lelia? They have a son named Gene. He's in the same class with Angie. They're 14. He's a really good basketball player. I'm just 9, and I sure do want to be able to play basketball as good as he does when I'm his age.

Mr. Ball drives a turpentine truck. He's a little short man with reddish hair and a red face. He looks like he'd just as soon kick your butt off as look at you. I'm scared of him. They said he came in the house the other night really drunk and fell down in his chair. There was a woman singing real loud on the radio. He told her to shut up but she wouldn't. He reached down under his chair and got his shot gun. He aimed it at the radio and blasted it into a hundred pieces.

Every Sunday afternoon a bunch of big boys usually go up to the stadium to play some basket-ball. Mr. W.F. Stone is the principle. He changed the locks on the doors cause so many of the boys had keys. Last Sunday afternoon I was walking by the stadium and saw Gene Ball trying to get through one of the windows. All the rest of the big boys had left cause they couldn't get in the stadium.

When Gene saw me walking by, he called me to come over there where he was. I couldn't imagine what he wanted cause he'd never spoken to me before in my life. He said he wanted to hold me on his shoulders so I could push up the window of the boy's dressing room. I crawled up on his shoulders and pushed it up. He told me to crawl in and come around to the side door and open it. He came in the door and found a basketball and started shooting. He wanted me to run and get the ball every time he shot and throw it back to him.

In a little bit we heard the side door open with a bang. We looked over there and this boy named Leland was standing in the doorway looking at us. His family was visiting with the Balls. He's about 2 years older than I am and is meaner than a mad dog. He walked in acting kinda crazy like he was up to no good. He started chasing me around the gym saying he was going to kill me. He was making weird noises that sounded like some kind of monster.

I yelled for Gene to please come help me, but he just kept right on shooting. For a long time I ran all over the gym with that crazy boy chasing right behind me. I jumped up on the stage. The curtain was pulled so that it was dark and spooky back there. I hid behind the piano. I heard him breathing real loud and making those crazy sounds. Light flashed up on the stage when he opened the curtain. "If I find you, I'm going to kill you," he growled. My heart was beating so fast and loud, I thought he might be able to hear it. I knew he was big enough and mean enough to tear me apart.

I was sitting there under the piano shaking all over. I couldn't see him but I could hear him breathing. Just before he reached down to grab me, I jumped up and ran as fast as I could. I jumped off the stage and ran across the basketball court for the door. Leland had locked it when he came in. I yelled out to Gene to please help me cause Leland was going to kill me. Gene said, "I wouldn't touch that little son of a bitch. He's crazy as hell." I didn't know what to do. I couldn't get the door open. But so far, I'd been able to outrun him.

One time when he got way behind me, I ran as fast as I could for the door and got it unlocked. I ran down the street to my house. I kept looking back to see if he was following me, but he wasn't. So I slowed down.

When Mama saw me she wanted to know what in the world was wrong with me. I told her what happened. But I'm not sure I should have.

Before I finished telling her the whole story, she started putting on her coat. She marched out the door, walking really fast over toward Mr. Ball's house. I could tell how mad she was by the way she walked. I thought she probably shouldn't be going over to Mr. Ball's house real mad like that. There's no telling what he would do. He probably had guns all over the place and might shoot her like he did his radio. But Daddy always said that Mama ain't scared of the devil himself.

When she came back to the house I asked her what she said to Mr. Ball. She didn't answer me.

Later on she told me not to worry cause it would never happen again.

I've been wondering for a while now what she said to Mr. Ball. I don't guess I'll ever know. But I bet she gave him some holy hell, as Daddy calls it. I think I'd rather have that crazy Leland chasing me all over the place than have Mama after me when she's mad.

I'll write you later when there's something else to tell you.

Love,
Tom

February 12, 1946

Dear Henry,

You'll never guess what I'm fixing to do. I'm going to get out of school early today cause I'm going to go to Athens with Angie and James and Sammy to see Elinor. You remember Elinor, don't you? She's Mr. and Mrs. Ware's granddaughter. You know they've been the head of the Pineview School ever since my daddy was a little boy. They had a daughter named Dorothy. She married Leon Smith. They are Elinor's parents. Elinor is 1 year older than Angie. When she comes to visit her grandmother, Angie is the only girl near her age she can play with.

Sammy and Elinor are 15. Angie and James are 14. And I'm just 9. But they treat me like I'm as old as they are. We're going on the bus from Hawkinsville to Macon then catch another bus to Athens. I've never been there but I know about it cause that's where the University of Georgia is. You know how much I love the Georgia Bulldogs. I listen on the radio to every football game they play.

The biggest news of all is that Elinor has gotten Angie a date with John D. Rockefeller. Angie said that he has more than a billion dollars. His daddy is one of the richest men in the whole world. I can't wait to meet somebody who is rich like that. He must have everything he wants.

Hey, Henry, I'm going to have to finish this letter when I get back cause it's time for them to pick me up. I gotta run.

Henry we just got back from Athens yesterday. I need to tell you what all happened. When we got there Elinor and her daddy met us at the bus station. Angie said he's the dean of Arts and Sciences at the University. Elinor's mother died when Elinor was little. Leon married Mary. She's a lot younger and real pretty too.

Mary fixed a good supper for us. But we couldn't think about what we were eating cause we couldn't wait for John D. Rockefeller to come by. After supper Leon went in the closet and pulled out his bassoon. He plays in an orchestra. When he played it sounded real funny. But I tried not to laugh.

Elinor told us that her daddy was in the Navy during the war. He spoke French. He worked at the Pentagon and was an expert on codes. He was trying to figure out the messages that the Germans were sending. He taught at the University of Chicago before he came to Athens. He's probably the smartest man I've ever been around. Elinor is pretty smart too. She was one of the Whiz Kids on the radio in Chicago when she was 12.

John D. Rockefeller got to Elinor's house about 10 o'clock. He's older than all of us. I think he said he was 17. He seemed pretty old to me. He made me think he might know everything in the whole world that was important. His clothes were really good looking. He was about the swankiest guy I'd ever seen in my life.

He wanted to take us to ride in his convertible. When we walked out the front door I couldn't believe how pretty his car was. It was a Chrysler Town and Country. It had real fancy wood on both sides. The color of the rest of the car was maroon. He put the top down but it was pretty cold. I'd never ridden in a convertible with the top down or with the top up either. We had on coats to try to stay warm. We got out on the Atlanta Highway and he floor boarded it. He pointed to the speedometer when it hit 100. I'd never been that fast in a car before. One time McCall Warren was driving a bunch of us to Hawkinsville and he hit 85. That was pretty fast for those old dirt roads around Pineview.

I was sitting in the back with James and Sammy. Angie was sitting by John D. Rockefeller. Elinor was sitting next to Angie. I saw him reach over and grab Angie's hand to hold. He was driving with just his left hand. I was thinking to myself that one day I would have a pretty girlfriend. I could hold her hand with my right hand and drive with just my left hand like John D. Rockefeller. That would be about the coolest thing in the whole world.

Sammy said he thought we might get killed driving over 100 miles per hour. I didn't even think about that cause I knew John D. Rockefeller would know exactly what he was doing. When he dropped us off back at Elinor's house, she and Angie started laughing. They said they were just playing a joke on me and James and Sammy. He was not really John D. Rockefeller. His name was Maynard Hazen and his nickname was Mobo.

Angie acted like she sure did like him a lot. She brought a picture of him back home with her and hung it up on her wall next to all the movie stars and she talked about Mobo all the time.

On Sunday. Leon and Mary decided they'd drive us in their car all the way back to Macon so we wouldn't have to take the bus. That was really nice of them. But I did a terrible thing on the way to Macon. I got car sick. I went to sleep and when I woke up I knew I was fixing to vomit. Angie yelled for Leon to stop the car. I jumped out of the back seat before the car even stopped and threw up everything I had in my stomach. It was so embarrassing, I wanted to die. But I couldn't help it.

I sure did have a good time in Athens. We got to ride all around the campus and see all the large buildings. It sure is a big place. I wish I could go there when I graduate from high school. But it's too big a place for a small town boy like me.

Love,
Tom

March 30, 1946

Dear Henry,

Guess what, Henry? We got new telephones. We don't have those old fashion ones anymore. You remember that big old wooden telephone that used to hang on the wall right behind the front door. You couldn't see it when the door was open. Mr. Wilson took all those old phones down. Now we got a new plastic one that's black. Mama's cousin in Rochelle who has a funny name put our new phone in. His name is Quattlebaum.

Mama told him to put our new phone on a little table in the dining room. It has a crank on the side of it to use when you want to call somebody. It's nice to be able to sit down in one of the dining room chairs when you're talking. I had to stand on a stool to use the old one.

The telephone switchboard has been down at Mrs. Wilson's house for as long as I've been alive. But now you don't have to call Mrs. Wilson every time you want to make a call. She always listened in on everybody when they would call somebody. One time Daddy got a call all the way from Macon. It was Fat Matthews. He was kinda like one of the bosses in the Internal Revenue Service where Daddy works. I heard Daddy say, "Get off the damn phone, Mrs. Wilson." I guess he didn't want her listening in on what they were saying.

I figured Mrs. Wilson had to listen in to every-body. How else would she know where everyone was all the time? Sometimes when I get home from school, I don't know where Mama is playing bridge. I'd jump up on the stool and turn the crank on the phone two or three times. Mrs. Wilson would always say, "Operator." I don't know why she'd say that cause everyone always knew it was Mrs. Wilson. I'd ask her where Mama was playing bridge. She'd tell me if they were playing at Juju's or Matibel's or Charlye's or Edith's or Lillian's. It was really good to have Mrs. Wilson to always know where Mama was all the time. Now with these new phones, I'm going to have to get out and look for her.

The other day I asked Mrs. Wilson where Mama was, and she said she saw her just a few minutes ago in Juju's car with Charlye and Matibel head-ing downtown. She told me to hold on just a min-ute so she could walk out on the porch and see if she could see them. She came back and said she saw Juju's car at the drug store. She said she was sure they were down there drinking a Co Cola. With these new phones, the operator is going to be down in Rochelle. How in the world is she going to know where Mama is all the time?

Sometimes when me and Irvin want to go swim-ming, we go down to Mrs. Wilson's house to see if she has heard of anybody who might be going. Other day she said, "You boys go out there in the yard and play. As hot as it is today, somebody will be calling soon." After while, Little Jane Lou called Mary Dennard and Sister to see if they wanted to go swimming. Mrs. Wilson told her to come by her house and pick us up. By the time she got there, Sammy and James and Angie had come down there looking for a ride to go swimming, too. Jane Lou and Sister and Mary Dennard acted real mad. They think they're so big 'cause they're teenagers and they don't like to hang around us.

If a person in Pineview ever gets a long distance call and they don't answer, Mrs. Wilson would always get in her car and ride around town looking for them. One time when Elbert was in the war he got a furlough to San Francisco. He called Jamie but she was at the picture show. Mrs. Wilson walked down there and found Jamie sitting with a bunch of girls. She got Jamie out of there in time to get back up to her house to say hello to Elbert. Jamie said she had to holler in the phone real loud cause he could hardly hear her. Nobody in Pineview had ever had a call as far away as San Francisco.

Daddy doesn't like telephones. He says that nobody should ever make a call unless it's an emergency. When he's at home he makes sure that none of us talk on the phone just to be talking.

Only 10 people in Pineview have one of the new phones. Hardly anybody would ever make a long distance call cause it costs so much money. One time Angie called Elinor in Athens. They must've talked a long time cause it cost more than a dollar. She really got in trouble when her mama found out about it.

On our new phone, our ring is two longs and one short. When anybody in Pineview makes a call or gets a call, all 10 phones ring at the same time. But you only answer if it's your ring. Daddy said some people probably pick up the phone and listen in on other people's conversations just like Mrs. Wilson has been doing all these years. He told me he'd better not ever hear of me doing anything like that. I have thought about it, but I'd never do it if Daddy is at home.

Irvin's ring is two shorts and one long. Edith's is one short, one long and one short. They're about the only 2 people I ever call cause Nona doesn't have a phone and Joan doesn't either.

When we're sitting around the house at night listening to the radio and the phone rings, Daddy always shouts, "Who in the hell is calling them at this time of night?" But if I hear the phone ring two longs and one short, I run as fast as I can to try to answer it before Daddy gets there. If he answers it, he hollers in the phone so loud it scares people to death. When he says "hello," he sounds like a mad person who just had somebody slap him in the face. Anyone who calls our house always hangs up unless the call is for him. Every time somebody hangs up when he answers it, he gets real mad and starts cussin. Some of my friends tell me they'd never in a 100 years talk to my daddy on the phone. He scares the living daylights out of them.

When Mr. Wilson took all the old wooden phones off the wall, Irvin kept his and brought it around to our house. So I got ours, too. We went down town to the scrap yard and found a bunch of haywire. We rigged up two wires running from each phone.

It worked too. We could talk on them from the barn to our garage. We had the best time cause we could talk on the phone as long as we wanted to. Daddy never knew we had them.

Well, Henry, that's about all the news I've got from Pineview. I hope you're having fun up there in heaven.

Love,
Tom

June 2, 1946

Dear Henry,

Little Jane Lou taught our Sunday school class yesterday. She and Sister just graduated from the University of Alabama. They're both 20 years old. I'm just 10 so they're twice as old as I am. Even though they are pretty old I still like them. I just wish they'd gone to the University of Georgia, so they could've been Georgia Bulldogs cause I love the Georgia Bulldogs.

I remember when Little Jane Lou graduated from high school. She was 16 and finished first in her class. That means she had the highest grades of anybody all the way through school. She must be really smart.

When you're the valedictorian you have to make a speech at graduation. Everybody in town always goes to everything they have at the stadium no matter if it's a graduation or a gospel quartet or a Halloween carnival or a donkey basketball game. I hope I'm not the valedictorian of my class cause I would be scared to death to have to make a speech in front of all those people.

Little Jane Lou must not be scared cause she knows how to make a speech really good. Nona said she uses a lot of expression. Edith started teaching her how to speak with expression when she was just 5 years old. Edith has been teaching me for a long time too.

I remember when Little Jane Lou was making her valedictorian speech, she started crying. Everybody looked at each other cause nobody knew why she'd be crying like that. She should've been happy to get out of high school. But she finally got herself together and finished her speech.

I heard Little Jane Lou telling Nona and Edith that Tommy Day Wilcox had just got drafted to go in the war the same day of her graduation. He is her sister Laura's husband. Little Jane Lou said while she was making her speech, she started thinking about Laura and how she was expecting a baby and all. It made her real sad. Edith asked her who wrote her speech for her. She said she used her mama's valedictorian speech when she graduated from college at GSCW in Milledgeville. I asked Edith what did GSCW stand for. She said it was the Georgia State College for Women.

Edith said that Charlye, who is Little Jane Lou's mama, was really smart, too. She said you had to be smart to graduate first in your class at GSCW like she did. Charlye's name before she married Rod was Ertzberger. Edith said that after Charlye graduated from college she tried to get a job teaching in Rochelle. They told her they'd love to have somebody as smart as she was teaching there but there would be no way in the world they could hire anybody with a name like Ertzberger.

I asked Edith why that was. She said it was in 1918 during World War 1. We were fighting the

Germans, and Ertzberger is a German name. So she got a job in Pineview teaching school. I guess they didn't care about what her name was in Pineview. Edith said when Charlye started teaching, she boarded at Steve Moore's house on the road going toward Cordele. She had to walk everyday to school. And that's over a mile.

Little Jane Lou's real mama is Charlye and her real daddy is Rod. But she went to live with Juju and Fletcher when she was a little girl and never came back to live with her mama and daddy again. Juju and Fletcher didn't have any children and they wanted somebody little to live with them. Juju's real name is Jane Lou. Some people call her Big Jane Lou. It's good that Fletcher's name is McLeod so Little Jane Lou can have the same last name. Fletcher and Rod are first cousins. Fletcher and Nona are first cousins too. I guess everybody in Pineview is kin to each other in one way or another.

Edith said that when Little Jane Lou was in the 6th grade, Fletcher gave her a horse for her birthday. When she got on the horse it took off running. She was screaming so loud that Rod heard her and ran out the door with shaving cream all over his face. He started yelling at her, "Pull back on the reins, pull back on the reins!" When she did, the horse stopped still.

I always thought Little Jane Lou was really something special cause she was the only girl I'd ever seen who could ride a horse. She rode that horse all over Pineview.

Daddy and Mama would take me to the horse races in Hawkinsville every year in March. There are always some big boys and girls parading their horses around on the track before the races. Little Jane Lou is usually one of them. She's always dressed up really pretty. She looks like she ought to be a movie star.

I guess that's all I have to write about today, Henry. I'll write more to you later.

Love,
Tom

July 4, 1946

Dear Henry,

You'll never believe what a horrible thing has happened in Pineview. Its got everybody in town talking about it. Midge Doster married a yankee. They got married last week. Nobody can believe she would've ever done a thing like that. Nona said, "Midge was old enough to know better. After all she's 31." She's been up in Atlanta working and met this man from Chicago. Nona said, "Midge is smart enough to know that nobody but yankees live in Chicago."

But, Henry, that's not the end of how bad it really is. Not only is he a yankee, but he's also a Catholic. And, Henry, that's not even the end of how bad it really is. To make it even worse, he's a Pollack. I didn't know what a Pollack was, but Nona said that Pollacks are people who come from Poland. I've never seen a yankee or a Catholic or anybody from Poland. I can't imagine what he must look like having 3 bad things like that against him.

Nona said Midge was always a pretty little girl, and all the boys liked her. "She certainly could've done a whole lot better than that. You just don't marry folks that are different from you. It's hard enough even if you marry your own kind," she said.

She said you're not supposed to hang around yankees either. They beat the South in the Civil War and were really mean about it too. Nona told me what the yankees did to her Granddaddy Barfield who lived near Round Oak, Georgia. She said he had a big house on a farm. He'd just finished ginning 500 bales of cotton, and it was all stacked out in the field when Sherman's Army came through. They set fire to every single bale of cotton and burned them all up. Then they went out in the field and shot all the hogs that her granddaddy had and cut the hams out to take with them. The rest of the dead hogs were left to spoil. They came in the house where his wife and children were hiding and took the silver and jewelry and stuff like that. Then set fire to the house. Nona's daddy was just a little boy at the time. He told Nona that his daddy was out there in the front of the burning house cussin' Sherman for everything he was worth. All those yankees rode off on their horses laughing at him. Nona said you should never ever trust a yankee and shouldn't ever hang around anybody named Sherman. Yankees and Shermans are some mean people.

Nona said that Catholics weren't like us either. They have a Pope that tells everybody in their church what to believe and what not to believe. I didn't say this to Nona, but it seems to me that the preachers in Pineview do the same thing. I think she must mean that Catholics don't believe in Jesus and God and they just pray to the Pope.

I started this letter 2 days ago. But a lot has happened in Pineview in the last 2 days. I had to tell you that Midge brought her new yankee husband to Nona's store yesterday to show him off to every-body. His name is Joe Panko. He's about the fun-niest looking man I've ever seen. His hair is falling out, and he looks like he's almost bald. His nose is weird too. It's kinda thin and pointed, and he wears wire rim glasses. Daddy said that none of us had ever seen a foreigner much less marry one. I guess when Joe Panko moved from Poland to Chicago he must've turned from a Pollack into a yankee. Everybody in town is talking about what a terrible tragedy all of this is, and how they feel so sorry for the family.

I don't know if you remember Midge or not. She is one of Uncle Philet and Aunt Ida's daughters. They have another daughter named Martha and two boys named Boots and Nonk. You know Aunt Ida. She is Papa's sister.

Daddy said that one time Uncle Philet tried to play a joke on Midge. She had been home for the weekend and was going back to Atlanta where she worked. Midge told Uncle Philet she wanted some turkeys to take back to Atlanta. She said they could live out in her backyard cause it was fenced in. Uncle Philet told her she was crazy to take live turkeys back in her car. He said he knew where he could find some turkey eggs. She could put them under a light bulb and hatch them out when she got back to Atlanta. Ephraim is the nigra man who works for Uncle Philet and Aunt Ida. Uncle Philet told Ephraim to climb up the chinaberry tree in their backyard cause there was a buzzard's nest full of eggs. He was going to give them to Midge thinking what a funny joke it would be when those eggs hatched out.   Ephraim had helped raise Midge since she was a baby and didn't like playing a joke on her like that. He told her what Uncle Philet had done. So when she started to drive off back to Atlanta, Uncle Philet told her not to forget the eggs. Midge said, "Papa, I decided not to take them since you said I shouldn't. So I got Ephraim to scramble those turkey eggs for your breakfast this morning."

Henry I'll let you know when I hear something else about what the yankee, Catholic, Pollack is doing while he's here in Pineview.

Love,
Tom

July 12, 1946

Dear Henry,

How are things up there in heaven? There's nothing to do here at night. Monday and Wednesday and Friday nights the gang goes to the picture show. Saturday I always spend the night with Nona. Other than that I just stay at home listening to the radio.

We always sit on the screen porch after supper in the summer and shell peas and butterbeans. Daddy gets an extension cord for the radio so we can listen to our programs on the porch where it's cooler. It gets pretty hot in our house during the summer. I wish we'd get an attic fan like some people have. It sucks all the hot air out of your house and pulls cool air from outside through the windows.

I get tired of shelling peas and butterbeans. We shell so many it makes my thumb hurt. When I complain, Mama keeps reminding me that I'll be happy to have them to eat next winter. She knows I like lady finger peas and crowder peas and black-eyed peas.

Daddy always says he's not shelling any butterbeans. He'll only shell peas. He says butterbeans are too damn hard to shell. Mama puts some newspaper in his lap and piles on a bunch of peas. He has a pan to put the peas in. She puts newspaper on the floor to throw the shells. She even makes my sister shell some peas and she's only 4. I'm 10, and I'm a pretty good sheller. When I get big like Daddy, I'm going to be like him and tell my wife I'm not shelling any butterbeans.

Everybody in Pineview sits on their front porch at night in the summer and does the same thing we do. We can hear the Clements talking next door and Nan and Sammy and Betty Jean next door to them. Ma-Me and Ruby and Joan are sitting on their porch across the street from us. Mrs. Gammage and Lelia sit on their porch across from our pecan trees. We all do the same thing except Daddy lets us listen to the radio while we're shelling. I guess none of the rest of them ever thought of that.

At Nona's house everybody on their front porches talks to each other. You have to talk pretty loud to hear Edith and Hendley. But you can talk to Guy and Alice and Angie on one side and Matibel and Joe L. on the other side. Everybody has a good time talking to each other even though you can't see them.

After we finish shelling all the peas and butterbeans, Mama puts them in the refrigerator in a dish pan. She takes them up to the canning plant where they put them in cans for us to eat next winter. The canning plant is in our school lunchroom where Sammy's mother is in charge of all the cooking. She's a really good cook, too. During school they always serve a meat and 2 vegetables with bread and dessert just like our health books teach us. My favorite meal is turkey and dressing with turkey giblet gravy and creamed potatoes and green beans and cranberry sauce. We always have that on the day before Thanksgiving and the last day of school before Christmas.

Mama and Daddy have a lot of programs they listen to on the radio every night. One of Mama's favorites is Fibber McGhee and Molly but her most favorite of all is The Jack Benny Show. He comes on the radio every Sunday night. She thinks he's really funny when he's talking to his wife Mary and Rochester. He's the nigra driver. Daddy doesn't care much for Jack Benny. He likes Inner Sanctum and The Squeaking Door and The Shadow. Those programs are too scary for me. Every time I listen to any of them I have trouble going to sleep. They make me have bad dreams, too.

Mama never misses Arthur Godfrey. He comes on in the middle of the day. I don't like listening to him. At night Mama and Daddy both like George Burns and Gracie Allen. I don't really like them either. They like Dinah Shore cause she sings all kinds of music. Mama especially likes Red Skelton. I do too. He plays all those funny characters that do all those crazy things like Clem Cadittlehopper.

In the winter time when I can't play outside on Sunday afternoons, we listen to the Quiz Kids. Daddy likes that show. I don't understand a lot of the questions they ask. Daddy likes to pretend they ask the questions to him. He tries to answer them before they do. Another radio program Mama and Daddy like is It Pays to Be Ignorant. I don't know why they like it. It seems pretty stupid to me. They sometimes listen to The Danny Kaye Show.

My favorite radio programs come on Saturday night when I'm at Nona's house. In the winter we sit by the fire. In the summer we sit on her porch and listen to Amos and Andy and Judy Canova and The Hit Parade. I always thought Amos and Andy were nigras. I couldn't believe it when Daddy told me they were two white men talking like nigras. That made me not like them as much.

I get more excited about The Hit Parade than any of the other shows. I have a pad I got at Nona's store. I use it to write down the songs they sing. It's the top seven songs of the country for that week. They always start off the program singing about Lucky Strike cigarettes.

> Be happy go lucky
> Be happy go Lucky Strike
> Be happy go lucky
> Go Lucky Strike today.

I've been listening to the Hit Parade as long as I can remember. Frank Sinatra used to sing most of the songs. Now Doris Day sings some and Frank Sinatra sings some. Different ones have sung the songs over the years like Dorothy Collins and Dick Haymes and Snooky Lanson and Gisele MacKenzie and Johnny Mercer and Dinah Shore and Eileen Wilson.

This year the song that has been the number 1 song for the longest time is The Gypsy. Another one that has been on The Hit Parade for a long time this year is Oh! What It Seemed To Be. Daddy likes to sing that one.

Here are some of the ones that I've got written down in my pad that have been making the Hit Parade this year:

Rumors Are Flying
They Say it's Wonderful
To Each His Own
Laura
Laughing on the Outside
Five Minutes More
A Gal in Calico
All Through the Day
Let It Snow, Let It Snow, Let It Snow
For Sentimental Reasons
Onezy, Twozy, I Love Youzy
Personality
The Whole World Is Singing My Song
You'd Be So Nice to Come Home to
You Won't Be Satisfied
Surrender
Day by Day
South America, Take it Away
Doin' What Comes Naturally
The Old Lamplighter
Shoo Fly Pie and Apple Pan Dowdy
Zip-A-Dee-Doo-Dah
Aren't You Glad You're You
I Don't Know Enough About You
You Keep Coming Back Like a Song

The Hit Parade always ends with all of them singing together.

> So long for a while
> That's all the songs for a while
> So long to your Hit Parade
> And the songs that you picked to be played
> So long.

When I was five years old, Mama and Daddy went to New York with Edith and Hendley. He'd just bought a brand new Pontiac. They drove all the way up there and saw some Broadway plays and stuff. I'll never forget what Daddy told me about going to Radio City Music Hall. He said they saw a radio program that had a picture on the front of the radio. You could see the program and not just hear it. I asked Daddy if that meant one day I could see Amos and Andy on a picture on the front of the radio. He said he wasn't kidding me. He said one of these days it might be possible that we could buy one of those things. I couldn't believe it. I told Irvin and Joan and Angie and everybody I knew that Daddy had seen a picture of the radio programs on the front of the radio.

I guess you've heard enough about all this Henry. So I'll write you more later on.

Love,
Tom

August 10, 1946

Dear Henry,

How're things in heaven? I bet it's really pretty up there. What's the weather like? It's so hot down here. Nona said its dog days. That's what makes it so hot and stuffy. I guess you know what dog days are since you're a dog.

I've got the sore eyes. Nona said it's caused by gnats. I'm sure you remember how those gnats get in your eyes and ears. Mama has been putting drops in my eyes every day. Nona said it won't do any good to put drops in my eyes cause nothing will get well until dog days are over.

They ginned the first bale of cotton last week. All the farmers want to be first cause the first bale gets ginned for free. The one who is first gets his picture in the Hawkinsville paper. Looney Peacock was the first one again this year. He lives in a house on the way to our farm.

Ruby Mann is my aunt. She's Joan's mother. Every day last week she took Joan and Betty Jean and Irvin and me to their farm to pick cotton. Their farm is on the Rochelle highway just on the other side of the nigra quarters.

I don't think I've ever sweated that much in my whole life. You have to wear a sack on your back to put the cotton in. Every time you fill it up, you take it to the end of the row to empty it on your cotton sheet. Everybody has their own sheet. I picked as hard as I could to try to beat the rest of them. The ends of my fingers are still hurting. Cotton bolls are sharp and can make your fingers bleed.

Joe is the nigra man who is in charge of the cotton pickers. He's the one that hollers out quittin time. That's when all the pickers know it's time to stop.

Yesterday the sun had already gone below the tops of the trees before he hollered quittin time. I looked at my sheet of cotton. I thought to myself that's the most cotton I've ever picked in my life. It was piled up so high that it almost covered the whole sheet. I figured that was going to make me a lot of spending money. We get paid 2 cents a pound. The man on the big truck came around with the scales. He weighed mine and yelled out 87. That's my record all right. I was hoping it'd be 100. Irvin had 85 pounds. Betty Jean only had 82. But when he weighed Joan's sheet, he called out 89 pounds. I couldn't believe she'd beaten me again. My pile looked a lot bigger than hers. I kidded her and told her she must've put a brick bat in her cotton sheet.

The man writes the amount we pick in a notebook. At the end of the week we get paid. My 87 pounds will be worth $1.74 and that's just for one day. I get a $1.50 allowance a week and I make $1.50 working at Nona's store on Saturdays. So I'm going to have a lot of money.

I don't know how nigras can pick so much. Most of them have 200 pounds or more every day. They start picking at sunup.   We don't get started til about 9 o'clock. Most of the nigras pick with both hands at the same time. They sing a bunch of old songs while they're picking.   I guess that makes them pick better.   I think if I picked all day and all night and sang the whole time, I could never pick 200 pounds.

I'll write you again soon.   I wish you could write me and tell me what goes on in heaven.

Love,
Tom

September 14, 1946

Dear Henry,

My most favorite thing to do in the whole world is play basketball. I love it and can't wait to get home from school every day to start playing. Daddy had Hosey put up a new goal for me. It's a real one that Daddy got from Sears Roebuck. It has a real net just like the ones at the stadium. He got Hosey to paint the backboard white. We measured the distance from the ground to the goal so it'd be exactly 10 feet. I'm so happy about it. Now I can shoot on a real basket.

My old goals weren't the right height. One was nailed to the side of the barn. It was pretty close to 10 feet. But the one on the other side of the court was nailed to the pecan tree. It was too low. But you couldn't raise it any higher cause a limb was in the way. I like playing full court with my 2 old goals, but I like having my new goal on the pole. Now I can run fast breaks without crashing into the side of the barn.

Sometimes Irvin plays with me. But most of the time I play by myself. That's the way I really like it. I have a league with 6 teams. Besides Pineview there's Rochelle and Abbeville and Pitts and Hawkinsville and Fitzgerald. I have a different shot that I shoot for each team. I got a notebook so I can keep all the standings written down just like they do in the newspaper with baseball teams. I always wear my watch so I can play 5 minute quarters. Each team gets a long shot. If I don't hit it then I back it up with a short shot.

Right now, here are the standings:

	Won	Lost	Games Behind
Pineview	12	3	
Fitzgerald	10	5	2
Hawkinsville	8	7	4
Pitts	7	8	5
Rochelle	7	8	5
Abbeville	1	14	11

When I hit a good shot for a team that I like a lot, I always cheer. I try to do it under my breath so no one will hear me and think I'm crazy. Angie said she has heard me cheering. So that's when I started holding the noise down.

Mama and Daddy always take me to every basketball game that Pineview plays at the stadium. I love watching the teams play. Of course I like it better when Pineview wins. Nona made me a sweatshirt that was white. She sewed Pineview Pirates on it in purple letters cause our school colors are purple and gold. The first time I wore it to a game, some big girl sitting behind me grabbed me by the shoulders and turned me around to show off my shirt to the other girls sitting with her. They all laughed. I never wore the shirt again.

Pineview usually has a pretty good team. We can always beat Abbeville and Chauncey. Sometimes we beat Rhine and Rochelle and Pitts and East Crisp but we hardly ever beat Vienna. They always have the best team around.

Daddy said that before I was born, Vienna had a high school basketball team called the Wonder 5. They won the state championship and then went to Chicago to play for the national championship. They lost by only 1 point. That must've been the best basketball team ever in the history of Georgia. The man who drives the truck for the Vienna Cleaners was one of the Wonder 5. I always look at him when he comes up on the front porch to get my daddy's suits and shirts. I can't imagine what it must've been like to have been on that team.

The first basketball goal I ever had was just an old metal rim from a syrup can that Daddy nailed on the side of the smoke house. I played with a small rubber ball. I got where I could throw it in the goal pretty good. But then after I got a little bigger, Daddy got me those goals that he nailed on the barn and the pecan tree.

I really hope someday I'll be able to play on the Pineview basketball team. That would be the greatest thing I could ever think of doing in my whole life.

I'll write more to you later, Henry.

Love,
Tom

December 9, 1946

Dear Henry,

Miss Cheek has given us a writing assignment. She wants us to write about any nigra we know. I thought I might write about Hosey cause he was my daddy's chauffeur on all his dates. Then I thought I might write about Jack Lawrence, but I still have bad feelings about him for shooting all my dogs when they get sick. Henry, as bad as I hate to say it, it's a good thing you got run over. That's gotta be a whole lot better than being shot.

I thought I might write about Mary, the wash-woman. Some people call her Yellow Duxie. She's the person who washes our clothes and carries them back to us in a pasteboard box on top of her head. But I decided the nigra I know most about is Duxie. Some people call her Black Duxie. She's got more funny sayings than any nigra I know of.

Here's my story:

DUXIE

Duxie is the nigra woman who works for my daddy's sister Edith. I call her Dook that rhymes with crook. I think she likes me, and I like her too. She is black and short and fat. She's got big eyes and a big rear end. She has a husband named Seaborn. They live out on Hendley's farm. Hendley is my uncle who is married to Edith, my daddy's sister.

Duxie walks to Edith's house every morning. It's more than a mile. She's the only person I know in Pineview who can walk a whole mile except me and Irvin. If we have to walk to Bluff Creek to go swimming, that's 3½ miles. Duxie walks to Mattie Richland to go to church. That's at least 2 miles.

Dook and Seaborn have a son named Buddy. Jamie and Sister and Boy are Edith and Hendley's children. They call him Butterbean.

Dook cleans up Edith's house and does the cooking. She doesn't cook breakfast cause Hendley is the rural mail carrier, and he has to leave the house early every morning about 6 o'clock. When Hendley gets home from the mail route about 12 o'clock, Dook has a good dinner fixed for him. Edith teaches school so she comes home to eat dinner with Hendley.

Dook is a really good cook. She cooks the best fried chicken of anybody I know of. Sometimes I watch her do it. She wets the chicken with milk then takes flour and salt and pepper and sticks it all over the piece of chicken. She keeps on wetting it and sticking flour on it so it will have a lot of crust. She gets a bunch of bacon grease from the Maxwell House Coffee can that sits next to the stove and puts it in the frying pan. It gets so hot it starts bubbling. Then she picks up the piece of chicken and sticks her fingers down in the hot grease to put the chicken where she wants it. After it has finished frying she picks the hot piece of fried chicken out of the frying pan with her fingers and puts it on the platter. I don't know why she doesn't use a fork or something. But her fried chicken is the best I've ever eaten. I think its cause she puts a lot of crust on it.

Sometimes when Jamie and Elbert come home and Sister and Elwyn and Boy and Frances and the children are all there, Dook cooks up a really big dinner. The last time they were all there for Christmas, Edith asked Daddy and Mama and me and Mary to come eat dinner with them. Dook told Edith she felt like she was having to cook for the chain gang.

I like Seaborn too. He gets drunk every Saturday night. He starts drinking in the afternoon and keeps on drinking until Miles McKinney puts him in jail. He is Pineview's only policeman. Hendley has to pay money every Sunday to get Seaborn out of jail. That jailhouse is not much bigger than our clothes closet. Me and Irvin went in it one time when it was unlocked. It stunk so bad, we couldn't stay in there.

Sometimes Seaborn comes into Nona's store late on a Saturday afternoon and buys Hoyt's Cologne. That's a perfume that a lot of the nigras use to make them smell good. Seaborn doesn't put it on. He drinks it. He got real sick a few weeks ago and was spitting up blood. Buddy took him to the doctor in Hawkinsville. Buddy has a car cause he lives in Cincinnati. Edith asked Dook what the doctor said about Seaborn. She said he had a roasted liver.

Nona said it's really called cirrhosis and you can't live very long with that.

Dook had never been out of Pineview her whole life except maybe to go to Hawkinsville or Rochelle. One day Buddy sent her a train ticket to visit him in Cincinnati. Dook called it Citchanati. She didn't much want to go cause she didn't know where it was or how far it was. Since Dook can't read or write, Edith made a sign for her to wear around her neck that had her name and where she was from and Edith's phone number. Edith packed her a lunch and took her to the train station.

We were all so glad when Dook made it back. She told Edith she was so scared she never got out of her seat. Edith said, "Well you had to get out of your seat to go to the bathroom. The trip took 24 hours." Dook said, "No M'am, I never went to the bathroom. I just held it in."

Edith asked her if she ate anything other than the lunch she'd given her. She said, "I ain't et nothing til I got to Buddy's."

Edith asked her if she went to sleep on the train. She said, "No M'am, I never closed my eyes."

Dook said it sure was good to see Buddy, but she ain't never gonna go back there again. Edith wanted to know why not. Dook said, "Cause it's too far. Do you know how far it is to Citchanati? It's way up there above the north."

Buddy wanted Dook to call him when she got back to Pineview. She told Edith she had already talked to him and he was glad she got home alright. Edith wanted to know how she called him and what phone she used. Dook said she hired Mr. Will Pope to take her to Hawkinsville. Edith wanted to know why she did that cause she could've used the phone at her house. Dook said, "You mean your phone will call all the way to Citchanati. Lord, Jesus I never knew there was a telephone in Pineview that could call that far."

Duxie came in one day and told Edith that Rosa Mae just had twins and had to go to the horsepital to get em born. Edith wanted to know why she went to the hospital cause most people had their children born at home. Dook said, "Miss Edith, when them two younguns was born, they were so little they had to keep 'em in an elevator."

During the war Seaborn heard you could get a good job down in Brunswick in the shipyard. He told Hendley one day that he was leaving to go see if he could get him one of them jobs. It was only a few days before Seaborn came back home. Edith asked Dook why he came back. She said, "Yes'm, he came back cause he didn't like it down there." Edith wanted to know why not. "Seaborn say he don't wanna live in no place where you gotta pay to walk the sidewalks."

"What are you talking about?"

"Yeah, Seaborn say they got a whole bunch of posts sticking up out of the sidewalks. He said he watched every person who got out of they car put money in them posts fore they could start walking. That's when he decided he better get out of there and come on home where it don't cost nothing to walk."

Dook came into Edith's house one day with a package under her arm.

"What you got?" Edith asked her.

"I went down to Mr. W. D.'s store and bought me some bamaramas."

"You bought what?"

"Somebody told me these bamaramas will be more comftable to walk around in."

"Let me see them," Edith said.

Dook opened the package and showed them to her.

"Those are ballerinas," Edith said. "But they look too little. Did you try them on?"

Dook sat down and tried to put one of them on. It didn't even cover half of her foot.

"I just picked em out and bought em." Dook said.

"Well you take them back down there to Mr. W. D. and tell him to get you some more that will fit you."

Seaborn saved up enough money picking cotton one year to buy him a car. Dook said he paid $100 for it. The only problem was that he'd never driven a car before.

When Dook told Edith about it Edith asked her, "Aren't you afraid to ride in the car with Seaborn? He doesn't even know how to drive."

She said, "Naw M'am, it's alright, Miss Edith, I just hold the door open with one leg hanging out so I can jump out."

Dook has a lot of funny sayings but the one she says a whole lot that has everybody in my family saying the same thing. "You gotta get some enjoy-cement out of life while you're living."

THE END

Henry, I hope you enjoyed my story. I'll be writing you later on.

Love,
Tom

March 31, 1947

Dear Henry,

I had to write a paper on any subject we wanted to write on. You know I've always liked politics a lot, so I decided to write about how Georgia got three governors. I turned the paper in to Miss Cheek. She's my fifth grade teacher. She gave the best three papers to Mrs. Ware to read. She teaches English in high school. She's in our gang that goes to the picture show together, so she's my friend. My paper was one of the three. Mrs. Ware told me to meet her after school was out. I went over to the two story red brick building where the high school is. It's the same building where my mama and daddy went to school. I was nervous cause I didn't know what she wanted to see me about.

I walked in. She told me to sit down. She said, "Tom, has anyone ever taught you about using good grammar when you write?"

I said, "Not really."

She said, "We're going to spend the afternoon here until you learn about how to write. You're a good writer, but you must learn proper punctuation."

She took my paper. We spent over an hour going over it. That paper had more red marks on it than you can believe. She told me to take it home and write it over with all the corrections. I took it back to her today, and she was real proud of me. So, Henry, I'm sending you what I wrote after all those corrections.

GEORGIA'S THREE GOVERNORS

My daddy says the state of Georgia is the laughing stock of the whole country because of having three governors. We had M.E. Thompson, Ellis Arnall and Herman Talmadge, all trying to be the governor at the same time.

My Daddy and Mama never liked any of the Talmadges and neither did Papa and Nona and Edith and Hendley. Daddy thought that Gene Talmadge got elected Governor by trying to make uneducated people think he was one of them. When Talmadge let a cow graze on the front lawn of the Governor's Mansion in Atlanta, Daddy didn't like that at all. He said it was just for show. He was trying to get the vote of the farmers. He said that a governor ought to have more dignity than that. Daddy said every time Talmadge ran for governor, half the people in the cemeteries where he came from in Telfair County always voted for him.

Daddy said when Talmadge was the Commissioner of Agriculture, he paid himself and his family a lot of money and used state funds to make personal trips, like to the Kentucky Derby. Some in the legislature got upset about what he was doing. They tried to get Governor Dick Russell to sue Talmadge to get the money back. Some of them even wanted to impeach him. But the governor turned it over to the Attorney General, and all the charges were dropped.

Daddy said when Talmadge was standing on the back of a wagon lectioneering to a bunch of people, one of the audience yelled out at him, "Hey, Gene, they say you stole money from the state. Did you do it?"

Daddy said Talmadge came right back and said, "Yeah, I stoled it. But I stoled it for you."

Daddy didn't like things like that. There's nobody in the whole world more honest than my daddy. Mama gets mad with him, because when he sells some of the pecans from the trees around our house, he puts it on his income tax return. Mama acts real disgusted and says, "Nobody in the world would do such a crazy thing as that."

Daddy likes to talk to me about politics, because he knows I'm really interested in it. He said someday I should run for Governor. I told him that maybe I would. Nona said, "Tom's too honest and nice to be in politics." I told Juju that I might run for governor some day. And she said, "I'll be the first one to give you a hundred dollar contribution."

Daddy gets into arguments when Rena and Syms come to visit. They live in Abbeville. Rena is Nona's sister, and Syms has a tag on his car that says "Governor's Staff." He's a big friend of Gene Talmadge. Daddy says he gets tired of hearing Syms say Gene this and Gene that just like Talmadge is his best friend. I like to listen to them argue.

Mama's mother, Ma Me, is also for Talmadge cause she's from Telfair County, where Daddy says all the dead people vote. When she and Nona come to our house for Sunday dinner it can sometimes be a problem. Ma Me is a big Methodist, and Nona is a big Baptist. They've got all kinds of differences.

Daddy said when Dick Russell ran for the U.S. Senate in 1932, Gene Talmadge decided he wanted to take Russell's place as governor. He won the election and served for four years. Daddy said the whole time he was governor if anybody ever crossed him, he had them fired. Like the time when the state treasurer and comptroller general refused to cooperate with him. Talmadge had the state militia physically remove them from their offices. They called him a dictator. But he still got re-elected, because he tried to make everybody think he was a friend of the common man. Daddy said, "There's one thing about it. There're a whole lot of common people in Georgia."

Daddy said that Talmadge got too big for his britches and tried to run against Dick Russell for the U.S. Senate in 1936. He got beat. Then in 1938, he ran against Senator Walter George and got beat again.

Daddy said when Talmadge got re-elected as governor in 1940, he got the board of regents to fire 2 professors at the University of Georgia, because they were making a fuss about wanting to educate negroes. When he fired those two professors, every white college in the state lost their accreditation.

This is how we got three governors. In the 1946 election the federal court said that Georgia's Democratic Primary was illegal because it was all white. Talmadge campaigned for governor that year by saying that no negro would ever vote in Georgia as long as he was governor. He got elected because Georgia has the county unit system. All the little counties in Georgia have two votes. The middle-sized counties have four votes and the biggest counties have six votes. James Carmichael got the most popular votes in the whole state. But Talmadge won the county unit vote, so he got elected. Talmadge died right after the election before he ever took office. M. E. Thompson was the Lieutenant Governor, so he claimed he should take the place of the Governor. But he hadn't been sworn when Talmadge died. Herman Talmadge was Gene's son. He got the legislature to elect him to be the next governor. Ellis Arnall was the governor for the past four years, so he refused to leave office until Georgia got a legitimate governor. So Georgia really got in a mess. We had three governors.

The Supreme Court ruled just a few days ago that the Lt. Governor, M.E. Thompson, would be the governor until the state can hold a special election in September, 1948. That made Daddy happy, because he likes M.E. Thompson.

THE END

You'll never guess what happened to me at school today. I went into the class room and leaned over to put my books under my seat. This big boy came up from behind and grabbed me. Before I knew it, he got me in a head lock. He was choking me and saying, "Your daddy's for the niggers cause he's against Talmadge." I could hardly talk and couldn't get loose. About that time Miss Cheek came in and wanted to know what was going on.

When he let me go, he said, "You tell on me, and I'll kill you."

Miss Cheek asked me what was going on.

I looked around at him. He was staring back at me with this mean looking face. I told her we were just playing.

I don't know what I should do Henry. You got any suggestions?

Love,
Tom

October 17, 1947

Dear Henry,

Marvin Talley got back from Warm Springs last week. He got polio last summer. A lot of people all over Georgia have gotten polio. Nona called it an epidemic. Me and Marvin have been in the same class since first grade.

When you get polio they send you off to Warm Springs. That's where President Roosevelt went when he got polio. Irvin said they put you in an iron lung. I don't know what an iron lung is, but I've seen a picture of one. It looks like a bomb. I guess they put you down in that thing where you have to stay forever to see if you die or get well.

I don't want to get polio cause if you live, you'll be crippled up for the rest of your life. Nobody knows what causes it except Mama. She says it's a bad disease that jumps on you if you don't take naps in the afternoon in the hot summer, or if you go swimming too soon after you eat.

Every day in the summer Mama makes me and my sister come in the house in the afternoon to take a nap. It just doesn't seem like that ought to have anything to do with having polio. Marvin said the doctors told him that polio was caused from tired muscles. So I guess it's a good idea to rest every afternoon to keep your muscles from getting too tired.

Resting gets old though.   No matter where I might be playing, Mama goes all over town looking for me. When she finds me, it's always the same thing. I tell her, "I'm playing right now, and I don't want to go home and take a nap." And she says, "All right, just be a cripple for the rest of your life. See if I care."

When I get home she already has my sister laying in the bed flat on her back. And we're not allowed to move around either. She won't even let me read a comic book.

Mama tries to keep me from going swimming. I told her that's taking things too far. I can lay in the bed for an hour or two in the afternoon. But in the summertime a boy has to go swimming. She says you shouldn't get real cold and go out in the hot sunshine unless you want polio. I argue with her. She always says, "All right, Mr. Hardheaded, just go right ahead and go swimming, and you'll be on crutches the rest of your life."

When Marvin got back to school this week I asked him what it felt like to have polio. He said he had a fever and was throwing up. But his daddy made him go out in the field to crop tobacco. He said that night he couldn't raise his right arm. His daddy took him to Dr. Baker in Hawkinsville. He told him he had polio. His daddy took him to Grady hospital in Atlanta. Marvin said they stuck a needle in his back bone. I told him that must've hurt a lot. He said it hurt like hell. The doctor at Grady Hospital sent him to Warm Springs. I told him it was too bad that President Roosevelt died. Marvin might've gotten to be in an iron lung right next to the President. Marvin said he didn't have to be put in one of those iron lungs cause that was for people who couldn't breathe.

Marvin said at Warm Springs they got hot wet blankets and wrapped around him every day to keep his muscles warm. They put him in a hot pool of water and told him he was not allowed to walk. They were afraid it might go from his arm down to his legs. When he got back to Pineview, his daddy had to learn how to give him therapy. Marvin came back to school with his right arm paralyzed. He was right handed too. He had to learn to write with his left hand. He had to learn to shoot a basketball with his left hand. He had to learn to swing a bat with his left hand. That polio is some bad stuff. I sure don't want it. Mama told me not to ever drink from the water fountain if Marvin used it.

I sure hope I don't get that polio cause I like to run and play basketball and baseball and swim and all those things. I sure do feel sorry that Marvin got that stuff. We're in the 5th grade now and he's been one of my friends for 5 years.

Love,
Tom

October 28, 1947

Dear Henry,

We had something really bad happen at school today. Some of the older boys were underneath the stadium with some girls. I don't know what went on. But Mr. Stone heard about it and called all the boys from the 6th grade to the 8th grade to go to the stadium for a meeting. None of the boys in my class in the 6th grade had any idea what the meeting was about. But I think some of the older boys knew what was going on.

We sat on the bleachers and Mr. Stone stood down on the floor. He's a big tall man. He's taller than any boy in the whole school. Somebody said he's 6 foot 6.

Mr. Stone said he'd heard there were some things going on between some boys and girls underneath the stadium yesterday. And he wanted to know if it was true.

Nobody said a word. We just kinda looked at each other. Some of the older boys snickered.

Mr. Stone said, "I want to tell you boys one thing, and I don't want you to ever forget it. I will not put up with that kind of behavior. Do you understand me? There will not be any kind of hanky panky going on at this school while I'm the principle. Do you hear me?" He yelled it out really loud like he was mad.

Nobody said a word.

He yelled louder. "I said do you hear me?"

Everybody said, "Yes sir."

"All right. I want to know which one of you boys was under the gym yesterday with those girls."

Everybody looked around at each other.

"All right. I'll start with the 6th grade. All you boys stand up."

We all jumped up in a hurry.

"I'm going to ask each one of you if you're guilty or not. I'll start with Marvin. Are you guilty?"

Marvin looked at me and then at Irvin and then at Vernon. We all just kind of shrugged our shoulders cause none of us knew what guilty meant.

Marvin said, "I don't know."

Mr. Stone yelled out. "What do you mean you don't know? You know whether or not you did it, don't you?"

"No sir." Marvin said. "I didn't do it."

"All right, Vernon, are you guilty?" Mr. Stone was talking in a really loud voice that made us all scared.

Vernon said he didn't do it either. And the same thing happened to me and to Irvin and Popcorn and Billy and all the other boys in my class. He went through all the boys in the 6th grade and then the 7th grade and then the 8th grade.

I don't know if any of them knew what guilty meant either. Finally Mr. Stone said, "I don't mind whipping every boy in this school if I have to. So somebody better tell me who did it."

Finally two of the boys in the 7th grade said they were under the gym but nothing bad went on.

Mr. Stone told them to come down there on the floor where he was standing. He picked both of those boys up by the seat of their pants and walked out of the gym holding them in the air. Their feet were just dangling cause they couldn't touch the ground. We all went out of the gym and watched. He walked them up the steps and into the school building. We all followed and stood out in the hallway when Mr. Stone slammed the door to his office.

We heard the paddle hit one of the boys on the butt cause he let out a yelp. Mr. Stone hit him with the paddle a bunch of times. Then he started whipping on the other boy. The rest of us were all standing out there in the hall when they walked out of the office. Both of them had tears in their eyes and tears rolling down their cheeks. They wiped their face off real quick with their shirt sleeves so none of us could see they'd been crying.

Henry I don't know what those boys did that was so bad. What's wrong with boys and girls going under the stadium together? If you have any idea I wish you'd let me know.

Love,
Tom

June 14, 1948

Dear Henry,

I just turned 12 about 2 weeks ago. Mama said I need to get baptized at the revival this month. I guess I'll join the Methodist church, but I go to the Baptist church almost as much as I do the Methodist. I go to Sunday School and church and MYF at the Methodist church.

But then I have to go to the Baptist Church in Pineview on 3rd Sunday and the Baptist Church in Finleyson on 1st Sunday. I have to go to Baptist Training Union every Sunday afternoon. A lot of the time either Nona or Edith is our teacher, so I have to be there.

My cousin, Joan, is going to be baptized at the revival. We agreed that we would go down the aisle together when they sing Just As I Am. We'll shake the preacher's hand and tell him we want to join the church. The preacher at the revival is always from some other town a long way off like Dublin or Eastman or somewhere like that. He doesn't have any idea who Joan is. He doesn't know me either, unless Mama has told him I'm her son.

Irvin joined the Baptist Church last week at their revival. Daddy said something about maybe I should join with Irvin. Mama said "NO." She told me that Nona probably put him up to saying that.

Henry, I'm writing this a few days later.

Last night was the end of the revival at the Methodist Church. That was the perfect time to go down the aisle and join the church. After supper last night I could tell that Mama and Daddy had been fussing. They weren't speaking to each other or even looking at each other.

Mama came up to my room and told me she wanted me to wear a white shirt and tie.

"A tie? Are you crazy? It's a 100 degrees out there. You want me to die of a heat stroke?"

"You do what I tell you, and don't you talk back to me."

I was in my room getting dressed and heard Daddy say to Mama, "I don't see why he can't join the Baptist Church." He might as well have spit in her face. She lit into him like a hive of hornets. I finally went back to their room where they were yelling at each other. I said really loud, "I'M NOT GOING TO JOIN ANY CHURCH AND THEN MAYBE BOTH OF YOU WILL BE SATISFIED."

That brought everything to a dead silence. I saw Mama look at Daddy like she could run a butcher knife through his stomach. She was red in the face and her hair was sticking out.

I ran out the back door and slammed it really hard. I walked to the church by myself. My stomach felt like it was tied up in a knot.

Mama and Daddy drove to the church. I went inside and sat down beside Joan. I saw Mama and Daddy come in. Daddy sat on the back row where he always sits in the Methodist Church. Mama went up to the front and sat down at the piano and started playing. She was playing a lot louder than she usually does.

When the preacher finished his sermon, he called out for the closing hymn. "Let's sing, Just As I Am. If anyone out there is feeling the call. If anyone out there loves Jesus and wants to give their life to Him, just get up out of your seat and walk down that aisle. Put your hand in my hand and say, Preacher, I love Jesus. I want to turn my life over to Him. I want to dedicate my life to doing God's work. I want to join this Methodist Church right here in Pineview, Georgia this evening."

Joan stood up. She turned around and looked at me. She wanted to know why I didn't get up, too. I shook my head. She looked at me real funny and went walking down the aisle by herself. I was so mad at Mama and Daddy I couldn't see straight. I wanted to go down that aisle with Joan. We'd been talking about joining the church together for a long time. And there I was sitting on the pew like a dunce.

I know what Nona said. And I believe everything that Nona tells me. She says that I have to have my body put down in the water to really be baptized and that sprinkling water on top of your head is just not enough. Then why can't Methodists put you down in the water? If that's the way Jesus was baptized by John, the Baptist, then why do Methodists have to be different and sprinkle people?

I walked home by myself. When I went in the house, I could tell Mama was mad and Daddy was mad. I was mad, too. My sister is only 6. She didn't know what was going on. I guess she probably wondered why everybody in the family would come home from church all mad at each other.

I said my prayers last night:

"Now I lay me down to sleep;
I pray the Lord my soul to keep,
If I should die before I wake,
I pray the Lord my soul to take.

And, God, how can I be a Methodist and be baptized under the water?

Henry, if you could find out from someone up there in heaven about this, I sure would appreciate you letting me know.

Love,
Tom

July 14, 1948

Dear Henry,

Mama warned me ever since the Hairs moved to town that I should never play with Joe Billy Hair. She said, "He'll get you in trouble if you do." Well, she was right. I've had a really bad thing happen to me that I have to keep secret from everybody else. Henry, you're the only one I can tell about it. It's about...it's hard for me to even say it to you. But it's about, you know, my thing. You know what I mean. You're a boy and you had a thing before you went to heaven.

It all started a few weeks ago when Joe Billy Hair wanted to know if he could go with me and Irvin down to Mr. Clements to get an ice cream. We were walking by his house. He was out in his front yard playing ball with all his brothers and sisters. I don't know how many there are. I think it must be a dozen. He's 16 and me and Irvin just turned 12. Mama said the Hairs are poor white trash, and it's a shame and a pity that the town allows them to live in Pineview around good, respectable people. That's one reason why she doesn't like for me to walk to church, 'cause it means I have to go in front of the Hair's house. There's always a big pile of junk in front of it.

When we got to the drug store, Joe Billy didn't have a nickel. So me and Irvin had to go in together to get one for him. We flipped for it and I lost. That meant I had to pay three cents and Irvin just had to pay two. I usually get strawberry. Irvin always gets chocolate. Joe Billy wanted vanilla with some chocolate syrup poured over his. Mr. Clements said that would cost a dime. We told him he better just settle for some plain vanilla.

After we ate our ice cream, Joe Billy wanted to go play in the cottonseed warehouse down there next to the Cook's house. To get inside, you have to pry the lock open. I don't like to do stuff like that. But it doesn't seem to bother Joe Billy. The warehouse is almost filled to the top with cottonseed. It's fun to jump around in there and roll down the hills of cottonseed all the way to the floor. Irvin said we'd probably get a good whipping if anybody caught us in there. But we kept playing for a long time.

We got really hot and sweaty and smelled like cotton. I was ready to get out of there and go get a cold drink, but Joe Billy said he had something he wanted to show us. I wondered what Joe Billy knew that we didn't cause I don't think he ever went to school.

He pulled his thing out of his pants and start playing with it. That wasn't anything I really wanted to see. He told me and Irvin to stand next to him with our backs to the wall and do what he was doing. I didn't want to but Irvin decided to try it. Joe Billy's thing got really, really big. I'd never seen anyone's thing get that big in my life, and I'd seen lots of them down at Pappy Jack.

He had his hand around it and was going up and down really fast. Mama told me I should never play with my thing. If I did, I would go blind or either crazy. I wanted to have good eyes and be able to see things. I sure didn't want to be sent off to Milledgeville like Bud, so I tried to never touch my thing except to pee.

A few days later, I was inside my room at home and something came over me. It was like nothing I'd ever felt before. I had an urge to want to try what Joe Billy had done in the cottonseed warehouse. I knew it was wrong, but I decided to try it anyway. I have to admit it did feel really good. But the worst thing in the whole world happened. Mama opened the door to my room.

"What are you doing?" She screamed.

"Nothing," I said.

She slammed the door. I knew I was in some big trouble cause she would probably kill me, and if she didn't, all of those bad things might start happening to me. But the weird thing about it was that she never mentioned it to me again.

About a week later, I could still see O.K. I didn't feel any different like I had gone crazy or anything like that. But my daddy surprised me one afternoon when he asked me to drive him out to the farm. I've been driving the car since I was eight, but he never asks me to drive him anywhere.

While I was driving along on the dirt road trying to keep the tires in the ruts of the sand beds, he said he needed to tell me something. I knew it must be something really serious. I took my eyes off the road and looked directly at him.

"We're going to have yours and Mary's tonsils taken out on Friday."

That was all he said. I didn't say anything but I wondered why we were going to do that. There wasn't anything wrong with my tonsils that I knew of. And I hadn't heard anything about my sister having bad tonsils or sore throats or anything like that.

"You know when boys your age have their tonsils out they really hit a spurt. It makes them grow taller. I've known boys who've had their tonsils out," he said, "and they'd start growing – sometimes 4 or 5 inches."

Well, that would be good, I thought. I wanted to be the best basketball player I could possibly be. I knew the taller I was, the better I'd be. But It never occurred to me that I might be a great basketball player if I had my tonsils out.

Dr. Gus Batts in Hawkinsville has always been our family's doctor, so he was the one who was going to do it. Daddy said that when you wake up from having your tonsils out, they give you all the ice cream you can eat. I thought that sounded pretty good.

Most of the students in my class have had their tonsils out. I didn't see any reason why I shouldn't have mine out, too. My sister is just 6. She has never been put to sleep before. But I had to have that butterbean taken out of my throat when I was in the third grade. I knew what it was like.

Dr. Batts took my sister to the operating room first. I sat there with Mama and Daddy. I was pretty scared, too. They brought her back to the room in about a half hour. She looked like she was dead.

They got me out of my bed and rolled me down the hallway into the operating room. They put me on a table that had a really bright light over it that made me squint my eyes like I was looking straight in the sun. The nurse held my legs down while they strapped them down to the table so I couldn't move them. Then they strapped my arms down so tight that it hurt. All of a sudden they plopped the ether over my nose that made me start squirming to get off that table and get out of there. But I couldn't budge. I could hear loud sounds like a train whistle blowing in my ears. Then I could feel the table begin to shoot backwards really fast with me on it. That's the last thing I can remember.

When the nurse was putting cold cloths on my forehead and calling my name, I was so groggy. I didn't want to wake up. I wanted to keep right on sleeping. Then I started feeling pain, not just in my throat where Dr. Batts had cut out my tonsils, but my thing was hurting really bad, too.

When I came to, I could see Mama and Daddy standing in the room. Mary was in the other bed beside me eating ice cream. I didn't want any damn ice cream. I just wanted to know why my thing was hurting so bad. I reached under the sheets to see if Dr. Batts had cut it off to punish me for what I'd done. Daddy stopped me. He said he'd explain everything to me later.

After awhile I had to pee in the bedpan. I was relieved to see that my thing hadn't been completely cut off – just the end of it had. Daddy said I couldn't touch it cause it had stitches in it. "If I touched it," he said. "It might get infected."

I guess I was lucky that Dr. Batts left some of it – just enough to pee out of.

After I got home, there was some kind of liquid medicine I had to pour over my thing every time I took a pee. When I walked it hurt. I had to try to keep it from rubbing against my pants.

Why didn't somebody tell me what Dr. Batts was going to do to me? Daddy called it circum something. I'm not sure what it's called. What I do know is that it hurts.

Later on, Daddy took me back to see Dr. Batts to take the stitches out. That was really embarrassing when he made me take my pants off in front of him. He pulled the stitches out. He said it looked like to him that everything seemed to be healing just fine.

Henry, I have taken a vow that I'll never ever touch my thing again. Especially if Mama is anywhere within a 100 miles. I know if she were to catch me one more time, there's no telling what she'd do. She might have Dr. Batts cut it all off and turn me into a girl.

I'll write more later.

Love,
Tom

September 12, 1948

Dear Henry,

You'll never believe who came to our house tonight! A Republican. He drove up in front in a little black '39 Ford Coupe to see Daddy. Me and my sister were looking through the venetian blinds so we could see what he looked like. We'd never seen a Republican before.

We could see the head lights of his little car parked by Daddy's black Buick. He got out of the car and stood there for a minute. We were real curious what he would look like. The front porch lights were on cause Daddy was expecting him. He didn't seem all that unusual. He was short and fat and had on a blue stripe suit and a hat. Daddy said his name is Jim Crummey from Rochelle. He's the only Republican in the county.

Daddy went out the front door acting all serious and business like. They shook hands, and Daddy got in the car with him. I sure hope nobody was watching. I wouldn't want anybody in town to think that Daddy was a Republican.

President Roosevelt was a Democrat. He's been President all my life until he died in 1945. Harry Truman was the Vice-President. He took over to finish out Roosevelt's term. He's a Democrat, too. I told my sister I bet they're talking about the election coming up this November.

I'd been hearing Daddy talk about Tom Dewey is the Republican running against Truman. Daddy said that nobody in the south likes Truman cause he's for civil rights. I asked him what that meant. He said that Truman is for the nigras having the right to vote and giving them equal rights with white people. That's the reason Senator Strom Thurman from South Carolina broke off from the Democratic Party and started a new party called the Dixiecrats. Daddy said that probably all the southern states would vote for Strom Thurman. So it looked like to him that Dewey would win the election.

Daddy talked to him for a long time just sitting in the car. I was glad he didn't ask him to come in the house. It's no telling what people would think of us if they knew a Republican came in our house.

They stayed in the car for about an hour. Daddy came back in the house and he drove off. Me and Mama and Mary were sitting in the living room listening to the radio and waiting to hear what he had to say.

Daddy walked through the living room and didn't say a word to anybody. He walked down the hall and out the back door. I knew what that meant. Either he had to pee or he was heading for the garage to get a drink of liquor. I walked back to the kitchen and looked out the window. He did both.

When I saw him coming back in, I ran up to the living room and sat down on the sofa next to Mama. Daddy sat down in his chair and leaned back. Mama was looking at him. Me and Mary were looking at him, too. But Daddy didn't say anything.

Finally Mama stood up. When she gives him that look, it means he better get up and go back in the kitchen with her right now or else. They walked back there together and sat down at the breakfast table. I told Mary to stay there and listen to the radio. She's just 6 and I'm 12, so most of the time she'll do what I tell her.

The door to the kitchen was cracked open enough that I could stick my ear in close enough to hear what they were saying.

Mama said, "What was that all about?"

Daddy said, "He wants me to vote for Tom Dewey."

"Is he crazy?" Mama raised her voice. "He wants you to vote for a Republican. You can't do that. If a person in Pineview were to vote for a Republican, they'd certainly find out who did it cause there'd only be one vote. Do you know what that would mean? We couldn't show our face in this town ever again."

Daddy said, "I think Dewey's going to win since Strom Thurmond has his Dixiecrat Party. Instead of all the southern states voting Democratic like they always have, they're going to vote for Thurmond. So it looks like Dewey is a shoo in.

"So what's that got to do with anything?" Mama asked him.

"He promised me a good job when the Republicans go in," Daddy said.

"But you got a good job," Mama said. "You could get fired if you voted for a Republican."

"Yeah, but I could also get fired if a Republican wins."

"Well, I can tell you one thing," Mama said. "I'm certainly not voting for a Republican. And you can do what you want to, but I'm not going to live with anybody who votes for a Republican." She slid her chair back and got up in a hurry. You can always tell when Mama is mad cause her hair sticks out like a cat's.

"Just get off your damn high horse for a minute," he yelled at her. "I told him no. I told him I wouldn't do it."

Mama sat back down.

"I told him I was voting for Harry Truman," Daddy said. "I said that everybody in my family had always voted for the Democrats. I wasn't going to be the first to break away from that tradition."

Mama didn't say anything. I could tell she was ashamed of the way she acted. I knew she wouldn't say it, but I think she was proud of him for saying what he just said.

Daddy pulled his pack of Camels out of his pocket and handed one to her. She didn't smoke much like he did, but every once in a while she did. She took one out of the pack. He lit it with his lighter.

She looked at him and said, "Fix me a drink, Edwin." Anytime she calls him Edwin, I know she's either mad with him or very serious about something. Normally she just calls him Ed.

Daddy got a little juice glass and went out to the garage and got her some liquor. He brought it back in and sat it down on the table in front of her.

I saw her sip it and make a face. Then she took another sip.

Mama and Daddy have argued and fought most all my life. But then they always seem to make up. I'm not going to ever fight with my wife when I get married.

Love,
Tom

September 30, 1948

Dear Henry,

Every single day at school we have to go to chapel. Miss Gussie Bragg always plays Glow Worm on the piano for us to march in the gym. All the folding chairs are set up on the basketball court next to the stage where Mr. Cornelius sits. He's the principal. The grammar school children march in the gym in a row and sit in the chairs out on the basketball court. The big boys and girls in high school always get to go up on the bleachers where the people sit when they come to watch basketball games.

I'm only 12 and in the 6th grade. We still have to sit in the chairs on the court with all the little children. We always sit as far back as we can. Usually on the back row. They have a rule that the whole class has to sit together with our teacher.

The first thing they do at chapel is have someone read a Bible Scripture. Mr. Cornelius asked me to read it one time. I was so scared I was shaking all over. Miss Gussie plays songs for us to sing like Home on the Range and Down by the Riverside and You are my Sunshine. Sometimes they have special entertainment like someone reading a poem or singing a solo or playing a musical instrument or something like that. Sometimes there will be traveling shows that come to chapel to perform, like magicians and clowns and gospel quartets and all kinds of things.

Mr. Cornelius always makes the announcements of what's going on in school and things we need to know. The one I hate the most is when he tells us that Miss Bessie Horne from the health department is coming to school to give every student from the 1st grade through the 12th a typhoid shot. I've always hated having to get a shot. But typhoid is the worst. It makes my arm so sore for 2 or 3 days I can hardly lift it. If you're right handed, she gives you a shot in the left arm. If you're left-handed, she gives it in the right arm. The last time we got our shots, one of the big boys in high school named Bartlett Barker walked past me in the hall and popped me with his fist on my left arm. I don't think I've ever had anything hurt me that bad in my life.

The other day at chapel Mr. Cornelius announced that every student in school would have to take a test for hook worms. We all looked at each other. Hook worms? We've never had to do that before. He said that a lot of people had hook worms, and it was something that was going around. We were all kind of laughing under our breath and snickering about it. We were wondering what kind of dirty person do we have in our school that would have something that only hogs and cows have?

Nobody in my class knew what kind of test you have to take. We didn't know if it was a blood test or what? Mr. Cornelius stood at the door of the gym when we all marched out. He handed out a little package to each one of us. All the people in my class were really laughing about it. When we got back to the classroom Miss Matibel, my sixth grade teacher, said we all had to read the instructions and do what it said.

When I got home that day, I was sitting out in front of our house on the steps letting the sun warm my body. My cousin Walt Mann came walking over and wanted to know what I was doing. I hardly ever hang around him. He's my sister's age.

"I'm just sitting in the sun," I said without even looking at him. "What does it look like?"

He asked me if I knew what we were supposed to put in that little metal can they handed out at chapel today.

I told him I hadn't read the directions, but I thought you were supposed to pee in it. He looked at me really funny. He acted like he couldn't believe that. "The can is too little to pee in," he said. "It's about half the size of a can of Shineola Shoe Polish."

Walt started walking back home and then turned around, "Are you sure?"

I said, "Just go pee in the can and don't worry about it."

"Somebody in my class said I was supposed to take a crap in it," he said.

I laughed so hard I almost fell off the steps. Whoever heard of such a stupid thing? You couldn't take a crap in a little can like that.

About that time Irvin came walking up. I told him what Walt Mann said about taking a crap in the little can. I was laughing so hard I could hardly tell Irvin what he said.

Irvin looked at me really funny. "But you do," he said.

"You do not," I argued.

"Yes you do," he said.

"I'm going in the house and ask Mama," I said. So I walked back to the kitchen where Mama was cooking and showed her the can and the instructions.

"Have you read them?" she asked.

"No," I said.

"Well, go read them, then come back and ask me if you have any questions."

I started reading them. It said some really nasty things about taking a bowel movement on a newspaper and scooping some of it in the can and sealing it. It was so gross I couldn't read the whole thing. I threw the instructions down on the floor and walked back out where Irvin was sitting on the front steps.

"Well, I guess you were right," I said.

About two weeks later, I was sitting at chapel next to my new girlfriend. Her name is Myrna Broadway. She asked me the other day if she could wear my ID bracelet I got for Christmas last year. I told her I'd think about it. I didn't want to say yes cause I really liked my ID bracelet a lot. But I finally gave it to her. Irvin was sitting by his girlfriend, Jo Horne. They've been liking each other for almost 2 years and wearing each others' ID bracelet.

When Mr. Cornelius got up to make his announcements that day, he said, "We've got the results back from the hook worm tests."

Some of the students sort of squirmed around in their seats and looked at each other real nervous like. Most of us in my class were laughing and pointing at each other.

He started reading off the names of the first graders that had tested positive. That's what he called it. He read the names of the second graders and so on. All the ones he named were little kids who lived out in the country on a farm where they worked around barns and animals and things. Then he got to our class. He cleared his throat and said the words that I'll remember the rest of my life. "The only one in the sixth grade is Tom Dennard." Everybody in my class looked at me and busted out laughing. My girlfriend acted like she wanted to get up and run away as fast as she could. Marvin Talley was sitting behind me. He punched me and said, "We just elected you president of the class. We need to have another election." Vernon Mashburn started calling me Wormy.

Mr. Cornelius yelled out, "Would all you students in the sixth grade please quiet down."

Henry, I've never been so mortified in my life. I felt like I wanted to die. How could I have hook worms? I don't even live on a farm? I've become the laughing stock of the class. What am I going to do?

Mr. Cornelius smiled at me really funny like when he handed me the package of treatment for hook worms. They were big old capsules I knew I could never swallow.

Henry, I was the only one in my class. How could that've happened to me? My girlfriend will probably never speak to me again. And I really kinda like her. I've already held her hand one time at the picture show. But I guess that's the end of that.

Love,
Tom

October 14, 1948

Dear Henry,

There's an old lady who lives right next door to Irvin. Her name is Miss Mattie Hunt. She's weird. Me and Irvin are scared of her cause some people think she carries a pistol in her pocketbook that she keeps in her lap all the time.

Sometimes when she's sitting on her front porch she calls us to come over there. We act like we can't hear her, so we don't answer. She always wants us to do things for her. But if we don't answer, she'll just keep right on calling until we go over there. Usually she wants us to go down to T.O.'s to get her a loaf of bread or a jar of mayonnaise or some bananas or something like that. Sometimes she wants us to pick up something inside her house that's heavy. We don't mind so much doing stuff like that. But she can be mean. She'll chew you out before you know it if you don't watch out. We mostly try to stay away from her.

The other day we were out in Irvin's backyard digging some worms for fish bait, and we heard her calling us. We didn't pay any attention to her, but she kept on hollering for us to come over there. We finally quit digging and walked over to her front porch.

"What do y'all know about these Indians scalping some people?" She asked.

Me and Irvin looked at each other. We thought she must've gotten a whole lot crazier since the last time we saw her.

Irvin asked her what she was talking about.

"I said have you heard anything about this?" She said in a loud voice. She picked up the newspaper and held it up for us to see. The headlines read INDIANS SCALP BRAVES.

We started giggling and laughing.

"What you boys laughing at? It's not funny!" She said.

"Miss Mattie, it's the world series," I said. "I listened to the game on the radio myself. The Cleveland Indians beat the heck out of the Boston Braves to win the world series."

"What kinda world series you talking about?" She asked.

"It's nothing but a baseball game, Miss Mattie," I said.

"Oh," she said. She threw the paper down on the floor and said, "You boys go on about your business."

Me and Irvin were snickering and giggling as we walked back over to his house. We looked at each other shaking our heads. Then we went back to digging fish bait again. We decided we're going to quit digging fish bait at Irvin's house. He lives too close to Miss Mattie Hunt. We got plenty of fish bait at my house.

Love,
Tom

October 30, 1948

Dear Henry,

Mr. Clements and Miss Thelma and James and Miss Fanny live next door to us. Mr. Clements and Miss Thelma are married. But I always thought it was funny that he calls her Miss Thelma, and she calls him Mr. Clement. That would be like Mama calling Daddy, Mr. Dennard. That would be about the funniest thing in the whole world. James told me that his daddy sleeps in a different room from his mama. I thought when you got married you were supposed to sleep in the same bed.

Their 2 children are Wilma Nell and James. Wilma Nell is 14 years older than I am. Her husband Herbert Fitzgerald was killed during the war. After that, she married Pope Williams. They live in Cordele. James is 5 years older than I am. He and Angie are the same age.

Mr. Clements runs the drug store downtown. Miss Thelma is the post mistress. Mr. Clements has a white, shaggy dog named Zip. When he drives home in the middle of the day for dinner, he gets out of his car while it's still moving, slams the door, and the car keeps right on rolling for another 10 or 15 feet before it comes to a stop. Zip always comes running down the steps from the front porch wagging his tail and begging for a pat on the head. Sometimes Mr. Clements will reach down and touch him on the back before he goes in the house. When he does, Zip goes crazy. He starts running around in circles like a mad dog. We can see all the comings and goings of the Clements cause our kitchen table sits next to the window facing their house.

Christine is their cook. She makes the best food. Sometimes James asks me to eat dinner with them. She makes fried pies, and they are good, too. I like the apple ones. But my favorite is pineapple.

Christine has 2 children: Roberta and Man. When Roberta and Hosey's son got married, Angie and James and Sammy took me with them to the wedding. That was the only time I've ever been to a wedding in a nigra church.

Mr. Clements's sister Miss Fanny lives with them. She has a wooden leg. James is always hiding her leg to play tricks on her. Miss Fanny sits on the front porch in a rocking chair and sings church hymns all day long. She told James that she was living in Miami during the really bad hurricane of 1926. She said she saw men running down the street and the wind was blowing them so hard, they couldn't stop running. They'd crash their bodies into the side of a house or a building just to be able to stop. She said a two by four was sailing through the air and came right through their front door just like it'd been driven in there with a sledgehammer. She said that snakes came out of the Everglades and were all over town and floating into peoples' houses.

Every Sunday morning Miss Thelma drives her car to pick up people to go to Sunday School and Church at the Pineview Baptist. She takes Miss

Fanny and picks up her sister Lelia. Lelia is the fattest woman in Pineview. Miss Thelma then goes to Miss Virgie Blue and Miss Sally Williford's house. They are sisters and live in their house right by themselves. Mr. Clements calls the car full of women the virgin bus. He goes to church, but he comes by himself. He's usually late and sits on the back row.

Mr. Clements goes to the picture show a lot, but not nearly as much as our gang. We go every Monday and Wednesday and Friday nights. If there's ever a scene in the film that shows a man and a woman kissing, he always gets up and storms out grumbling under his voice like he's really disgusted.

I've been going to his drug store just about every day for as long as I can remember. That's the only place in town where you can buy ice cream. He has vanilla and chocolate and strawberry. One scoop of ice cream on a cone is a nickel. Two scoops is a dime. I really like a crook. That's 2 scoops of vanilla ice cream in a glass with a squirt of chocolate syrup on the top. You have to eat that with a spoon. A crook costs a dime though. So I have to save up for special occasions like that. My favorite drink is a Co Cola. It costs a nickel. But a lot of times in the summer when I'm really thirsty, I get a Pepsi or a Royal Crown except I call it an RC. They're both in a 12 ounce bottle and they cost just a nickel too, just like a coke. On the radio they sing, "Twice as much for a nickel, too. Pepsi Cola is the drink for you."

I went in the drugstore the other day to get some ice cream and a coke. James was keeping the store for his daddy. He took me upstairs to a big room where the Masons used to hold their meetings. He showed me an old skeleton that was in a black wooden box shaped like a coffin. He said the Masons used it in their initiation. The room was really dirty with lots of spider webs and stuff. We went back downstairs and James showed me some of the big brown medicine bottles his daddy uses to fill prescriptions. He made me sniff the Chloroform. It smelled awful. He said if I got too much of it, it would probably put me to sleep. Then he said he wanted to show me something special. He went over to a counter that had a pasteboard box up underneath it. He pulled it out and opened the box. He asked me if I knew what it was. I looked, but all I could see were some little packages in a tinfoil wrapper that had Trojans written on them. I told him I didn't have any idea what they were. He said they were rubbers. Then he told me what they're used for. James is 17. I'm just 12. He knows a lot of things that I don't. He showed me his billfold and told me where he carried one of those rubbers. He said it was a really big thing to pull out your wallet in front of other boys in school so they could see the circle on the outside of your wallet. "All boys know what that means. It makes other boys think you're really something," he said.

A few weeks later, I went in the drug store to get my daily ice cream and coke. Mr. Clements was walking out the front door when I was walking in. He said he had to run out to his farm. He asked me if I would keep the store for him until he got back.

Before I had time to say anything, he got in his car and drove off. I was standing there in the store not having any idea what to do if somebody walked in. I kept thinking what if somebody wanted some medicine or a prescription filled.

A little bit later a girl came in wanting a strawberry ice cream. She was little, probably about 8. I didn't know who she was and I know every single person in Pineview. I scooped up a cone of strawberry ice cream and gave it to her. She asked me if this was my daddy's store. I told her no I just worked there. She handed me her nickel. I put it in the cash register. I've been working at Nona's store on Saturdays ever since I was 5 years old. I know how to wait on customers real good. But I never have used a cash register before. Nona just has a drawer that you pull out to put the money in.

I sat around for awhile but nobody came in. I got a spoon and tasted the chocolate. It reminded me of the Exlax I used to have to take. I tasted the vanilla and then the strawberry. I like strawberry the best. When I go off with Daddy and Mama sometimes we stop at Howard Johnsons and they have lots of different kinds.

I wandered around the store then thought about those rubbers James showed me. I thought the other boys in school would really think I was something if I had a circle on my wallet. They'd really be jealous like James said.

I went back of the counter and found the box where Mr. Clements hid them. I got one out and looked at it. I didn't have any idea what it costs.

I only had a dime and a quarter in my pocket. I thought there's no way it could cost more than a dime. So I put my dime in the cash register. I fixed the rubber inside my wallet so that it would be next to the outside and the circle would really show up.

For the next few weeks I came up with all kinds of excuses to pull my wallet out in front of the other boys at school. But nobody ever paid any attention to the circle on my wallet. Then one day a few weeks later one of the older boys in high school saw my wallet. He elbowed his friend standing next to him and started laughing like crazy. He said, "Look what Tom has in his wallet." They both laughed so hard I thought they might split their sides. My face turned really red. They started teasing me saying, "What you think you're going to do with that thing?" They started laughing a lot more really loud. When I got home from school that day I took the rubber out of my wallet and went out in the back yard. I got the shovel out of the garage and dug a hole. I buried it so deep I knew no one would ever find it.

The day I was keeping the store for Mr. Clements to go to his farm, he finally came back after about an hour. When he walked in I was sitting at one of the tables where customers usually sit to eat their ice cream and drink their coke.

"Did you sell anything?" he asked.

"Just some ice cream," I said.

"How much did you make?" he asked.

"15 cents," I said.

He went over behind the counter and started mumbling and doing some work. He never said anything else to me. I went out the front door and walked back home.

I would never in the whole world tell him or anybody else where that money really came from.

Now every time I see those big boys at school, they point at me and start laughing. I hope I never see one of those rubbers ever again in my whole life.

Love,
Tom

December 8, 1949

Dear Henry,

I don't have much time to write cause I gotta get to school. But I had to tell you the news about the Bank of Finleyson getting robbed. Finleyson is one mile north of Pineview. They have the only bank anywhere around, so all the people in Pineview use it.

The paper said 3 young men came in the bank just after the bank opened. Two of them had shot guns and the other one had a pillow case. They held a gun on Mr. Clarence and Lucille Tippett and told them to gimme all your money. Mr. Clarence told them the vault where they keep the money was on a timer and couldn't be opened until 9 o'clock. One of the boys asked Mr. Clarence to show him the vault to prove to them he couldn't open it. So the robber just took what money was in the drawer. It was over $1,000.

Beth Hardy's daddy runs a grocery store next to the bank. He saw the boys running out of the bank holding the shotguns and the pillow case. He jumped in his car and chased them up the road toward Hawkinsville. Mr. Hardy said he was gaining on them until they ditched their car and went running into the woods. He saw an older man waiting on them in a black '35 Dodge. The three boys jumped in the car and took off in a big hurry.

The paper said 35 men including the sheriffs from Pulaski, Houston, Crawford, and Crisp counties, and the state patrolmen from Cordele, Americus, Perry, and Tifton, FBI agents, and GBI agents had all formed a search party. The paper said, "Bloodhounds bayed and sniffed the cold air late into the night in efforts to tract down the trio, but they lost the trail."

The robbery was the headlines in the Atlanta Journal and the Macon Telegraph yesterday morning. When Sam brought the papers, Daddy got them off the porch and came back to the kitchen to show us. He said Finleyson has never made any newspaper ever in his lifetime about anything, and this time they made the damn headlines in both papers.

This morning's papers had articles on the front page that said that the robber's get-away car pulled up beside the barn of Pookie Bozeman. He's a nigra man who lives in a tenant house between Finleyson and Hawkinsville. One of the bank robbers came up on the front porch of his house and knocked on the door. Pookie said, "Who is it?" But nobody answered. The robber then knocked the front door down. Pookie got his pistol and shot at the robber.

"You've shot the law," the man said.

According to a quote from Sheriff Jim Hill of Hawkinsville, "Bozeman said he thought the bullet had hit the man in the right shoulder. The companion of the wounded man shot back into the house grazing the head of the Negro tenant. Bozeman described the wounded man as being small and slender and wearing a leather jacket. Later, Bozeman found $916 stashed out beside his barn."

Sheriff Hill further said, "Officers are making a thorough search of all farmhouses in the belief the quartet may be in hiding. All doctors in Pulaski and nearby counties have been asked to call the sheriff if the wounded man comes to them for treatment."

How about that, Henry? They haven't found the robbers yet. Why is it that Pineview has never made the headlines ever, but Finleyson made it in both papers?

Love,
Tom

November 30, 1951

Dear Henry,

Starting the 10th grade this year, Pineview had the best basketball coach we've ever had. In the 9th grade we had the worst. Last year's coach was Mr. Nash. We lost the most games ever. Just to show you how much he knew, at the first practice he lined up everybody against the wall and chose the ten tallest boys to be on the team. He'd never even seen any of us shoot a single shot at the goal. We should've known right then and there that we'd never have a good team when you have a coach that does some idiotic thing like that.

Irvin got picked to be on the starting five before the coach ever saw him play. He has never ever beaten me a single time in a one-on-one game. He really doesn't care all that much about basketball like I do. I've been playing it just about every day of my life. Irvin says I'm a fanatic. I probably am.

It just so happened I was the 10th tallest boy in the lineup. I grew 5 inches in the 8th grade from 5'3" to 5'8". I think I'm about 5'10" now.

I sat on the bench most all of last season and watched the tallest boys try to make a team. It was so crazy. Some of us on the bench were a lot better than those guys. But the coach never figured it out.

All of us on the bench were thankful Mr. Nash was not rehired. Coach Cooey is the new coach. He's from Perry, Florida. He played for the University of Florida and knows more about basketball than anyone I've ever known. He started the year by first making us get in shape. I don't think I've ever run so many laps and sprints in my life. He said he wanted us to be in shape to play a whole game without getting tired.

He can shoot a jump shot from anywhere within 30 feet of the goal and the ball seems to always strip the net. He's got a right handed hook and a left handed hook that never misses. It amazes me what he can do with a basketball. I've never seen anyone that good. All the players really like him. He coaches the girls' team. They all love him, too.

When he first came to town in August, he rented a room at Nan's house. Sammy was off at college, so Coach stayed in his room. He left after a couple of months and got a room with Lizzie and Robert Brown. I'm not sure why he left, but I think it might've been that he ate too much. Nan is really a good cook. She is one of the lunch room cooks, and they have some really good food.

Lizzie and Robert had a separate place in their house where he had a little kitchen, so he did his own cooking. A lot of the players on the team who lived out in the country would sometimes spend the night with him. He would cook a huge amount of food. He asked me to eat supper with him once or twice, but I never spent the night there.

When I ate with him, it was usually after the two of us had played basketball all afternoon. We ate like starved animals. We never talked about anything but basketball. It was his whole world and mine, too.

Just about every afternoon after school, I stayed at the gym and shot baskets with Coach. He taught me a lot of things I didn't know about shooting and how to fake out the guy who was guarding me. We sometimes played a one-on-one game, but I was no match for him. I'm just 15. He's probably about 30. And at least 4 inches taller.

Both the boys and girls have had the best teams this fall we've ever had. We've only lost a couple of games and the girls are undefeated.

But, Henry, you're not going to believe what I'm going to tell you. The other day when my class was marching from the schoolhouse to the cafeteria, one of the senior boys on the team and our best player, called me over to where he was eating. I couldn't imagine what he wanted. Seniors boys don't ever say a word to 10th graders off the basketball court.

"Coach is gone," he said. He had a look in his eyes that let me know something was really bad wrong.

"Gone? What do you mean gone?" I asked.

"You'll find out," he said. He started back eating while I just stood there not knowing what to think. I couldn't believe it. I thought it must be a joke. But then the bigger boys would never try to joke around with us.

I went back and sat down at our table. I was staring at the wall. Some of my classmates asked me why I was not talking. It wasn't like me, they said. But at that particular time I felt like Popcorn, the biggest guy on the team, had just socked me in the stomach as hard as he could.

I was thinking that any man who could play the game of basketball the way Coach did was someone I wanted to be like. I have two more years of high school. I wanted him to coach me into becoming a really good player. I've improved so much since he's been working with me. I want to play in college and then be a coach as long as I can.

I didn't say anything to anybody in my class about what I'd been told. They all thought I was nauseated or had the flu or something. I really did feel sick to my stomach and didn't eat anything on my plate. When we went back to the classroom, my homeroom teacher called me up to her desk and said, "Tom, you need to go to the principal's office."

For what? I hadn't done anything to make me have to go to the principal's office.

Mr. Cornelius is baldheaded, about six feet tall, wears glasses and always has on a suit and tie. Even though I'm halfway scared of him, I still like him. He has a lot of respect for all the students, and we respect him, too.

"Tom," he said with a stern look. "I think it's best for you to take the rest of the school day off."

"Why?"

"I've spoken with your mother about this," he said, looking over his glasses. "She'll explain it to you."

"Is something wrong?" I wondered if maybe my daddy had died. He'd been sick. Nona was getting older. Could she be the one?

"Your mother will explain it to you," he said. "Just get your books and go on home. We'll get your homework assignments to you later."

My heart was pounding. I ran every step of the way home. I slammed the front door, ran through the living room and down the hallway to the kitchen. Mama was sitting at the breakfast table acting real somber like somebody had died.

"What is it?" I yelled.

She didn't say anything.

"What's wrong?"

"Mr. Moore is waiting to talk to you."

"Mr. Moore? What about?"

He's the preacher at the Methodist Church. His daddy is the Bishop of the Methodist Church of Georgia. Mr. Moore is blind, but can walk all over town with his walking cane. He's not always perfect though. One time I saw him walk square into the trunk of one of the pecan trees in our yard.

I ran to the parsonage where he lived next door to the church. He was sitting in a rocking chair on his screen porch holding his white walking cane between his legs.

"Have a seat, young man." I was glad he couldn't see the look on my face.

"Tell me about your coach," he said.

I told him what I knew – that he was a great coach and had been helping me so much with my game after school.

He then asked me, "Has he ever laid a hand on you?"

I stared at him for quite a while. I had no idea what he meant. Of course, when you play a one-on-one basketball game, you have your hands on each other a lot of the time. When I didn't answer, he asked again, "Has he ever touched you in places where he shouldn't?"

"No, we've just played basketball together," I said.

"You do know he's a homo, don't you?"

I'll never forget that question for the rest of my life. I had absolutely no clue what he was talking about.

When I left the parsonage after satisfying him that I'd never been harmed by the coach in any way, I went home. My mother was on the phone talking to Mr. Moore. I knew she'd be quizzing me next. I grabbed my daddy's dictionary he uses for working crossword puzzles and ran to my room. I looked up the word "homo." The dictionary said it meant "same or like." I figured I must've misunderstood him, so I looked up "hemo." It meant blood. Oh, my God. Is Coach a bloodsucker!

Mama asked me all kinds of questions that were stupid as usual. After she finished with me, I called Dicky Cook to come over. Dicky didn't play much basketball because he was too short.

"Did you know Coach is a homo or hemo or something like that?"

Dicky had no idea what I was talking about either. He hadn't heard any of the news.

Later that afternoon I ran into Billy Mann and some of his buddies. They were laughing about it and making fun of me and Coach. They told me a lot of things I didn't really want to hear. I can't believe that Coach would've ever done anything like that with any of the boys on the team. Why would anybody want to do anything like that with another person?

In typical fashion no member of my family ever breathed a word about it. After Mama satisfied herself that Coach had not touched me in the wrong places, it became a dead issue.

I found out later that he had touched some of the 8th graders in the wrong places. I don't really understand it. I don't guess I ever will. Mama and Daddy have always taught me not to think about things you don't understand, so I'll try to forget it.

After Coach left, Mr. Cornelius took over the team. He'd never coached any sport in his whole life. He had no idea what to do. We started losing games that we never should've. We began the season with so much hope, and now it looks like we'll never make it through the tournament

This is a sad story. I had to write to somebody. There's no one I can talk to about this except you.

Love,
Tom

May 1, 1952

Dear Henry,

I'm going to be 16 in 30 more days. I'll be getting my driver's license. I just have a learner's license now. It's not like it's such a big deal. I've been driving Daddy's car for at least 8 years. It'll be nice having a license in my billfold though. Then I won't have to get scared every time I see a state patrol car.

I'll be finishing the 10ᵗʰ grade in 3 weeks. Mrs. Scarborough has been my homeroom teacher this year. She's a good teacher. I really like her a lot. But the teacher I like best is Mrs. Bellflower, my English teacher. She wears really tight sweaters. She and her husband live at Nona's house. I go over sometimes in the afternoons to get her to help me with my English papers. I don't know how old she is, maybe 27 or 28.

I have a new girlfriend now. Her name is Pat Palmer. When they opened up Bowen's Mill a couple of weeks ago, a bunch of us went down there to go swimming and bowling and dancing. I asked Irvin and his girlfriend, Jo Horne, to go with us, but I think they wanted to be alone. It's O.K. I like being alone with Pat, too. She sits close to me. I put one arm around her and drive with the other hand.

We have a good time diving off the high dive. It's really high. It must be 20 feet up in the air.

I'm not a very good bowler. Most of the time I can beat the girl I take with me, but I can't beat Jo Horne, and Irvin can't either. She puts all the boys to shame. She can break 100.

We like to put nickels in the jukebox and dance. Pat can dance better than any girlfriend I've ever had. Sometimes there are some older students, maybe 17 or 18, who are in there dancing. We don't like to dance in front of them. They'd probably make fun of us.

I get concerned when grownups ask me, "What you gonna do when you grow up?" I just don't know for sure. Edith tells me I need to be a doctor or a lawyer or something like that. Sometimes when I think about what I really want to do, the only thing I can ever come up with is to be a basketball coach.

There're so many other things I want to know. Where will I go to college? Who will I marry? Where will I live? Will I go to heaven when I die? When I think about all those things, it kinda scares me.

Mama tells me, "No matter what you do, you've got to get out of this town." She said I should never live within 100 miles of any of my relatives. I guess she should know. Her parents live across the street from us. Daddy's parents live behind us. Her two brothers and their families live next door. Daddy's sister and her family live only two houses away, and most of my cousins live in Pineview, too. In fact, I'm probably related in one way or another to practically everybody in town.

Mama says I have to start a new life someplace else. "Look at your daddy. Look at your 2 grand-daddies. They were unhappy because they didn't go out and find their own life. They took the easy way out and stayed in this little town. If they'd gotten away from here, they could've had a good life. Just because your great, great granddaddy was a farmer doesn't mean his sons and grandsons should all be farmers. We're all different. Everybody needs to get out and find what's best for them. And that's what I want you to do."

"But Pineview is where my Dennard ancestors have lived since the early 1800's," I tell her.

I don't have a person to talk to that I can say all the things on my mind. You were the best dog I ever had. I've always felt like you knew me and understood me better than anybody else in the whole world. That's the reason I've written you so many letters.

Most people would think I'm crazy to write letters to a dog that's dead. That's the reason I've never told anybody about writing them. No one but you and me could understand it. But I know your spirit has always been with me. And I know it'll always be with me.

I want to try to be the best person I can, so that when I die, I can go to heaven and be there with you. I have a feeling deep down that someday you and I will be together again, and we can play every day like we used to.

Love,
Tom

EPILOGUE

I placed the last letter in my lap, closed my eyes, and leaned back on Daddy's pillow. It still has the smell of Vitalis Hair Tonic. A multitude of thoughts raced through my mind. So many things have happened since those letters to Henry – graduating from college, my marriage to Marie, our three children, my law practice, the building of the hostel, travels to foreign countries, and other events I could never have foreseen when I was writing those letters.

I'm sad my daddy's gone. I know he expects me to take care of Mama. She'll miss him, for certain. After all, they've been together for 45 years. But she's pretty tough, and she's a survivor. I'm sure she'll make it.

Mama walked into the room, "What are you doing laying up there in your daddy's bed?"

"I was just reading some old letters."

"Well, I need for you and the boys to come help me move a dresser."

"O.K. I'll be there in just a second."

I pondered over the letters before putting them back into the manila envelope. I thought about the dog we have now named Rufus. He's about as close to me as any member of my family. I could easily see one of my children writing letters to him after he's gone.

Over the years, I've learned that dogs are very special creatures. They're many times more intuitive and loving than other animals – never critical and always willing to return a bountiful supply of love for just a little pat on the head. Why shouldn't their spirits live on after death? Should a creature so loving be denied the rewards of an afterlife?

I'm now more convinced than ever that Henry was well aware of every word I wrote to him. He may not have read my written words, but he sensed the feelings as they poured from my heart.

"Tom! Are you coming or not?"

"O.K., Mama. I'll be there right now."

Ecclesiastes 3:19-21 – *"Man's fate is like that of the animals; the same fate awaits them both: As one dies, so dies the other. All have the same breath; man has no advantage over the animal. Everything is meaningless. All go to the same place; all come from dust, and to dust all return. Who knows if the spirit of man rises upward and if the spirit of the animal goes down into the earth?"*

Job 12:7 – *"But ask the animals, and they will teach you..."*

APPENDIX

DENNARD FAMILY TREE

Dennard is a French name. There is a town on the English Channel in Brittany, in northern France, named DiNard. One might assume that Dennard is a corruption of the name DiNard, but we don't know that for sure. I went to the town. It is near St. Malo. I tried to do some research there in the library and went through various cemeteries. But being limited by the language, I didn't find anything about the Dennards.

It is believed that the Dennards were French Huguenots who came to the Americas in the early 1700s. The Huguenots were French Protestants who were members of the Reformed Church established in 1550 by John Calvin. An edict had been issued in France to exterminate all Huguenots under the guidance of Cardinal Richelieu, with the blessing of Pope Gregory. King Louis XIV brought forth a large scale persecution of the Huguenots during his reign (1643-1715.) Many were burned at the stake. At least 250,000 fled France looking for religious freedom. Between 1618 and 1725 between 5,000 and 7,000 French Huguenot refugees reached the shores of America, particularly in the Carolinas.

The earliest record found of a Dennard in America is in 1733 when Martin Dennard signed a petition to locate the capital of North Carolina at New Bern, which is the area where a large group of French Huguenots had settled in 1707.

The next thing recorded of a Dennard is when Thomas Dennard signed as a witness to a deed conveying property in Granville County, North Carolina, on March 4, 1746. Thomas Dennard later gave a mortgage to Phillip Dill on July 26, 1766, which was recorded in New Bern, Craven County, North Carolina. He mortgaged all his household effects and cattle. It mentions that his cattle are branded with the following mark: 王

In January, 1772, in Tryon County, North Carolina, Thomas Dennard, William Dennard and Jacob Dennard are mentioned along with a group of other men charged to lay out a road from Tates Ferry to Charleston.

It is believed that Thomas Dennard was born around 1726 in North Carolina and died in South Carolina around 1786.

One of Thomas Dennard's sons was John Dennard, Sr., who had 3 sons: William Dennard, Jacob Dennard and John Dennard, Jr. John Dennard, Sr., the father, and all 3 of his sons served in the American Revolutionary War. In his Revolutionary War record, John Dennard, Sr. uses the same mark(王) in signing some of his papers that was used by his father, Thomas, in branding his cattle.

Thomas's son, Jacob, is our direct ancestor, and was born in 1750 in Edgefield District, South Carolina. He married a woman from Virginia in 1772 by the name of Harriet Byrd. She was supposedly from the prominent Byrd family of Virginia. They had eleven children: Shadrack, Isaac, Rebecca, Byrd, Kennedy, Thomas, William, John, Jared, and two daughters. I don't have the daughters' names. Jacob moved to Twiggs County, near Milledgeville, Georgia, and later died in 1810 at the age of 60.

Jacob's son, Byrd, was our direct ancestor. He was born in 1780 in Twiggs County, Georgia. He married Rhoda Marshall and died in 1835 at the age of 55. He and Rhoda had seven children: Marshall, Hartwell, Rhoda, John, Anne, James, and Mary.

Jacob's son, John, was our direct ancestor. He was born in 1812, also in Twiggs County. He married Martha Denson, and they had eight children: Anne, Joe, Polly, James, Tom, Ben, Robert, and Fanny.

John reputedly won a land lottery and had over 10,000 acres of real estate in middle Georgia in what is now Wilcox and Dooly Counties between the Ocmulgee River, north of Abbeville, and the Flint River, north of Cordele. I'm guessing he acquired this property in the land lottery of 1833.

My daddy told me that John could neither read nor write but worked really hard all his life. He had slaves who are buried in back of his house, located on my daddy's farm. His house sat about 100 yards back of the north side of the road between Pineview and Abbeville, just before the curve where Boots Doster lived. There is an old well there, and both my grandfather (Papa) and my daddy took me on several occasions to show me the old well. John was Papa's grandfather. Papa was eight years old when John died. He said that John worked in the fields along with his slaves and always worked as hard as they did. My daddy told me that John was working on a fence the day he died on Christmas Eve, December 24, 1887. He was considered to be an old man when he died at the age of 75. His burial site is enclosed with a chain link fence inside a pasture in front of Boots Doster's house. At the time of this writing, a Dennard Reunion is held on the second Sunday in October every year in Pineview, and all the descendants of John's eight children are invited to attend.

John's son, James, was my great grandfather. He was born on his father's farm on September 15, 1849. James served in the Georgia Legislature for many years, and, according to my daddy, was a "real sport." He was not into farming. He was more of a fancy-dressing, ladies' man. He ordered his clothes from Brooks Brothers in New York, shipped to him by train. Frequently picking up his packages from the Hawkinsville Depot, he wore the latest in fashion: good-looking suits, ties, shirts, shoes, and top hats, according to my daddy.

James was only 12 years old when the Civil War started, but he served his time during the latter stages of the war. I don't know where he was stationed or where he fought. However, it is said that after the war, he brought a girl back home with him to Pineview. She was from New York, and thus a Yankee. She was promptly "run out of town on a rail."

James's first wife was Katie Blue, and she died during their marriage without having any children. He then married her sister, Martha Blue, and they had three children: Joseph A. Dennard, Thomas Jefferson Dennard, and Ida Dennard, who married Philetus Doster. James's wife, Martha, died when Ida was a baby and Tom was a small boy. James then married Flora McLeod, and they had no children.

On the Fourth of July, 1892, at the age of 42, James shot himself and died immediately. He is buried at the Cedar Creek Church Cemetery on Highway 129 north of Abbeville. I asked Nona one time why he killed himself. She said he was "despondent" over the deaths of his wives and didn't know how to raise those small children. I always remember her saying the word, "despondent," because I didn't know what it meant.

Joseph (always referred to in my youth as Uncle Joe) was married at the time of his father's death, so he took Tom and Ida, his little brother and sister, to live with him and his wife.

Tom was my grandfather. I always called him Papa. He was born on February 21, 1879, in Pineview. He married Leona Barfield of Abbeville in October, 1901. He was 22. She was 17. I always called her "Nona." They had two children: Jamie Edith Dennard born on December 27, 1902, and my daddy, Thomas Edwin Dennard born on September 28, 1904.

Edith married John Hendley McLeod of Pineview, and they had three children: Jamie, Ann (called

"Sister") and John Hendley McLeod, Jr. (called "Boy.")

Jamie was born on March 27, 1922. She married Elbert Hickman of Rochelle, and they had one daughter, Carol Ann Hickman. Carol was born October 4, 1960, and died without children on August 5, 2000.

Sister was born April 29, 1924. She married Elwyn McKinney of Hawkinsville and they had 3 sons: John Elwyn McKinney born February 19, 1950; William Grady McKinney born September 19,1953; Jamie McLeod McKinney born September 27,1961.

Boy married Frances Ingram of Hawkinsville. They had 3 children: Brenda Faye McLeod McKaig born July 2, 1948; Mary Frances McLeod Pierce born July 26, 1950; and John Hendley McLeod III born January 21,1953.

On November 12, 1933, my father, Thomas Edwin Dennard, married Marilu Mann from Pineview, always known by everyone as "Coot." They had two children: Thomas Edwin Dennard, Jr., born May 30, 1936, and my sister, Mary Mann Dennard, "Mary," born January 7, 1942.

I married Marie Louisa Burton, "Marie," from Toccoa, Georgia, on March 24, 1962. Our 3 children: Susan Marie Dennard, "Susan," born November 12,1963; Thomas Edwin Dennard III, "Ted," born December 9,1965; Jefferson Burton Dennard, "Jeff," born January 5,1968.

Susan married Robert Hunt Dunlap, Jr., "Hunt," on September 20, 1986; They have 4 children Robert Hunt Dunlap, III., "Hunter" born May 18,1989;

Burton Dennard Dunlap, "Burton," born June 19, 1991; Thomas Sutton Dunlap, "Sutton," born September 9, 1998; Hannah Marie Dunlap, "Hannah," born December 11, 2003.

Ted married Carolyn Cooper Jenkins. "Carolyn," on December 02, 2004; Ted and Carolyn have 2 children: Thomas Edwin Dennard, IV, "Wynn," born August 3, 2006; and Bluford Jenkins Dennard, "Blue," born December 1, 2007. Carolyn has two children of a previous marriage: Carolyn Cooper Hall, "Cooper," born November 27, 1997, and Elizabeth Rivers Hall, "Rivers," born June 5, 2000.

Jeff married Whitney Bourne on November 03, 2001. They had two children: Avery Marie Dennard, "Avery," born April 24, 2002; Sarah Ellis Dennard, "Ellis," born January 30, 2004. Jeff married Cindy Janus on June 6, 2009. They have one son: Miles Heron Dennard, "Miles," born December 27, 2010.

My sister, Mary Mann Dennard, "Mary," was born January7, 1942. She married Ed Vernon Hungerford, "Skip," on May 30, 1964. Their two children: Mark Vernon Hungerford, "Mark," born April 3, 1970; Mary Catherine Hungerford, "Catherine," born June 8, 1974.

Catherine married Michael Anthony Scott, "Michael," on July 27, 2002. They have 2 children: Chloe Madeline Scott, "Chloe," born June 8, 2004 and Owen Wesley Scott, "Owen," born January 15, 2006.

How did Pineview get started?

When Papa and Nona married in 1901, they lived near a sawmill in front of the old John Dennard place and behind where Boots Doster lived. Papa was teaching school. In the mid to late 1890's, Papa attended the University of Virginia for a period of time with the intention of going to law school. But he left before he finished and came back to Pineview. The only excuse he gave for dropping out of school was that he'd left because of a girl.

In the early 1900's a rail line was laid between Hawkinsville and Ocilla. Families began moving close to the rail line, so a depot was built. There had been a community called Pineview that had a post office about two miles east of the present town. It was located on property that was owned during my lifetime by Calvin Stone.

Papa and Nona moved into the new town of Pineview around 1905. Three streets extended east of the depot, and people began building houses along those streets. Before long, the town not only had a depot, but also a post office. Papa named it Pineview and served as its first mayor.

When I was a young boy, Pineview had around 500 inhabitants. My daddy said, "That meant counting all the dogs."

For easy access without having to read the text, the following is a list of my male Dennard ancestors as far back as I know:

Thomas Dennard, born 1726, died 1786, age 60

Jacob Dennard, born 1750, died 1810, age 60

Byrd Dennard, born 1780, died 1835, age 55

John Dennard, born 1812, died 1887, age 75

James Hartwell Dennard, born 1849, died 1892, age 43

Thomas Jefferson Dennard, born 1879, died 1944, age 65

Thomas Edwin Dennard, born 1904, died 1978, age 74

Thomas Edwin Dennard, Jr., born 1936 (Author of this book)

Boy and Nona

Edith

Angie

JuJu

Hosey

Nona

Dummy

Mary and Me

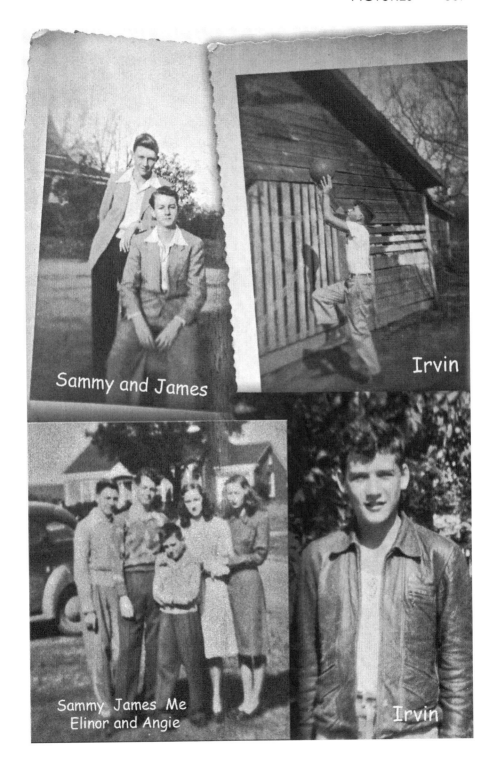

Sammy and James

Irvin

Sammy James Me
Elinor and Angie

Irvin

Big Irvin and Daddy

Papa

Daddy